CVIC

T5-CVI-486

T5-CVI-486

JUL   2023

TIMELINES
OF NATURE

TIMELINES OF NATURE

DK LONDON
Senior editor Amanda Wyatt
Senior art editor Smiljka Surla
US editor Jennette ElNaggar
Editors Penny Arlon, Zaina Budaly, Steven Carton, Elizabeth Cook,
Jolyon Goddard, Susan Kelly, Mani Ramaswamy, Isabel Thomas
Designers Emma Clayton, Tory Gordon-Harris, Hoa Luc, Anna Pond, Rhys Thomas
Illustrators Peter Bull, Stuart Jackson-Carter, KJA, Naomi Murray, Gus Scott
Retoucher Steve Crozier
DK media archive Romaine Werblow
Senior picture researcher Laura Barwick
Managing editor Rachel Fox
Managing art editor Owen Peyton Jones
DTP coordinator Pushpak Tyagi
Production editor Gillian Reid
Senior production controller Meskerem Berhane
Jacket designer Surabhi Wadhwa-Gandhi
Jackets design development manager Sophia MTT
Jackets senior DTP designer Harish Aggarwal
Senior jackets coordinator Priyanka Sharma
Publisher Andrew Macintyre
Art director Karen Self
Associate publishing director Liz Wheeler
Publishing director Jonathan Metcalf

Authors
Steven Carton, Tim Harris, Rob Hume, Tom Jackson, Dr. Sarah Jose,
Dr. Anthea Lacchia, Georgia Mills, Douglas Palmer, Nicola Temple

Lead consultant
Dr. Nick Crumpton

Consultants
Sophie Allan, Dr. Chris Clennett, Douglas Palmer

First American Edition, 2023
Published in the United States by DK Publishing
1745 Broadway, 20th Floor, New York, NY 10019

Copyright © 2023 Dorling Kindersley Limited
DK, a Division of Penguin Random House LLC
23 24 25 26 27 10 9 8 7 6 5 4 3 2 1
001–334048–June/2023

All rights reserved.
Without limiting the rights under the copyright reserved above, no part of this publication
may be reproduced, stored in or introduced into a retrieval system, or transmitted, in any form,
or by any means (electronic, mechanical, photocopying, recording, or otherwise),
without the prior written permission of the copyright owner.
Published in Great Britain by Dorling Kindersley Limited.

A catalog record for this book is available from the Library of Congress.
ISBN 978-0-7440-8148-0

DK books are available at special discounts when purchased
in bulk for sales promotions, premiums, fund-raising, or educational use.
For details, contact:
DK Publishing Special Markets,
1745 Broadway, 20th Floor, New York, NY 10019
SpecialSales@dk.com

Printed and bound in China

For the curious
www.dk.com

THE SMITHSONIAN
Established in 1846, the Smithsonian—the world's largest museum and research complex—includes
19 museums and galleries and the National Zoological Park. The total number of artifacts, works of art, and
specimens in the Smithsonian's collection is estimated at 154 million. The Smithsonian is a renowned research
center, dedicated to public education, national service, and scholarship in the arts, sciences, and history.

MIX
Paper | Supporting
responsible forestry
FSC™ C018179

This book was made with Forest Stewardship
Council™ certified paper—one small step
in DK's commitment to a sustainable future.
For more information go to
www.dk.com/our-green-pledge

A note on timings

The earliest events in this book took place a very long time ago. Some dates may be followed by BYA (billion years ago), MYA (million years ago), or YA (years ago).

Where the exact date of an event is not known, "c." appears before the year. This is short for the Latin word *circa*, meaning "around," and indicates that the date is approximate.

When seasons are mentioned, for example in an animal's life cycle, we mean the season for that hemisphere—for example, for an animal in the northern hemisphere, summer is around the middle of the year.

Finally, climate change is affecting the life cycles of plants and animals. The timings given in this book are correct at the time of going to print but may be changed in future printings.

PLANTS AND FUNGI

CONTENTS

ANIMALS

EARTH

Our home in the universe is planet Earth, which formed from a dense ball of gas and dust in the solar system about 4.5 BYA. Earth boasts the most diverse collection of natural features of anywhere in the solar system—from vast oceans, lakes, and rivers full of liquid water to bone-dry deserts. Earth's surface is continually changing, a result of shifting continental plates that have created massive mountain ranges and cause volcanoes to erupt violently without warning. Earth is also the only place where life as we know it has been able to take root.

The Big Bang

The universe started with a bang about 13.8 billion years ago. It was not an actual bang—there was no sound—but it was big, and the Big Bang is the name used to refer to the events that created the universe. At first, the entire universe—which is all of space and everything in it—was only a tiny speck of pure energy. It grew larger incredibly fast, and the universe is still expanding today.

James Webb Space Telescope

The James Webb Space telescope was launched into space in 2021. It can look farther into space than any telescope humans have made before, and it enables astronomers to look into the past. It can see parts of the universe that are 13.6 billion light-years away, which means it is seeing that far back in time as the light has taken that long to reach us.

Primary mirror

Sunshield

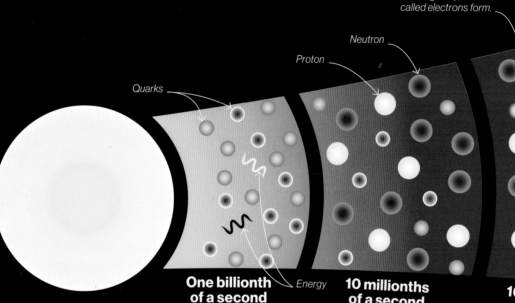

Atomic nuclei

Lighter particles called electrons form.

Neutron

Proton

Quarks

Energy

0 seconds

Bang!
An explosion creates the whole universe in an instant. At first, it is tinier than a pinhead and is extremely hot and full of energy. In a fraction of a nanosecond, the universe expands faster than the speed of light to the size of a grapefruit.

One billionth of a second

Cooling down
As the universe expands, it cools slightly. The basic forces of nature, including gravity, begin to emerge. These forces shape the energy into quarks, particles that are the building blocks of matter—the substance from which every material in the universe is made.

10 millionths of a second

Heavy particles
In the still-scorching temperatures and compressed space, the quarks zip around extremely fast. As the universe continues to expand and cool, the quarks slow down and cluster together. These clusters turn into protons, which have a positive electrical charge, and neutrons, which are neutral.

10 thousandths of a second

Lighter particles
The universe's temperature has cooled significantly, allowing smaller, lighter particles to form, including electrons. Electrons have a negative electrical charge, which makes them naturally move toward protons.

3 minutes

Going nuclear
The universe is now cool enough for protons and neutrons to cluster together. As the universe cools further, the jumble of particles slowly form atomic nuclei (the centers of atoms).

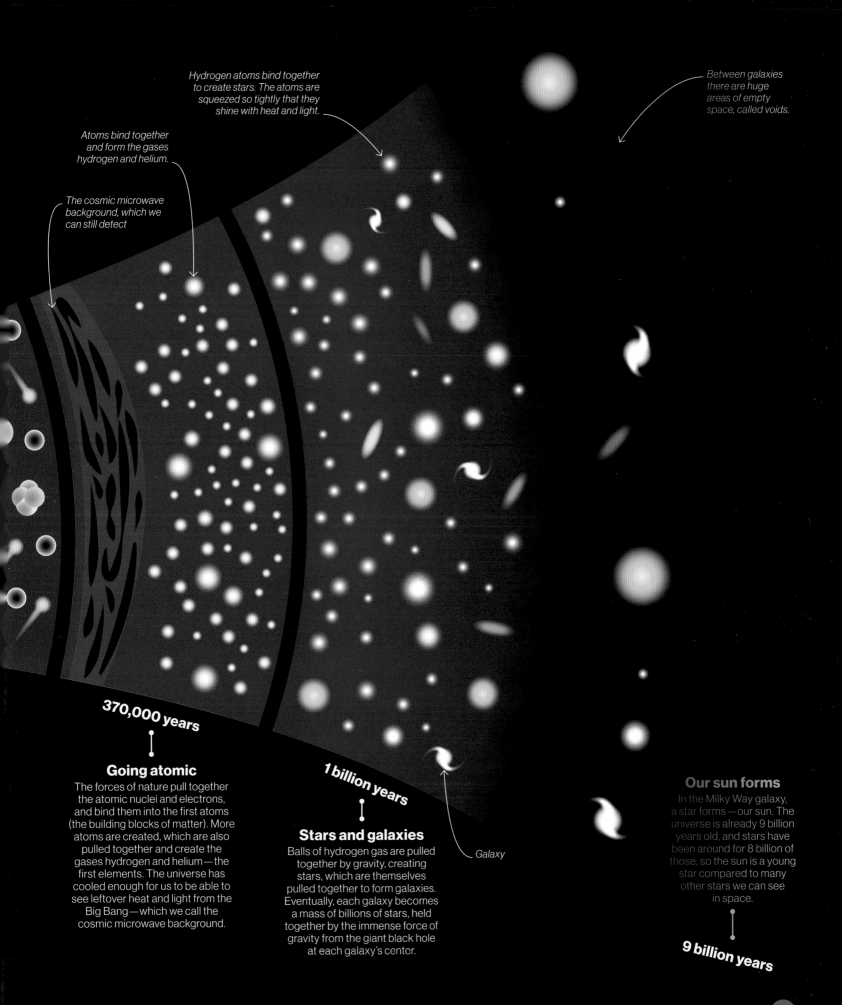

Hydrogen atoms bind together to create stars. The atoms are squeezed so tightly that they shine with heat and light.

Atoms bind together and form the gases hydrogen and helium.

The cosmic microwave background, which we can still detect

Between galaxies there are huge areas of empty space, called voids.

370,000 years

Going atomic
The forces of nature pull together the atomic nuclei and electrons, and bind them into the first atoms (the building blocks of matter). More atoms are created, which are also pulled together and create the gases hydrogen and helium—the first elements. The universe has cooled enough for us to be able to see leftover heat and light from the Big Bang—which we call the cosmic microwave background.

1 billion years

Stars and galaxies
Balls of hydrogen gas are pulled together by gravity, creating stars, which are themselves pulled together to form galaxies. Eventually, each galaxy becomes a mass of billions of stars, held together by the immense force of gravity from the giant black hole at each galaxy's center.

Galaxy

Our sun forms
In the Milky Way galaxy, a star forms—our sun. The universe is already 9 billion years old, and stars have been around for 8 billion of those, so the sun is a young star compared to many other stars we can see in space.

9 billion years

c.4.57 BYA

Collapsing cloud

The motion of the swirling nebula creates dark, cold regions where the gases and dust are packed together more closely. One of these regions begins to shrink, as the material inside is compressed into a smaller and smaller space under the pull of its own gravity.

c.4.5699 BYA

Protostar

A spinning ball of gas forms at the center of the cloud. The gas inside is being squeezed harder and harder by gravity as more gas is pulled into it. This squeezing makes the gas ball very hot, and it eventually forms the core of what will become our sun. This protostar blasts out jets of electrically charged gases from its poles.

Unknown

Death of a star

It is thought that the story of our sun begins with the death of a much larger, giant star. Small stars like our sun have a different life story from giants, which are less common. Giant stars die in an immense explosion called a supernova. At some point, billions of years ago, the shockwave of a supernova hits a nearby nebula (a cloud of gas and dust), making it start to slowly spin and swirl.

Birth and death of our sun

The sun is the star closest to us—a vast ball of hot gas that started shining just under 4.6 billion years ago, a few million years before Earth and the other planets of the solar system formed around it. The sun has not always existed. Just as it had a beginning, so too will it have an end, which will happen many billions of years from now.

Inside the sun

The sun's heat and light is produced by a process called nuclear fusion that takes place deep inside the star's core. During nuclear fusion, atoms of hydrogen are squeezed together so tightly that they merge, making larger atoms of helium. This releases huge amounts of energy in the process. The sun fuses 5.5 million tons of hydrogen gas every second. When the hydrogen runs out, it will fuse the helium instead and become a red giant.

The sun's huge weight pushes down on the core, squeezing the hydrogen inside so much that it fuses together and forms helium.

Dark sunspots are relatively cool areas on the surface caused by the star's magnetic field. The temperature of a sunspot is about 8,132°F (4,500°C), instead of 10,832°F (6,000°C) on the brighter areas.

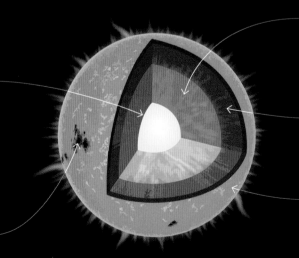

The heat released from fusion takes 170,000 years to travel through the radiative layer of the star to the convection layer.

The convection layer is thinner and cooler than the radiative layer.

Once the sun's energy arrives at the surface, it shines out into space at the speed of light, reaching Earth eight minutes later.

Planets form

The jets of electrified gas gradually push away the cloud of gas that surrounds the new star, allowing the sun's light to shine out into the universe—it is now a true star. All that is left from the original cloud is a disc of debris circling the sun's equator, that eventually forms the planets and other objects in the solar system.

A normal star

The sun today is a very typical star. It is a little larger and hotter than the average star in the Milky Way galaxy, and it is about halfway through its life. It is getting gradually brighter and bigger as it ages. It is 30 percent brighter today than it was when it just formed.

3.5 billion years from now

The end of Earth

The sun is 40 percent brighter than it is now. Its extra heat gradually blasts away Earth's atmosphere and oceans, making our planet a bare, lifeless rock with a surface temperature of more than 572°F (300°C).

5.4 billion years from now

Red giant

The sun has run out of hydrogen fuel and is now fusing helium. It has ballooned to 2,300 times the width of today's sun and has become a red giant. Eventually, after burning up most of its fuel, it will shrink down to a subgiant—although this is still 10 times bigger and 50 times brighter than today's star.

Unknown

White dwarf

At the core of the planetary nebula is a small star called a white dwarf. This is about as wide as Earth, but it weighs about 200,000 times more, because it contains half of the sun's original material. The white dwarf is what remains of the sun's core. Although it is not burning fuel any more, it is still very hot and will keep shining for trillions of years.

6 billion years from now

Planetary nebula

After puffing up to a red giant and shrinking back down to a subgiant many times over, eventually the sun has run out of fuel completely. Half of the star's original material forms a cloud of gas and dust called a planetary nebula.

Life of a giant star

Our sun is by far the largest object near us, and it is huge. But in the universe, our sun is actually a small, or dwarf, star. Dwarf stars are not very big and not very hot compared to other stars. Stars that are at least 8 times bigger than our sun are called giant stars. These giants burn very hot and last for only a relatively short time, when compared to dwarf stars.

Gas cloud

All stars form in a nebula. A nebula is a vast cloud of gas mixed with specks of dust and ice that floats in space. The size of the nebula and how much material it contains affects how big the star can be.

Birth

Red supergiant

A giant star fuses its hydrogen fuel incredibly fast—much faster than a dwarf star does. As it runs out of hydrogen, the star begins to fuse helium, which causes it to swell up into a red supergiant that is at least 100 times wider than before. The biggest red supergiant known in the universe is 1,800 times bigger than our sun!

50 million years later

Supernova!

Eventually, the supergiant runs out of fuel and the energy pushing outward is overwhelmed by gravity pushing inward. It can no longer keep its shape. In less than a second, the star collapses. The gases that are left over smash together in a violent explosion called a supernova. The light from a supernova is so bright that it can outshine even galaxies.

10–30 million years later

The supernova leaves behind a cloud of gas and dust called a remnant.

Star beginnings

New stars form in a part of the nebula called a globule, which has more dust in it than elsewhere. The material in the globule has its own pull of gravity, which makes it collapse into a smaller ball of gas. The gas is not spread out evenly, so as it collapses, the unevenness makes it spin around.

Protostar

This core of gas pulls more material from the nebula down in to it, causing it to grow bigger and hotter. It forms a protostar, which is not yet big enough to produce a lot of heat and light.

Gases fall on to the surface of the protostar with enough force for small amounts of heat to be given out.

2 million years later

30,000 years later

A shining star

Now a giant star, its core is so tight that it causes a reaction called nuclear fusion. This reaction produces a huge amount of heat and light. As the cloud around the star has gone, the star can be seen shining brightly. It is now a "main sequence" star—which means that it is fusing hydrogen into helium at its core and is stable.

Polar jets

The spinning of the protostar creates a magnetic field around it. The forces of magnetism create jets of heat and gas that blast out of the poles. These polar jets blow away the gases around the new star.

100,000 years later

1 million years later

1 million years later

1 million years later

Black hole

The most massive stars end up as black holes. The force of gravity of a black hole is so strong that not even light can escape its pull, and that is why it is black. The black hole forms a second after the supernova, but takes millions of years to grow.

The black hole sucks in everything nearby–even other stars. This material heats up as it falls in, creating an outer glowing disc.

Neutron star

Smaller giant stars may collapse into neutron stars. Here the atoms have been squashed so they all form a solid lump of subatomic particles called neutrons. A neutron star is only about the size of a city, but one spoonful weighs as much as Mount Everest.

Star types

Stars are not all the same—they differ greatly in size, brightness, color, temperature, and life span. These features are usually related—a typical giant star is incredibly hot and bright but has a short life span. More massive main sequence stars turn into supergiants and die in supernovas. Smaller main stars, like our sun, become red giants, and then they leave behind small stars called white dwarfs.

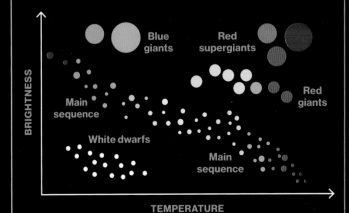

Blue giants

Red supergiants

Red giants

Main sequence

White dwarfs

Main sequence

BRIGHTNESS

TEMPERATURE

How the solar system formed

Our solar system started its life about 4.6 billion years ago as a cloud of gas and dust. There are different ideas as to how and when the system came into being, but the current best theory says that some of the material at the center collapsed inward, began to spin, and gradually became our sun. The unused material farther out from the center eventually became the eight planets, and billions of other rocky and icy objects—from comets and asteroids to dwarf planets and moons.

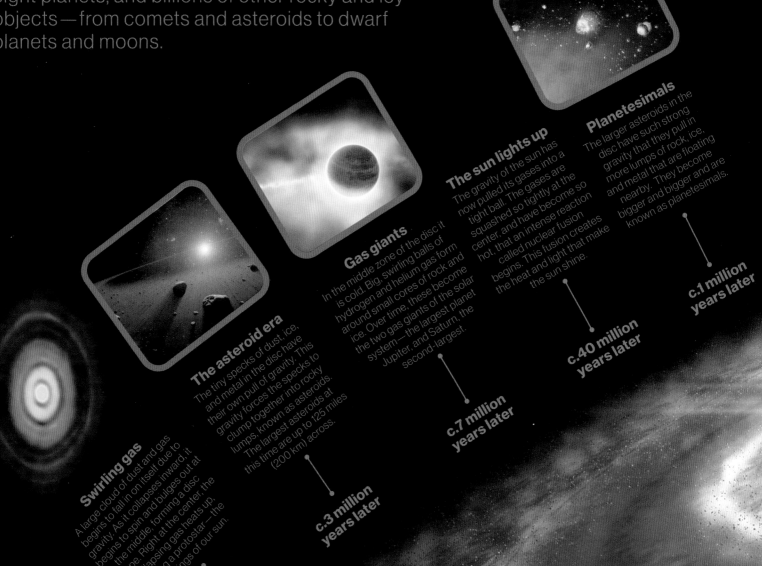

Swirling gas
A large cloud of dust and gas begins to fall in on itself due to gravity. As it collapses inward, it begins to spin and bulges out at the middle, forming a disc shape. Right at the center, the collapsing gas heats up, forming a protostar—the beginnings of our sun.

c. 4.6 BYA

The asteroid era
The tiny specks of dust, ice, and metal in the disc have their own pull of gravity. This gravity forces the specks to clump together into rocky lumps, known as asteroids. The largest asteroids at this time are up to 125 miles (200 km) across.

c. 3 million years later

Gas giants
In the middle zone of the disc it is cold. Big, swirling balls of hydrogen and helium gas form around small cores of rock and ice. Over time, these become the two gas giants of the solar system—the largest planet Jupiter, and Saturn, the second-largest.

c. 7 million years later

The sun lights up
The gravity of the sun has now pulled its gases into a tight ball. The gases are squashed so tightly at the center, and have become so hot, that an intense reaction called nuclear fusion begins. This fusion creates the heat and light that make the sun shine.

c. 40 million years later

Planetesimals
The larger asteroids in the disc have such strong gravity that they pull in more lumps of rock, ice, and metal that are floating nearby. They become bigger and bigger and are known as planetesimals.

c. 1 million years later

URANUS

NEPTUNE

Ice giants
Close to the sun, the planets that will become Uranus and Neptune form. They gradually migrate farther away from the sun. They are made of frozen ice, gas, and dust, gathered around cores of rock and ice. These "ice giants" are the third and fourth biggest planets.

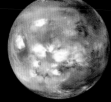

MARS

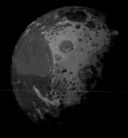

EARLY EARTH

Solar jets
As the young sun continues to grow bigger and hotter, it sends out powerful jets of gas. These jets blast away the cloud and dust that surround the sun and also any gases clinging to the smaller planetesimals. The sun is now a fully fledged star.

Rocky planets
Closer to the sun, the planetesimals continue to grow by crashing and clumping together, though the sun's heat melts much of their ice. Four worlds, the rocky planets Mercury, Venus, Earth, and Mars, come into being, formed mainly of rock and metal.

Bombardment
The giant planets move farther out into the solar system. This movement knocks millions of asteroids (rock and metal) and comets (ice, frozen gases, and dust) toward the sun, with many bombarding Earth and other rocky planets.

Earth's water
Many icy comets hit Earth, and as they land, they leave water behind, which becomes part of Earth's atmosphere. Earth has now cooled down enough for the water to fall as rain, and permanent oceans form on the surface.

c.29 million years later

c.10 million years later

c.10 million years later

c.500 million years later

c.100 million years later

Solar system objects
Astronomers have so far mapped over a million objects in our solar system other than the planets. These include asteroids, comets, and dwarf planets. Powerful telescopes are finding more and more all the time.

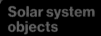

Asteroids
There are more than one million asteroids in a belt that orbits the sun between Mars and Jupiter. The asteroids are mainly rock and metal.

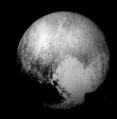

Dwarf planets
Planets that are big enough to be round, but too small to be the only object moving in their orbit, are known as dwarf planets. Pluto is the largest dwarf planet.

Comets
Comets are balls of icy rock. Some can take thousands of years to orbit the sun. When near the sun, they grow long tails of gas and dust.

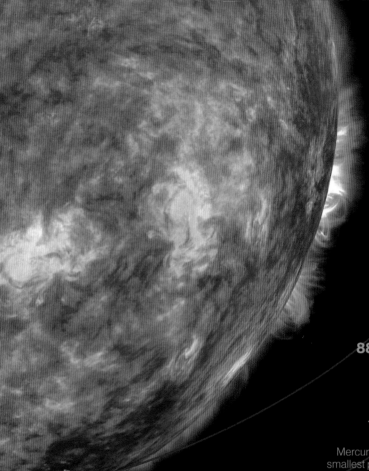

Venus

In many ways, Venus is Earth's twin planet as it is similar in size and density. It is very different in other ways, however. Its thick, cloudy atmosphere traps heat, causing Venus to be the hottest planet in the solar system. It reaches temperatures of 867°F (464°C) — hot enough to melt most plastics and some metals.

225 Earth days

88 Earth days

Mercury

Mercury is the solar system's smallest planet and is the closest to the sun, orbiting it at an average of 36 million miles (58 million km) away. The sun's intense heat has blasted away most of Mercury's atmosphere.

Unlike other planets, Venus spins in a clockwise direction.

The sun is 864,938 miles (1,392 million km) wide. It is a huge ball of hot gas that makes up 99 percent of the whole mass of the solar system.

Mars

This small planet is about a third of the mass of Earth. Its weak gravity can only hold on to a thin layer of atmosphere, so Mars is a cold and dry world.

687 Earth days

365.3 Earth days

Earth

Our planet is the largest of the inner four rocky planets. It is about 93 million miles (150 million km) from the sun. At this distance, water can stay as a liquid, which is crucial for living things. Any closer and the water would boil into steam; further out and it starts to freeze into ice.

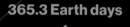

The length of a day

A planet's day is the length of time it takes to spin around once on its axis. The gas giants Jupiter and Saturn spin the fastest—their days are shorter than Earth's. Mars's day is about the same as Earth's, while Venus spins so slowly that its day is longer than its year!

Saturn is slightly tilted, which means it has seasons, just like Earth.

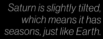

| **Mercury** 59 Earth days | **Venus** 243 Earth days | **Earth** 23.9 Earth hours | **Mars** 24.6 Earth hours | **Jupiter** 9.93 Earth hours | **Saturn** 10.7 Earth hours | **Uranus** 17.2 Earth hours | **Neptune** 16 Earth hours |

Planet orbits

Everything in the solar system—from huge planets to tiny icy comets and rocky asteroids—is held in place by the gravitational pull of the sun. Each of the eight planets of the solar system moves in an orbit—a counterclockwise path it takes around the sun. The time it takes to complete one orbit around the sun is that planet's year, which can be measured in Earth days (23.9 Earth hours). The farther a planet is from the sun, the longer it takes to travel around it.

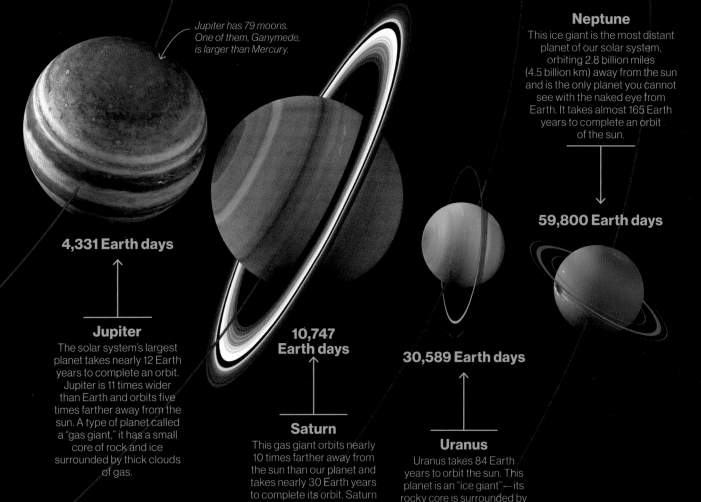

The majority of asteroids orbiting the sun are found between Mars and Jupiter in the main asteroid belt.

Jupiter has 79 moons. One of them, Ganymede, is larger than Mercury.

Neptune
This ice giant is the most distant planet of our solar system, orbiting 2.8 billion miles (4.5 billion km) away from the sun and is the only planet you cannot see with the naked eye from Earth. It takes almost 165 Earth years to complete an orbit of the sun.

59,800 Earth days

4,331 Earth days

Jupiter
The solar system's largest planet takes nearly 12 Earth years to complete an orbit. Jupiter is 11 times wider than Earth and orbits five times farther away from the sun. A type of planet called a "gas giant," it has a small core of rock and ice surrounded by thick clouds of gas.

10,747 Earth days

Saturn
This gas giant orbits nearly 10 times farther away from the sun than our planet and takes nearly 30 Earth years to complete its orbit. Saturn is famous for its rings. They are made from billions of chunks of ice and are 167,800 miles (270,000 km) across but never more than 328 ft (100 m) thick.

30,589 Earth days

Uranus
Uranus takes 84 Earth years to orbit the sun. This planet is an "ice giant"—its rocky core is surrounded by a mixture of liquid ices. Uranus is unusual because it spins on its side, not upright like the other planets.

The birth of the solar system

Our solar system forms when a cloud of dust and gas collapses inward and creates the sun. Dust and ice particles combine and build up to form the planets revolving around the sun, including Earth.

c.4.6 BYA

Theia approaches

Attracted by Earth's gravity, a Mars-sized planet called Theia approaches a young Earth, which is still hot, molten, and irregularly shaped. At this time, Earth is almost as big as it is today and its interior has separated into a core and a mantle.

Theia traveled toward Earth as fast as 31,400 mph (50,500 km/h).

c.4.45 BYA

Young Earth

Giant collision

Theia smashes violently into Earth, vaporizing (turning into gas) a large part of both planets. It hits Earth at an angle and material from both planets is blasted out into space.

c.4.45 BYA

How the moon formed

Humans have always been fascinated with the moon, Earth's only natural satellite. Its origin has long puzzled scientists. There have been many theories, but the most widely accepted is the "giant-impact hypothesis," according to which the moon was formed from material thrown into space when another planet collided with Earth billions of years ago. This theory is supported by studies of moon rocks, showing that they have a very similar composition to rock found inside Earth.

c.4–3.9 BYA

Asteroid bombardment

The moon and Earth suffer a barrage of asteroids, or space rocks. The moon's crust is punctured, with parts of its interior mantle blasted across its surface. This dramatic period is known as the Late Heavy Bombardment.

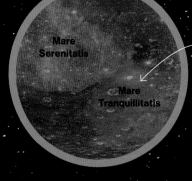

Mare Serenitatis

Mare Tranquillitatis

This enhanced-color photograph highlights the differences in rock composition of two neighboring lunar "seas."

Asteroid shower

A shower of asteroids hits the far side of the moon, leaving craters on its surface. Scientists think that the total mass of the asteroids was 30 to 60 times larger than the meteorite that killed off the dinosaurs when it hit Earth 65 MYA.

The heavily crater-marked far side of the moon always faces away from Earth.

Lunar "seas"

Huge basins dug out by asteroid strikes are flooded with lava from the moon's interior. Early astronomers mistook these areas for oceans and called them *maria*, Latin for "seas." Volcanic eruptions continue for a further 2 billion years, but they become less frequent.

c.3.8–3 BYA

c.800 MYA

Two hours after impact

A shower of hot material from the impact is propelled into space. This debris includes fragments from both Theia and Earth's crust and mantle.

c.4.45 BYA

Ring of debris

The debris from the impact arranges itself into a ring and starts orbiting Earth. This ring is thought to have included both vaporized and molten rock.

The pull of Earth's gravity kept the debris in orbit.

c.4.45 BYA

Clumped debris

Over millions of years, the debris in the ring is pulled together by gravity to form a huge mass of molten material—the moon is formed. Over the next 150 to 200 million years, the moon cools and a crust forms over its surface.

The material in the ring gradually combined into a mass that became the moon.

c.4.425 BYA

Moon rocks

Rocks from the moon sometimes land on Earth as meteorites. Others have been brought back by uncrewed exploratory spacecraft or astronauts on lunar missions. The rocks give scientists a lot of information about how the moon was formed. Harrison Schmitt, pictured here, is the only geologist to have walked on the moon.

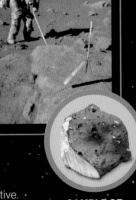

SAMPLE OF MOON ROCK

Still active

The moon is far from inactive. It experiences moonquakes (lunar earthquakes) and faulting, in which the huge blocks of rock forming the crust shift positions.

Present day

Mare Frigoris

Archimedes

Mare Serenitatis

Aristarchus

Eratosthenes

Mare Crisium

Copernicus

Mare Tranquillitatis

Mare Fecunditatis

Ptolemaeus

Mare Nectaris

Mare Nubium

Mare Humorum

When the sun is directly behind the moon, we cannot see the moon.

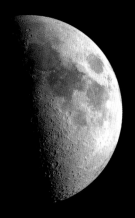

New moon   **Waxing crescent**   **First quarter**   **Waxing gibbous**

Phases of the moon

Lit by sunlight, our moon is the brightest natural object in the night sky. As it orbits Earth every 29.5 days, the moon appears to change shape, caused by it being lit up at different angles by the sun. We call these changes in the moon's shape "phases." How the moon moves across the sky is different depending on whether you are looking at it from the northern or southern hemispheres, on either side of Earth's equator.

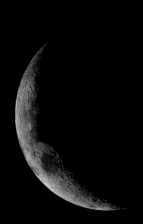

New moon   **Waxing crescent**   **First quarter**   **Waxing gibbous**

Northern hemisphere

In the northern parts of the world, the moon rises in the east, before moving south and eventually setting in the west. People in the northern hemisphere see the north pole of the moon at the top.

Lunar north pole

Full moon

Waning gibbous

Third quarter

Waning crescent

Southern hemisphere

Below the equator, the moon rises in the east, but then moves into the north sky and then sets in the west. People in the southern hemisphere see the south pole of the moon at the top.

Lunar south pole

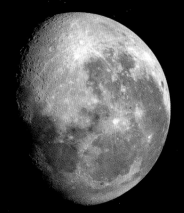

Full moon

Waning gibbous

Third quarter

Waning crescent

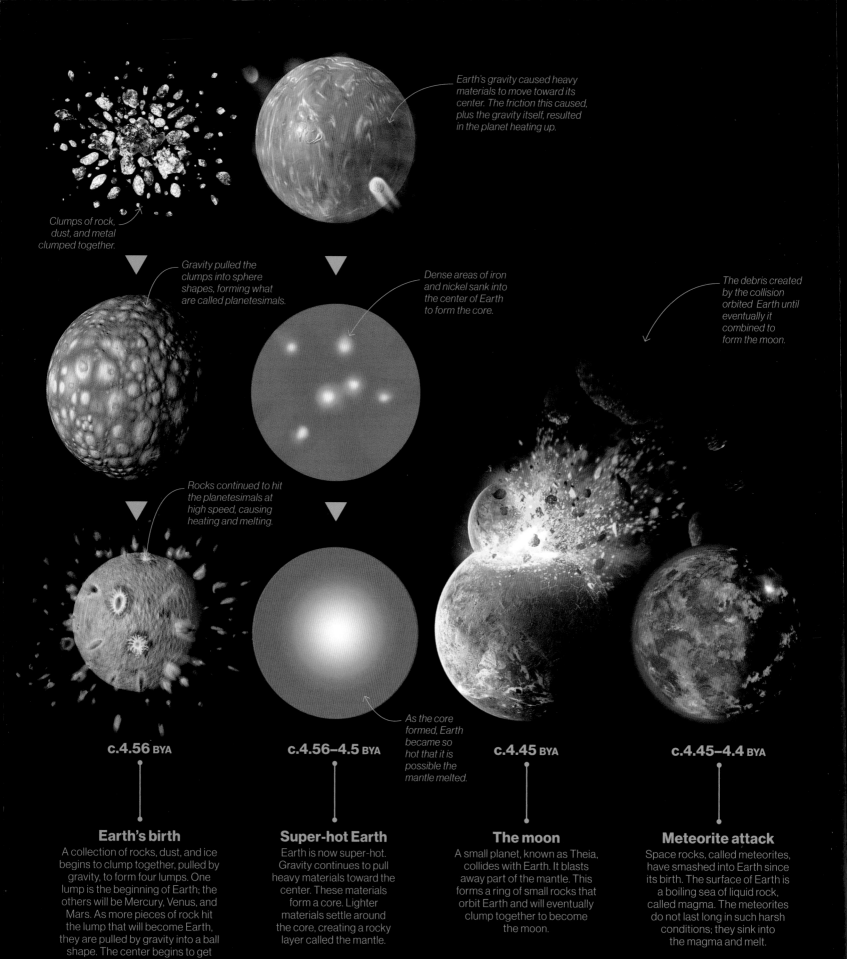

Clumps of rock, dust, and metal clumped together.

Earth's gravity caused heavy materials to move toward its center. The friction this caused, plus the gravity itself, resulted in the planet heating up.

Gravity pulled the clumps into sphere shapes, forming what are called planetesimals.

Dense areas of iron and nickel sank into the center of Earth to form the core.

The debris created by the collision orbited Earth until eventually it combined to form the moon.

Rocks continued to hit the planetesimals at high speed, causing heating and melting.

As the core formed, Earth became so hot that it is possible the mantle melted.

c.4.56 BYA

c.4.56–4.5 BYA

c.4.45 BYA

c.4.45–4.4 BYA

Earth's birth

A collection of rocks, dust, and ice begins to clump together, pulled by gravity, to form four lumps. One lump is the beginning of Earth; the others will be Mercury, Venus, and Mars. As more pieces of rock hit the lump that will become Earth, they are pulled by gravity into a ball shape. The center begins to get

Super-hot Earth

Earth is now super-hot. Gravity continues to pull heavy materials toward the center. These materials form a core. Lighter materials settle around the core, creating a rocky layer called the mantle.

The moon

A small planet, known as Theia, collides with Earth. It blasts away part of the mantle. This forms a ring of small rocks that orbit Earth and will eventually clump together to become the moon.

Meteorite attack

Space rocks, called meteorites, have smashed into Earth since its birth. The surface of Earth is a boiling sea of liquid rock, called magma. The meteorites do not last long in such harsh conditions; they sink into the magma and melt.

How Earth formed

Our planet may have just the right setup for plants and animals to thrive, but its past is a whole different story. From scalding oceans of liquid rock covering its surface to ice ages that caused it to freeze over completely, Earth has experienced some violent and extreme phases. It is difficult to know exactly what happened billions of years ago, so clues about Earth's formation come from studying meteorites and moon rocks. Though they reveal much, a lot remains to be discovered.

Inside Earth

If you could slice through Earth, like an apple, and look at the inside, you would find three main layers: the crust at the surface, the fluidlike mantle beneath, and the core at the center. As you travel through the layers, it gets hotter and hotter. It is thought that Earth's core is hotter than the surface of the sun!

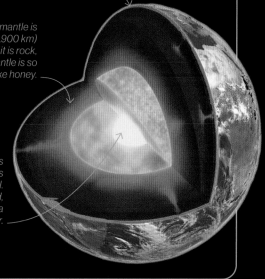

The crust, Earth's outer rocky layer, is up to 43.5 miles (70 km) thick. It is made of solid rock and minerals.

The rocky mantle is 1,800 miles (2,900 km) deep. Although it is rock, much of the mantle is so hot that it flows like honey.

Earth's core is made of the metals iron and nickel. The center is solid, surrounded by a liquid outer layer.

Earth's crust started to become land surfaces, and seas began to grow around them as rains fall.

Earth today is sometimes called the Pale Blue Dot, but at this time in its life it was a pale orange dot.

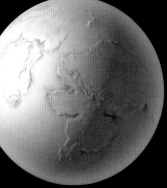

c.4.4–4 BYA

c.3.85–3.5 BYA

c.2.2 BYA

c.900–800 MYA

Cooling down

The bombardment of meteorites slows down and Earth starts to cool. Liquid magma on the surface becomes solid and forms the crust. For the first time, water—transported to Earth by meteorites—can exist on Earth in liquid form. Giant volcanoes send gases up into the air from the mantle, creating a blanket around Earth called the atmosphere.

The atmosphere

Sunlight interacting with gases on Earth leads to a pale, orange haze surrounding the planet. This atmosphere acts like an umbrella, shielding Earth from the sun's harsh rays, and cooling the planet down. But the gases beneath the atmosphere keep the planet from getting too cold, making conditions just right for life to evolve.

Snowball Earth

The first in a series of ice ages happens. During these events. all or part of Earth freezes. About 2.2 BYA the planet freezes over completely, creating what is sometimes called "snowball Earth." Scientists do not know why these ice ages occur; they might be triggered by a lack of greenhouse gases in the atmosphere or perhaps a slight change in Earth's orbit around the sun.

Rodinia

Oceans cover most of Earth. Exposed land combines into the first huge continent, known as Rodinia. Oxygen helps life to develop in the oceans. For the next 800 million years, the land will shift and life will flourish to form the home planet we know today.

Early Earth

In its early years, Earth is super-hot. As gravity pulls heavy materials into the core, the surface becomes so hot that rocks turn to liquid.

c.4.45–c.4.4 BYA

History of Earth's climate

The "climate" is the name we give to the weather conditions that are usual in a place over a long period of time. Over its history, Earth has had massive swings between hot and cold climates, which experts believe is partly to do with the gases in the atmosphere. Certain gases, called "greenhouse" gases, trap heat from the sun, heating Earth up like a greenhouse. When there are fewer greenhouse gases, temperatures are cool enough for a lot of ice to appear, and ice ages begin.

More ice ages

At least two more ice ages affect Earth during this time, but it is possible that the planet may not be entirely frozen over. Slow-moving rivers of ice, known as glaciers, flow as far away from the poles as the equator. Scientists know this by studying clues in rocks.

c.850–c.630 MYA

Plants affect climate

Earth is in a 30-million-year-long ice age, possibly caused by the first plants appearing. Plants take in carbon dioxide (CO_2), which is a greenhouse gas, from the atmosphere. This causes the temperature of Earth to drop.

c.460–c.430 MYA

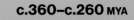

Mosses were one of the earliest land plants to appear on Earth.

c.360–c.260 MYA

As cold as ice

Temperatures drop dramatically, and the whole of Earth's surface is covered with ice. If you were to view it from space, Earth would look like a giant snowball.

c.2.2 BYA

Ice and snow covered Earth's surface.

Karoo ice age

Earth is in the grip of another ice age. This one is named after the Karoo region of South Africa, where rocks show historic evidence of ice. Again, the continued spread of land plants, which take in the greenhouse gas CO_2, may be the reason for the freeze, with giant ferns growing about 65.6 ft (20 m) tall.

Tropical Earth

Massive volcanic eruptions pump CO_2 into the air. This traps heat, and Earth warms up. Earth is on average about 18°F (10°C) hotter than today. Though there is no ice left anywhere on the planet, life—including the dinosaurs—flourishes at this time.

c.250–c.66 MYA

Carbon warming

Earth heats up once again. Billions of tons of CO_2 enter the atmosphere, warming the planet by as much as 14.4°F (8°C). This may be due to volcanic eruptions, a comet crashing into Earth, or sediments on the sea floor releasing carbon and another greenhouse gas, methane.

c.55 MYA

Global warming

Earth has been heating up since 1850, a trend we call "global warming" or "climate change." Scientists agree that this is caused by humans burning fossil fuels (gas, coal, and oil), which releases the greenhouse gas carbon dioxide (CO_2) into the air. Global warming is devastating for all life on Earth—it destroys animal and plant habitats, causes rising sea levels and flooding as it melts polar ice, and leads to unpredictable weather patterns.

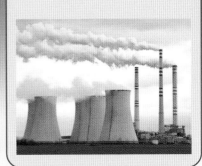

Earth's climate now

Today, global temperatures are rising and glaciers around the world are melting, causing sea levels to rise. Humans, burning fossil fuels, have contributed to the release of more greenhouse gases into the atmosphere. Average global temperatures on Earth have increased by 1.8°F (1°C) since 1880, with most warming happening since 1975.

Present day

c.66 MYA

A huge, floating platform of ice, called an ice shelf, forms where a glacier meets the ocean.

c.34–c.14 MYA

c.2.58 MYA–c.10,000 YA

The last ice age ended around 10,000 YA.

Asteroid attack

A 6-mile (10 km) wide asteroid smashes into Earth. It propels a giant cloud of dust into the atmosphere, blocking out the sun and causing temperatures to drop. The impact leads to the extinction of the dinosaurs and many other animals and plants.

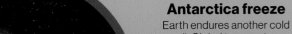

The latest ice age

It is thought that Earth slightly shifts its position, or tilts differently, during this time, causing the climate to go through very cold and warm periods. This causes the poles to either freeze or melt depending on where the sun's rays hit Earth.

Antarctica freeze

Earth endures another cold spell. Global temperatures drop by about 14.4°F (8°C). The land, on tectonic plates, shifts around and Antarctica repositions to where it is today. A cold ocean current starts to flow around it, allowing glaciers to grow. Antarctica has been frozen ever since.

Woolly mammoths roamed the land during the latest ice age.

Solstice

Toward the end of June, the North Pole is tilted as close to the sun as it gets. This marks the solstice—the longest day of the year for the northern hemisphere and the shortest for the southern hemisphere.

June

Last days of fall

Fall is coming to a close in the southern hemisphere. Hibernating animals prepare for their long winter sleep, as leaves begin to turn orange, red, or brown before falling from the trees.

May

Life returns

The northern hemisphere is starting to tilt more toward the sun, which means the days are becoming longer there. Spring is in full swing—plants and animals are coming to life after the long, dark months of winter.

April

Equinox

Around March 21, the sun is directly above the equator, which means that night and day are of equal length in both hemispheres—this is called an equinox.

The equator is an imaginary line between the northern and southern hemispheres.

March

June is the sunniest month for the northern hemisphere.

Earth spins in an counterclockwise direction.

July

Hot summer days

Even though the days are beginning to shorten, the temperatures are high in the northern hemisphere. The strong sunshine from spring and summer has warmed the land and oceans, and this heat keeps the northern hemisphere warm.

August

End of winter

The last month of winter has arrived in the southern hemisphere. The days are beginning to get longer and warmer but still not enough for hibernating animals and many plants to spring to life.

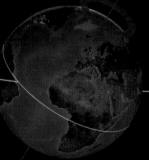

September

Equinox

The day and night are once again the same length, as the equinox arrives around September 23. In the southern hemisphere, the days will get longer, with the opposite happening in the northern hemisphere.

The seasons

As Earth spins in its counterclockwise orbit around the sun, it goes through a cycle of changes caused by the tilt of its axis (an imaginary line running from pole to pole on which Earth spins). There are four stages, or seasons, to this cycle: winter, spring, summer, and fall. Whichever hemisphere of Earth is tilting toward the sun receives more sunshine, and therefore warmer weather. This means that when it issummer in one hemisphere, it is winter in the other.

Shortest month

It is the shortest month of the year. In the southern hemisphere, February also marks the last month of summer, and the days are getting shorter.

February

New Year

At the start of the calendar year, the northern hemisphere is tilting away from the sun. The days are short and cold.

January

Southern hemisphere

Northern hemisphere

Earth's axis is tilted 23.5°—this means that there are times of the year when the North Pole is further away from to the sun than the South Pole. This is why there are seasons.

December

Summer heat

When the sun is high in the sky, its energy is more concentrated because it is spread over a smaller area. This is why it feels hotter at the equator, and during the summer. In summer, the sun also spends longer in the sky than in winter, so it has longer to heat the parts of Earth tilted toward it.

Sun's rays spread over a wider area do not feel as hot.

At the equator, sunlight is more concentrated on a smaller area, which feels hotter.

Solstice

The second solstice of the year happens in December. This time, it is the turn of the South Pole to be as close to the sun as it gets—bringing with it the longest day of the year in the southern hemisphere and the shortest day in the northern hemisphere.

November

Last days of spring

In the southern hemisphere, late spring blends into early summer, causing the air and the land to heat up dramatically. Animals are thriving, and some early crops are ready for harvest.

October

Fall

The days become shorter and the temperatures drop in the northern hemisphere, and plants and animals prepare for the winter. Tree leaves turn oranges, reds, and browns as they die and fall.

Lights in the sky

About 200 nights a year, streams of green and pink light, known as auroras, shimmer across the night skies above the northern and southern extremes of Earth. There is nothing quite like these auroras—natural events in which electrically charged particles released by the sun, known as the solar wind, interact with gases in Earth's upper atmosphere to create an amazing light show. The aurora borealis—also known as the "northern lights"—happens in the north, while the "southern lights," or aurora australis, happens in the south.

The science of Earth's structure and history is called geology. Geologists have discovered that our planet's natural history stretches back billions of years. To make it easier to understand this long history, they have created the geological timescale. This system divides up the past into chunks of time, with each chunk beginning and ending with a worldwide event, such as a mass extinction. The following timeline shows the geological timescale from the arrival of complex life to the Quarternary period—the time that we are in now.

Geological time

The geological timescale has different terms for spans of time. The longest is the supereon—there is only one, the Precambrian. Below the level of the supereon is the eon—there have been four of them so far in Earth's history. Eons are divided into eras. The current eon has three eras—Paleozoic, Mesozoic, and Cenozoic—which show the main stages in the evolution of life. Each era is further divided into periods.

- SUPEREON
- EON
- ERA
- PERIOD

MESOZOIC

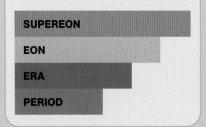

c.201.3 MYA–c.145 MYA
Jurassic
Forests are growing across much of the warm world, including at the poles. Giant dinosaurs devour these plant foods—and big predators appear, too. Pterosaurs become the first vertebrate animals to fly.

c.251.9 MYA–c.201.3 MYA
Triassic
This is a hot and dry time, and the first dinosaurs evolve. They are fast-running two-legged animals, balanced by their long tails. Small, hairy animals begin to appear—the ancestors of today's mammals.

c.298.9 MYA–c.251.9 MYA
Permian
Four-legged vertebrates, such as giant reptiles, now roam Earth. This period ends with the biggest mass extinction in Earth's history, where about 95 percent of ocean animals, and 70 percent of land animals, become extinct.

CENOZOIC

c.145 MYA–c.66 MYA
Cretaceous
Famous dinosaur species, such as Tyrannosaurus rex and Triceratops, dominate Earth. A meteor strike at the end of the period kills all the non-avian dinosaurs and pterosaurs, but some mammals and birds survive.

c.66 MYA–c.23 MYA
Paleogene
The world's climate begins to cool down, and warm-blooded mammals and birds now include the largest animals on Earth. Among them are the "thunder beasts" or brontotheres, which are distant ancestors of horses and rhinos.

c.23 MYA–c.2.58 MYA
Neogene
The climate is drying out at this time, and the jungles and forests are shrinking and being replaced with grasslands. The first humanlike animals, the distant ancestors of today's people, evolve to live in the African grasslands.

PALEOZOIC

c.4.6 BYA–c.541 MYA
Precambrian

The supereon includes the times when Earth is young and very hot, when it cools into a water planet, and when simple life forms such as bacteria develop. Complex life appears at the end of the Precambrian.

c.541 MYA–c.485.4 MYA
Cambrian

Animal life is evolving very fast in the oceans, a process called the "Cambrian explosion." The largest animals are creatures such as the hunter *Anomalocaris*, which is a relative of today's crustaceans.

c.485.4 MYA–c.443.8 MYA
Ordovician

Earth's climate starts very warm but cools to an ice age. The sea is home to all life, such as trilobites, sea scorpions, and long, straight shellfish called orthocones.

c.358.9 MYA–c.298.9 MYA
Carboniferous

The first treelike plants have evolved and formed vast forests. Plants have absorbed a lot of carbon dioxide from the atmosphere, making the planet colder. The oxygen levels have increased, which enables insects to grow huge, such as this bird-size dragonfly.

c.419.2 MYA–c.358.9 MYA
Devonian

Most of Earth's land is clustered close together, leaving a vast ocean called Panthalassa (which means "all sea") covering the rest of the planet. This is the age of fish, including *Dunkleosteus*, a predator the size of today's killer whale with a thick, armored skin.

c.443.8 MYA–c.419.2 MYA
Silurian

There are many shallow seas and islands at this time. The first plants and animals start to live on land along the shores and in swampy areas. These land animals are relatives of today's insects, arachnids, and millipedes.

c.2.58 MYA–Present day
Quaternary

This is the period Earth is in today. It has been marked by several cold periods known as ice ages, where large areas of the planet are covered in ice and home to woolly mammoths and rhinos able to survive the cold.

The Anthropocene

Humans have had a very big impact on planet Earth. Evidence of our activities, such as plastic pollution, can be seen in all parts of Earth—from the deepest seabeds to the polar ice caps. Geologists consider that modern humans have caused so much change to the climate and environment of the planet that we are in a new geological age called the Anthropocene—the "age of humans."

PLASTIC WASTE

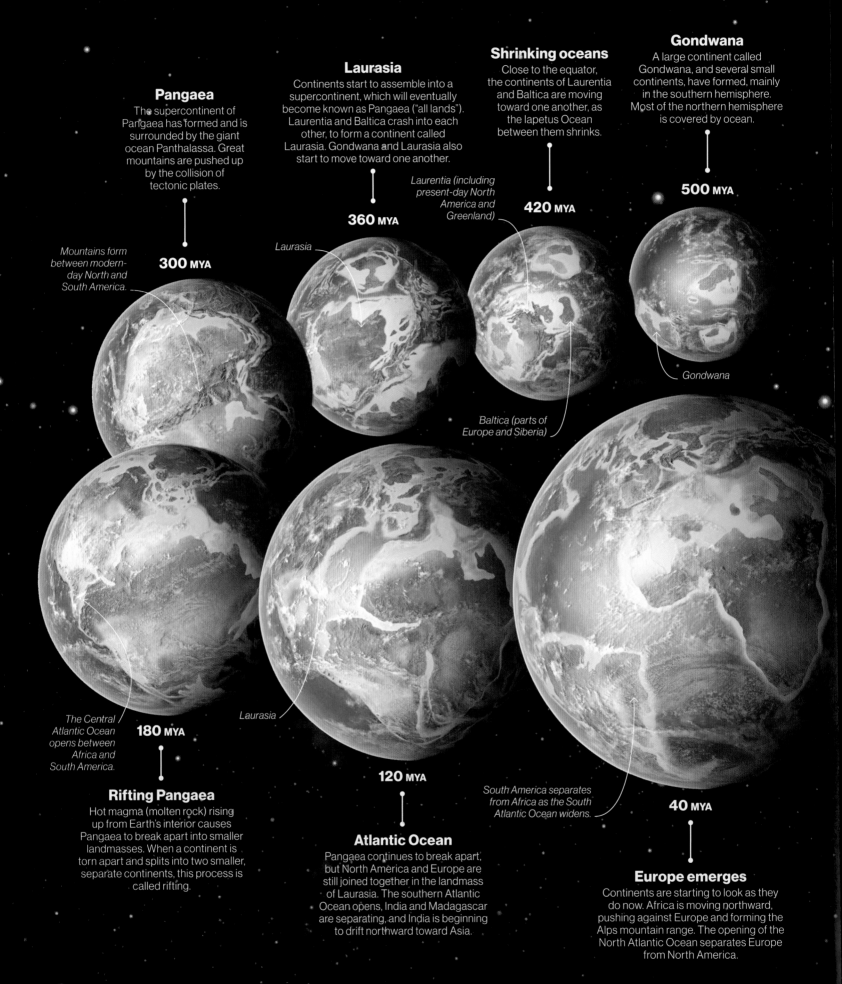

Gondwana
A large continent called Gondwana, and several small continents, have formed, mainly in the southern hemisphere. Most of the northern hemisphere is covered by ocean.

500 MYA

Shrinking oceans
Close to the equator, the continents of Laurentia and Baltica are moving toward one another, as the Iapetus Ocean between them shrinks.

Laurentia (including present-day North America and Greenland)

420 MYA

Laurasia
Continents start to assemble into a supercontinent, which will eventually become known as Pangaea ("all lands"). Laurentia and Baltica crash into each other, to form a continent called Laurasia. Gondwana and Laurasia also start to move toward one another.

360 MYA

Laurasia

Pangaea
The supercontinent of Pangaea has formed and is surrounded by the giant ocean Panthalassa. Great mountains are pushed up by the collision of tectonic plates.

300 MYA

Mountains form between modern-day North and South America.

Gondwana

Baltica (parts of Europe and Siberia)

Rifting Pangaea
Hot magma (molten rock) rising up from Earth's interior causes Pangaea to break apart into smaller landmasses. When a continent is torn apart and splits into two smaller, separate continents, this process is called rifting.

180 MYA

The Central Atlantic Ocean opens between Africa and South America.

Atlantic Ocean
Pangaea continues to break apart, but North America and Europe are still joined together in the landmass of Laurasia. The southern Atlantic Ocean opens, India and Madagascar are separating, and India is beginning to drift northward toward Asia.

120 MYA

Laurasia

South America separates from Africa as the South Atlantic Ocean widens.

Europe emerges
Continents are starting to look as they do now. Africa is moving northward, pushing against Europe and forming the Alps mountain range. The opening of the North Atlantic Ocean separates Europe from North America.

40 MYA

Continents on the move

Like a jigsaw puzzle, Earth's outer rocky layer, or lithosphere, is broken up into more than a dozen tectonic plates that float around on hot, partly molten rock. These plates sometimes collide or move apart from each other, moving at roughly the rate of a growing fingernail. Over millions of years, these tiny movements add up to huge changes in the appearance and positions of the continents.

The Arabian Peninsula joins Europe (above) to Africa (below).

Present day

Recognizable Earth

The seven continents are in the positions we are familiar with. Australia has shifted to its present location; India has collided with Eurasia, giving rise to the Himalayas. The Mediterranean Sea separates Africa from Eurasia. This is only temporary, though, as the continents are always moving.

Tectonic plates

Earth's outer rocky crust is divided into seven major and eight minor plates, which fit together like a giant ball-shaped jigsaw. The edges of the plates, called plate boundaries, are where most earthquakes and volcanic eruptions occur. These events happen because tectonic plates are constantly moving over Earth's surface and colliding with each other. This movement is driven by Earth's internal heat, which makes the hot, slightly soft, rock in Earth's mantle move gradually over millions of years.

THE NES CANYON BETWEEN THE EURASIAN AND AMERICAN TECTONIC PLATES

Pacific Ocean

On the other side of Earth from Africa is the Pacific Ocean. This vast ocean covers almost 30 percent of Earth's surface. It began to form 190 million years ago when lava welling up from deep inside the planet tore open a section of crust. The Pacific Ocean is now getting smaller by a tiny amount every year, as the tectonic plate it sits on is slowly being churned up by other plates.

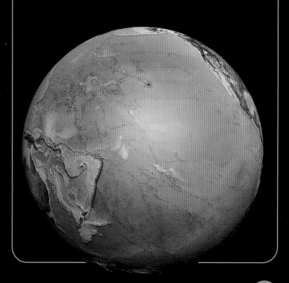

35

Marine fossils

Shells of ancient sea creatures, such as these ammonites, have been found high on the mountains in the Himalayas. These fossils are from the floor of the Tethys Ocean, which existed between India and Asia more than 70 million years ago.

c.180 MYA

India breaks away

The ancient supercontinent of Pangaea breaks up into separate tectonic plates, driven by the slow, churning movement of hot rock deep inside Earth's interior. Around 130 MYA, the plate carrying India tears away from what will eventually become Africa and begins to drift north.

Pangaea

Indian plate

c.70 MYA

India on the move

India moves toward Eurasia, Earth's largest continent at the time, at a speed of about 3.5 in (9 cm) a year. Between them is the ancient Tethys Ocean. The floor of this ancient ocean is part of the same tectonic plate as India but is weaker and thinner than the land.

Eurasia

Tethys Ocean

India drifted northward.

c.45 MYA

Shrinking ocean

The Tethys Ocean has been gradually shrinking for millions of years as the tectonic plates carrying India and Eurasia move together. As India approaches Eurasia, its northward drift slows down.

Eurasia

India drifted toward Eurasia and eventually crashed into it.

The Himalayas

Stretching 1,700 miles (2,700 km) across India, Nepal, Bhutan, Pakistan, and China are the Himalayas—the world's highest mountain range. Ten of the tallest mountains on Earth are located there, including the most famous peak of all, Mount Everest, which stands 29,028 ft (8,848 m) high. Mount Everest's peak was once on the ocean floor, but as Earth's tectonic plates moved and collided, the land was forced upward. Today, these towering mountains continue to grow even bigger.

c.40 MYA

Subduction

The floor of the Tethys Ocean is pushed deep under the Eurasian plate in a process called subduction. The subduction unleashes vast forces, causing earthquakes and volcanic eruptions. The Eurasian plate crumples and buckles under the strain, causing the land to rise and mountains to form.

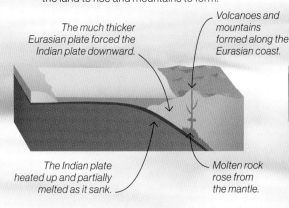

The much thicker Eurasian plate forced the Indian plate downward.

Volcanoes and mountains formed along the Eurasian coast.

The Indian plate heated up and partially melted as it sank.

Molten rock rose from the mantle.

c.30 MYA

Colliding continents

The landmass of India finally crashes into Eurasia, slowing the process of subduction. The Tethys Ocean disappears, but rock and sediment from the sea floor piles up in an "accretionary wedge" that will grow to form the Himalayas. As the continental crust thickens, molten rock can no longer reach the surface and volcanoes stop erupting.

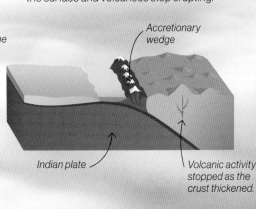

Accretionary wedge

Indian plate

Volcanic activity stopped as the crust thickened.

Present day

The Himalayas

The "accretionary wedge" piles up further to form the Himalayas. The Indian plate continues to push north at about 2 in (4 cm) a year, lifting the Himalayas by about 0.4 in (1 cm) a year. Today the Himalayas are the highest mountain range on Earth.

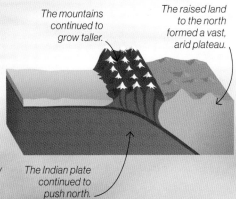

The mountains continued to grow taller.

The raised land to the north formed a vast, arid plateau.

The Indian plate continued to push north.

Dormant volcano

Krakatau, a 5.6-mile (9 km) long volcanic island rising 2,600 ft (800 m) above sea level, is a familiar landmark to thousands of ships and people living in Indonesia's Sunda Strait. For more than two centuries, the volcano has been quiet, and local people do not expect it to erupt again.

Before 1883 **May–August 1883** **August 26, 1883** **August 27, 1883** **August 27, 1883** **August 28–29, 1883**

Eruptions begin

Krakatau springs to life. Ash and steam spew from the volcano, rising 7 miles (11 km) into the air. Tremors are felt in the city of Batavia (present-day Jakarta), 100 miles (160 km) away. The tremors die down by the end of May, but smaller eruptions continue, spreading showers of pumice (solidified lava) across the ocean.

Gigantic explosion

The biggest eruption occurs around 10 a.m. The volcano blasts rocky fragments into the atmosphere with the explosive force of a 200-megaton bomb. A black cloud of debris and ash rises up to 50 miles (80 km) into the sky, blocking sunlight and plunging the region into darkness for three days.

Island destroyed

Quiet returns once more to the island. But when daylight breaks through the following day, Krakatau looks very different. Two-thirds of the island has collapsed under the sea and has been replaced by a gaping underwater hollow, about 980 ft (300 m) deep, called a caldera.

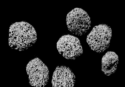

Krakatau rages

Volcanic activity intensifies. In the early afternoon, the first of a series of violent eruptions shakes the mountain. A column of black smoke and debris rises from the volcano into the sky, and the sea becomes violent. Eruptions, high waves, and storms continue into the night.

Tsunamis

The explosion causes part of the volcano to collapse, triggering a series of devastating tsunamis (tidal waves) up to 120 ft (37 m) high. The waves wipe out towns and villages on the distant islands of Java and Sumatra, killing more than 36,000 people.

Krakatau before 1883

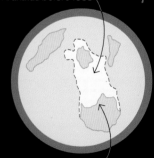

Krakatau after 1883

The story of Krakatau

Where the plates that make up Earth's crust crash together, they can create chains of highly explosive volcanoes. None is more famous than Krakatau (often known as Krakatoa), an Indonesian volcanic island that is part of the 24,900-mile (40,000 km) chain in the Pacific Ocean known as the Ring of Fire. In 1883, Krakatau erupted with a deadly force equivalent to several nuclear bombs. The blast, heard 1,900 miles (3,100 km) away in Australia, was one of the loudest noises in recorded history.

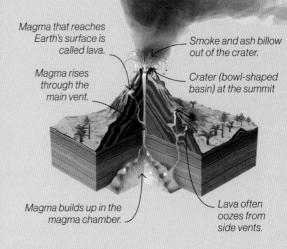

Magma that reaches Earth's surface is called lava.

Smoke and ash billow out of the crater.

Magma rises through the main vent.

Crater (bowl-shaped basin) at the summit

Magma builds up in the magma chamber.

Lava often oozes from side vents.

How volcanoes work

Volcanoes are openings in Earth's crust out of which magma (hot liquid rock) and gases escape. Volcanoes such as Krakatau have steep sides, made up of past flows of lava and ash. They erupt violently because the sticky lava blocks the volcano's openings, causing a buildup of pressure.

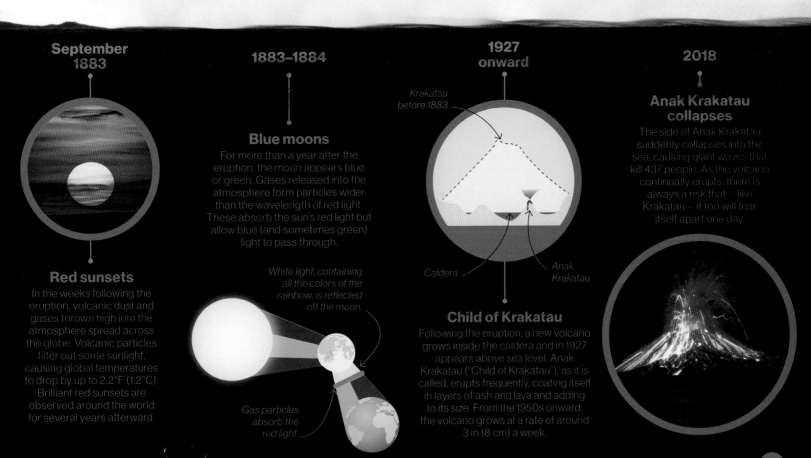

September 1883

Red sunsets
In the weeks following the eruption, volcanic dust and gases thrown high into the atmosphere spread across the globe. Volcanic particles filter out some sunlight, causing global temperatures to drop by up to 2.2°F (1.2°C). Brilliant red sunsets are observed around the world for several years afterward.

1883–1884

Blue moons
For more than a year after the eruption, the moon appears blue or green. Gases released into the atmosphere form particles wider than the wavelength of red light. These absorb the sun's red light but allow blue (and sometimes green) light to pass through.

White light, containing all the colors of the rainbow, is reflected off the moon.

Gas particles absorb the red light.

1927 onward

Krakatau before 1883

Caldera

Anak Krakatau

Child of Krakatau
Following the eruption, a new volcano grows inside the caldera and in 1927 appears above sea level. Anak Krakatau ("Child of Krakatau"), as it is called, erupts frequently, coating itself in layers of ash and lava and adding to its size. From the 1950s onward, the volcano grows at a rate of around 3 in (8 cm) a week.

2018

Anak Krakatau collapses
The side of Anak Krakatau suddenly collapses into the sea, causing giant waves that kill 437 people. As the volcano continually erupts, there is always a risk that—like Krakatau—it too will tear itself apart one day.

The Grand Canyon

For millions of years, the powerful Colorado River has carved its way through the landscape of the US, wearing away layers of sandstone, limestone, shale, and the remains of prehistoric animals and plants to form the Grand Canyon. Today, this awe-inspiring rock formation in Arizona stretches 277 miles (446 km) and in places reaches a depth of 1.1 miles (1.8 km).

c.1.7 BYA

Vishnu mountains

Long before there is life on land, the ancient Vishnu mountain range occupies the site of the Grand Canyon. It is taller than the Himalayas, but over millions of years the mountain range is eroded to stumps. These rocky remains will form the bottom layer of rock in the Grand Canyon.

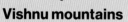

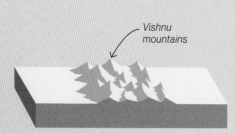

Vishnu mountains

c.1.25 BYA– c.230 MYA

Layers of rock

The ocean covers the remains of the Vishnu Mountain. Over hundreds of millions of years, the sea deposits layer after layer of sediment, forming alternating bands of sedimentary rock, including sandstone, limestone, and shale. The rock layers preserve fossils from the ancient sea.

Ammonite shells on the sea floor were fossilized in the rocks.

Layers of sedimentary rock

c.80– c.60 MYA

Rising land

The whole of western North America is pushed up by a collision between the tectonic plate forming the Pacific sea floor and the plate forming North America. A vast plateau (a high, flat area of land) called the Colorado Plateau forms, and the Rocky Mountains rise to its northeast.

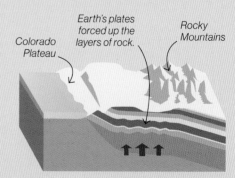

Earth's plates forced up the layers of rock.

Colorado Plateau

Rocky Mountains

Sedimentary rocks

About 80 percent of the rocks found on Earth are sedimentary. The Grand Canyon is made up of these types of rocks, which are formed in layers (strata) over millions of years. When water, ice, and wind deposit their minerals, they are compressed and become sedimentary rocks as more layers build up on top.

Sediments are deposited on the seabed.

Rock pieces are squashed together to form strata (layers).

c.6 MYA

A new river

The Colorado River forms as glaciers melt on the nearby Rocky Mountains. Because of its high starting point and steep course, the flowing water erodes the land with great power, wearing away the layers of soft sedimentary rock. At first it forms a small river valley.

The Colorado River flows quickly thanks to its steep slope, speeding up the process of erosion.

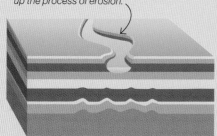

Present day

Growing canyon

The Colorado River has now cut all the way down to the remains of the Vishnu mountains, forming a canyon. The canyon is still growing, its walls widening as rain and winter ice eat away at them. The alternating layers of hard and soft rock erode at different rates, which is why the Grand Canyon has a stepped appearance.

Steps formed as layers eroded at different rates.

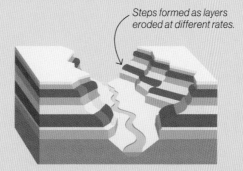

Future

Drying up

Climate change, agriculture, and dams have weakened the Colorado River. If the trend continues, it might dry up at some time in the future. If that happens, the main force of erosion would come to a halt and the Canyon would stop growing.

As Earth's temperature rises, the Colorado River dries up.

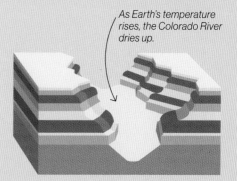

The Giant's Causeway

In County Antrim in Northern Ireland, about 40,000 steplike rock columns dot 4 miles (6 km) of the coastline—a formation known as the Giant's Causeway. According to Irish legend, this unusual place was built by a giant called Finn McCool, but it is actually the result of a dramatic lava eruption tens of millions of years ago. The varied-height columns are made of basalt, a type of rock that forms when volcanic lava cools. Once solidified, the rock was gradually worn down into the stepping stones that jut out into the sea today.

c.85 MYA

Moving plates

The moving of tectonic plates away from each other causes the breakup of the ancient continent of Laurentia. This causes Greenland to separate from Europe and a new ocean, the Atlantic, to open between them.

c.60 MYA

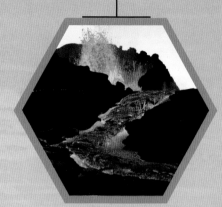

Lava flows

As Earth's crust (the planet's rocky top layer) is stretched and thinned, magma (molten rock) rises up from below and reaches the surface. In the area around Northern Ireland, huge volcanoes and long cracks in the crust cause vast flows of lava over huge distances.

Irish legend

The name "the Giant's Causeway" comes from Irish mythology. Legend has it that the rock columns formed one end of a causeway (bridge) between Ireland and Scotland. Two enormous giants, Finn McCool and Benandonner, were due to fight. To reach his enemy across the Irish Sea in Scotland, McCool built the causeway, using rocks he found along the coastline. The other end of the mythical causeway is thought to be at the island of Staffa, where similar rocks can be found.

FINGAL'S CAVE ON STAFFA, SCOTLAND

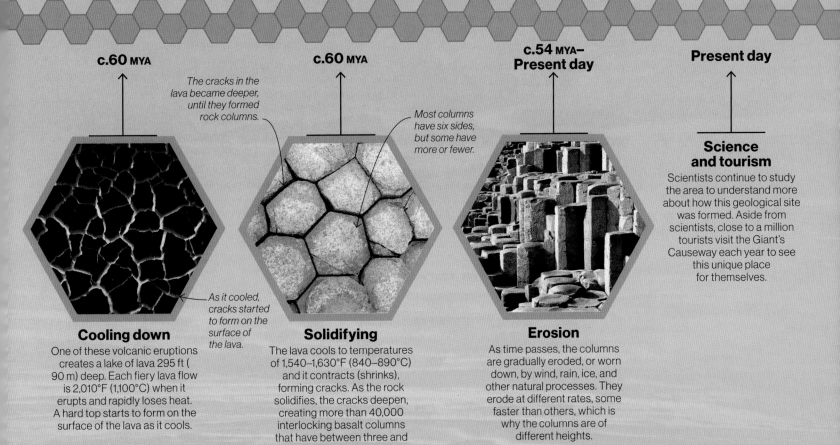

c.60 MYA

The cracks in the lava became deeper, until they formed rock columns.

c.60 MYA

Most columns have six sides, but some have more or fewer.

c.54 MYA– Present day

Present day

Science and tourism

Scientists continue to study the area to understand more about how this geological site was formed. Aside from scientists, close to a million tourists visit the Giant's Causeway each year to see this unique place for themselves.

Cooling down

As it cooled, cracks started to form on the surface of the lava.

One of these volcanic eruptions creates a lake of lava 295 ft (90 m) deep. Each fiery lava flow is 2,010°F (1,100°C) when it erupts and rapidly loses heat. A hard top starts to form on the surface of the lava as it cools.

Solidifying

The lava cools to temperatures of 1,540–1,630°F (840–890°C) and it contracts (shrinks), forming cracks. As the rock solidifies, the cracks deepen, creating more than 40,000 interlocking basalt columns that have between three and seven sides.

Erosion

As time passes, the columns are gradually eroded, or worn down, by wind, rain, ice, and other natural processes. They erode at different rates, some faster than others, which is why the columns are of different heights.

Oldest rocks

The ancient volcanic deposits of the Nuvvuagittuq Greenstone Belt in Hudson Bay, Canada, are some of the oldest rocks on Earth. Their exact age is still being debated, but the rocks record a part of Earth's earliest crust (hard outer layer). This crust is thought to have formed when Earth cooled enough to allow rock to harden at the surface.

c.4.4 BYA

Tiny crystals

Earth's oldest known material is a mineral called zircon, found in the Jack Hills of Western Australia. The oldest crystals appear only a few hundred million years after Earth formed 4.6 billion years ago.

One of about 200,000 zircon crystals from the Jack Hills.

c.4.375 BYA

Rocky wonders

Have you ever seen hot lava spewing out of an erupting volcano, or stood at the boundary between two tectonic plates? Do you know where to find exceptionally preserved fossils, or where billion-year-old rocks and grains are hidden? Here, we explore some of the most spectacular and famous geological formations around the world. From Earth's most ancient rocks to hot springs and volcanoes, geological wonders are found across the world.

Rock recycling

Earth endlessly recycles its rocks. Igneous rocks, such as basalt, form when molten magma or lava cools. These may erode over time to form soft sedimentary rocks, such as limestone and sandstone. Alternatively, they may turn into metamorphic rocks if put under intense heat and pressure underground. If the conditions change, these metamorphic rocks may later melt to form igneous rocks again.

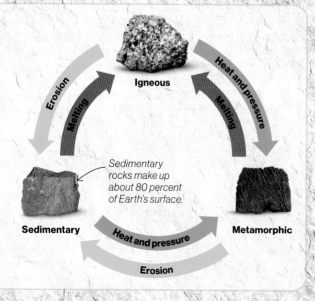

Erosion · Melting · Heat and pressure · Melting

Igneous

Sedimentary rocks make up about 80 percent of Earth's surface.

Sedimentary · Heat and pressure · Erosion · **Metamorphic**

Supervolcano

About 2.1 million years ago, the first major eruption of the Yellowstone supervolcano in Wyoming blankets western North America in ash. The volcano is still active today and sits within Yellowstone National Park, which is home to geological features such as pools of bubbling hot mud, geysers, and hot springs. The Grand Prismatic Spring, shown here, gets its amazing colors from tiny bacteria in the mineral-rich water.

c.2.1 MYA

Ancient mountain

At 9,220 ft (2,810 m), Mount Roraima is the highest peak in South America's Pakaraima mountains. It stands along the border of Brazil, Guyana, and Venezuela and is known as a tabletop mountain, or *tepui*, because of its flat summit. Its pinkish, quartz-rich sandstone is one of the oldest geological formations on Earth.

Quartz crystals

c.2 BYA

Stone forests

In south China's provinces of Guizhou, Guangxi, Yunnan, and Chongqing, giant towers of limestone that rise high above the surrounding plains start to form at this time. This karst landscape of limestone is dissolved away by slightly acidic rainwater to form extensive cave systems, gorges, and steep cone-shaped hills.

c.270 MYA

Plate boundary

Plates are massive slabs of rock that float around on Earth's surface, occasionally colliding or breaking apart. Iceland sits at the boundary between two tectonic plates, the North American plate and the Eurasian plate, and it forms around this time. It is one of the only places in the world where a plate boundary, the Mid-Atlantic Ridge, is visible on Earth's surface.

c.33 MYA

Ancient fossils

The Solnhofen Limestone in Bavaria, Germany, is famous for its exceptionally preserved fossils. When the waters of the ancient lagoons here dry up, their muddy sediments turn into limestone. The remains of hundreds of different animal species that sank to the bottom are preserved by the limestone. The fossils include jellyfish, dragonflies, and a dinosaur with feathers called *Archaeopteryx*, pictured here.

c.155 MYA

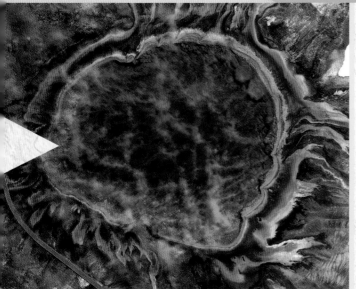

Volcanic islands

The Hawaiian islands, in the Pacific Ocean, are one of the best places on Earth to see the forces of the planet in action. Here, streams of hot magma from deep beneath Earth's surface burst out of volcanoes as eruptions every day. Over time, the magma cools down and hardens, forming a dark, volcanic rock called basalt.

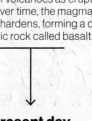

Present day

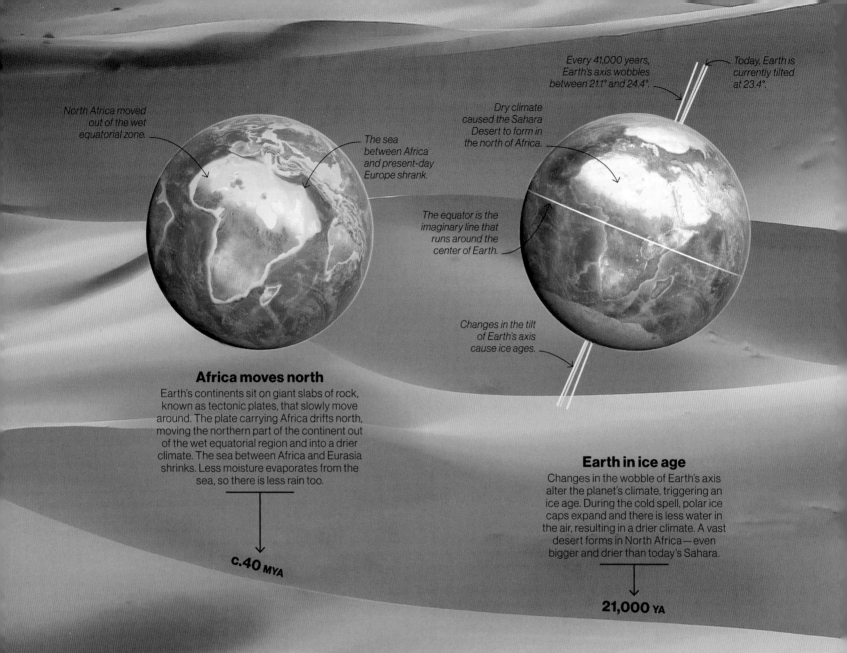

North Africa moved out of the wet equatorial zone.

The sea between Africa and present-day Europe shrank.

Every 41,000 years, Earth's axis wobbles between 21.1° and 24.4°.

Today, Earth is currently tilted at 23.4°.

Dry climate caused the Sahara Desert to form in the north of Africa.

The equator is the imaginary line that runs around the center of Earth.

Changes in the tilt of Earth's axis cause ice ages.

Africa moves north

Earth's continents sit on giant slabs of rock, known as tectonic plates, that slowly move around. The plate carrying Africa drifts north, moving the northern part of the continent out of the wet equatorial region and into a drier climate. The sea between Africa and Eurasia shrinks. Less moisture evaporates from the sea, so there is less rain too.

c.40 MYA

Earth in ice age

Changes in the wobble of Earth's axis alter the planet's climate, triggering an ice age. During the cold spell, polar ice caps expand and there is less water in the air, resulting in a drier climate. A vast desert forms in North Africa—even bigger and drier than today's Sahara.

21,000 YA

The Sahara Desert

A vast landscape of golden sand, where only the toughest plant and animal species survive, the Sahara Desert in North Africa is the largest hot desert on Earth. Deserts are Earth's driest places, so it is surprising to imagine that the area now covered by the Sahara Desert was once filled with greenery. Today the desert is slowly expanding in a process known as desertification.

The Great Green Wall

In order to prevent the Sahara Desert from expanding south, people have been planting a 4,970-mile (8,000 km) long wall of trees across the Sahel region as part of an initiative called the Great Green Wall. By helping to regenerate nonfertile land, this movement is fighting the effects of desertification, and creates jobs.

People planting trees to slow down desertification

Savannas and forests covered northern Africa.

Tropical rainforests covered central Africa.

Scrublands filled western and eastern Africa.

Southern Africa was dry and parts were covered in deserts.

Key

- Tropical rainforest
- Scrubland
- Savanna
- Semidesert
- Extreme desert

The area of extreme desert is too dry for most animals and plants.

Areas of semidesert are dry but wetter than the extreme desert.

In northern Africa, winds blow sand to the southwest.

Green Sahara

The most recent ice age ends, causing warmer and wetter weather across the world. A monsoon season develops in Africa, bringing heavy rain to the Sahara in summer. The desert turns green with vegetation. There are rivers, lakes, grasslands, and forests where giraffes, hippos, and rhinos roam. Human civilization begins to flourish.

11,000–5,000 YA

Drying up

Summers in the northern hemisphere turn slightly cooler due to a change in Earth's orbit (the northern summer no longer coincides with the point when Earth is closest to the sun). As a result, the African monsoon weakens and the Sahara dries out. Lakes and rivers disappear, and people abandon the desert.

5,000–2,500 YA

Winds from southern Africa blow sand to the northwest.

The Sahara is expanding into areas that were once semidesert.

Desert expansion

Today, the Sahara Desert is expanding north and south in a process called desertification. The main causes are deforestation and overuse of agricultural land—when vegetation is removed, the land dries out and the wind blows the soil away. Global warming may be making the problem worse.

Present day

Desert oasis

An oasis is a wet area in a desert where lush vegetation grows. Oases are important sources of food and water to animals and people. In the Sahara, they occur where ancient water trapped underground is close to the surface.

How the Amazon River Basin formed

The Amazon River in South America is the largest river in the world—it spans 30 miles (48 km) at points during the rainy season. It winds its way eastward through the Amazon rainforest for 4,101 miles (6,600 km) to reach the Atlantic Ocean. The area over which it moves, known as a drainage basin, took millions of years to form.

c.40– c.20 MYA

Huge sea forms
Rivers in the northwestern part of the continent flow eastward into an inland sea. This sea then empties into the Caribbean Sea in the north and the Pacific Ocean in the west.

The inland sea emptied into the Caribbean Sea.

Caribbean Sea

Rivers flowed into the inland sea.

c.12 MYA

The Andes rise
A tectonic plate is sinking beneath the South American plate and pushing against it. The pushing causes the Andes mountains to rise higher. They block the rivers flowing off the west coast of South America, causing the inland sea to fill up, widen, and become a swampy lake.

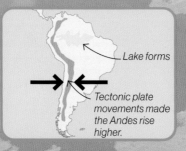

Lake forms

Tectonic plate movements made the Andes rise higher.

c.8– c.7 MYA

Sea and sediment
A land barrier on the east side of the swampy lake causes rainwater and sediment (rock, sand, and mud) from the north and south to flow eastward in a series of small rivers. These form the beginning of the Amazon Basin.

Land barrier

Early Amazon basin

Oxbow lakes

When a bend in a river is cut off from the main river, it becomes an oxbow lake. The lake starts out as a meander, and then the meander gets cut off as the river finds a shorter course. This happens when erosion and the buildup of sediments work on different parts of the river.

Erosion occurs on the outside of bends, and sediment piles up on the inside.

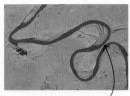

As the meander increases, the land in the middle narrows.

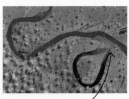

The bend is cut off and forms an oxbow lake.

c.4– c.3 MYA

Draining into the Atlantic

In the west, the amount of sediment in the lake grows and raises the level of the water. In the east, the origins of the east-flowing rivers eventually erode the natural barriers between the two sides. Both processes result in the two bodies of water joining up, and water can now flow from the Andes all the way to the Atlantic Ocean.

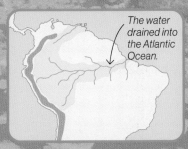

The water drained into the Atlantic Ocean.

c.25,000– c.15,000 YA

Ice ages

Parts of the region freeze during ice ages. The inland swampy lake dries up, leaving behind winding streams and lakes. The Amazon River Basin takes on its present shape.

North America

Amazon River Basin

South America

Present day

The river today

These days, the Amazon River Basin covers more than 35 percent of the area of South America and lies across nine countries. It starts in the Andes and winds its way across the continent, with many smaller rivers flowing into it, before it empties into the Atlantic Ocean. A dense tropical rainforest has sprung up around it.

The river's course today

Dragon Caves

Caves can often look otherworldly, but they are usually the result of a few simple processes happening over a long period of time. The Coves del Drac ("Dragon Caves" in English) on the coastline of Majorca, Spain, were formed by coastal erosion, changing sea levels, and water dissolving limestone. As water drops on the cave roof evaporated, they left behind minerals. Over time, these minerals formed long deposits that hang from the roof (known as stalactites), or drop down and pile up on the floor (stalagmites).

The Victoria Falls

On the border between Zimbabwe and Zambia, the Victoria Falls (*Mosai-oa-Tunya*—"the smoke that thunders" in the local Tsonga language) make up the world's largest curtain of falling water, up to 5,600 ft (1.7 km) long when the Zambezi River is in full flood. The falls have formed over millions of years, created by a sequence of powerful geological processes that continue today.

c.180 MYA

Basalt forms

The giant continent Gondwana starts to break apart. Volcanoes erupt, spewing out molten lava, which cools and solidifies into a hard rock called basalt. In the Victoria Falls area, these basalt layers are 980 ft (300 m) thick.

c.110 MYA

Fissures form

Gondwana continues to break apart, causing further eruptions. As the basalt cools down, huge cracks called fissures open up in the rock and are gradually filled with soft rock, sand, and mud (sediment). These cracks later become a sequence of waterfalls.

Fissures (cracks) formed in the basalt.

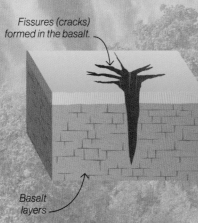

Basalt layers

c.15 MYA

Giant lake

Uplift (rise) in the landscape blocks the course of the upper Zambezi River as it makes its way to the ocean. This causes a giant inland lake to form in what is now central Botswana.

Giant lake

Upper Zambezi

Lower Zambezi River

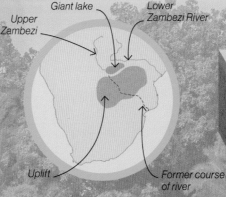

Uplift

Former course of river

c.5 MYA

The first falls

Water builds up in the lake and spills out, linking the upper Zambezi and lower Zambezi River and flowing across the basalt. The water erodes (wears away) the soft sediments inside the basalt fissures, creating the first Victoria Falls, around 80 miles (130 km) from the current falls.

The basalt was eroded block by block.

The life cycle of waterfalls

Waterfalls form through a process of erosion (wearing away of rock) when a river flows over a band of hard rock that has softer rock lying underneath. The rushing water erodes the soft rock faster than the hard rock, slowly creating an overhanging ledge. Water drops down over the ledge, continuously eroding the rocks over which it flows. Eventually even the hard ledge collapses, moving the waterfall upstream.

Harder rock

Softer rock

Riverbed steepens
As the water erodes the softer rock beneath the hard rock, the riverbed steepens. Stones pushed along by the flow help erode the rock further.

Overhanging ledge

Plunge pool

Overhang formed
The soft rock disintegrates, creating a ledge of hard rock above. The falling water creates a depression in the rock below called a plunge pool.

The hard rock in the ledge wears away.

Chunks of rock break off, eroding the plunge pool further.

Overhang collapses
With nothing to support it, eventually the ledge collapses into the plunge pool. Gradually, the position of the waterfall begins to move upstream.

| c.5 MYA– c.250,000 YA | c.100,000 YA– Present day | 2019 | 10,000 years' time |

The falls retreat
The waterfall gouges out a gorge (steep valley) in the basalt, and the position of the falls slowly moves upstream. As the falls retreat, they eventually meet another fissure and form a new gorge, over which a wide curtain of water tumbles—a new Victoria Falls. Around 500,000–250,000 YA the falls are 9 miles (15 km) from their current position.

Zigzagging gorges
Water continues to wear away the rock at a rate of 40–80 mm (1.5–3 in) per year, leaving a series of narrow, zigzagging gorges. Each of these gorges, visible from today's falls, would once have contained a massive waterfall. The falls are now in their eighth position.

The falls run dry
The rise in global temperatures causes the worst drought in the region for a century. The Zambezi is reduced to a trickle and for the first time the falls run dry. Scientists fear these seasonal droughts, caused by climate change, will become more frequent.

The next falls
If the falls continue to retreat at their current rate, in around 10,000 years the river will excavate the full length of a new gorge. The next line of falls is already visible along a fault line (rock fracture) called the Devil's Cataract.

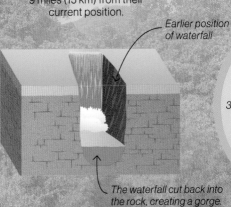

Earlier position of waterfall

The waterfall cut back into the rock, creating a gorge.

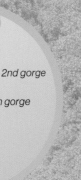

Current Victoria Falls

2nd gorge

3rd gorge

4th gorge

5th gorge

THE DEVIL'S CATARACT

Origin of life

There is no agreement on our earliest evidence of life on Earth. The current earliest possibility are tiny grains of iron-rich minerals, possibly from 4.28 BYA, found in Canadian rocks. They look very similar to structures produced by undersea microbes today.

Complex cells

The first cell to house a nucleus, known as a eukaryote, develops. All complex organisms, including fungi, animals, and plants, are eukaryotes. The oldest known eukaryote fossils are millimeter-size *Diskagma* fossils—a possible fungus—which lived on land in South Africa.

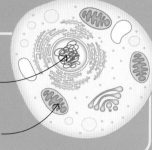

The nucleus sits at the center of the cell.

Mitochondria generate energy for the cell.

c.2.2 BYA

c.2.1 BYA

Chloroplasts

The first chloroplasts appear in algae. Plants use chloroplasts to convert sunlight into energy in a process known as photosynthesis.

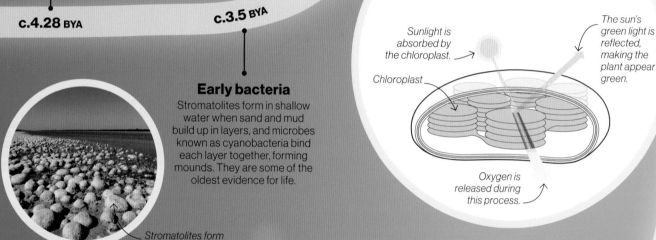

Sunlight is absorbed by the chloroplast.

The sun's green light is reflected, making the plant appear green.

Chloroplast

Oxygen is released during this process.

c.4.28 BYA

c.3.5 BYA

Early bacteria

Stromatolites form in shallow water when sand and mud build up in layers, and microbes known as cyanobacteria bind each layer together, forming mounds. They are some of the oldest evidence for life.

Stromatolites form in salty lagoons.

Bacteria invade land

Microbes from Earth's oceans start migrating on to land. They produce oxygen, a mineral that releases sulfur, and a substance known as molybdenum into the oceans. This increase in sulfur boosts the spread of life in the oceans.

c.1.2 BYA

Evolution of life

Over 4 billion years, life has evolved from microbes (bacteria) in the oceans to occupy most of Earth's surface. Central to life is DNA (deoxyribonucleic acid), a molecule that stores a living organism's genetic information, and allows organisms to evolve (change) over generations. This process of evolution has produced an enormous diversity of organisms and transformed Earth's climate, soils, and landscapes.

Multicellular life

Red algae are the oldest known multicellular organisms to convert sunlight into energy through photosynthesis and also the oldest known organisms to reproduce sexually. Fossil evidence of red algae was discovered in marine rocks in the Canadian Arctic.

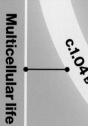

c.1.04 BYA

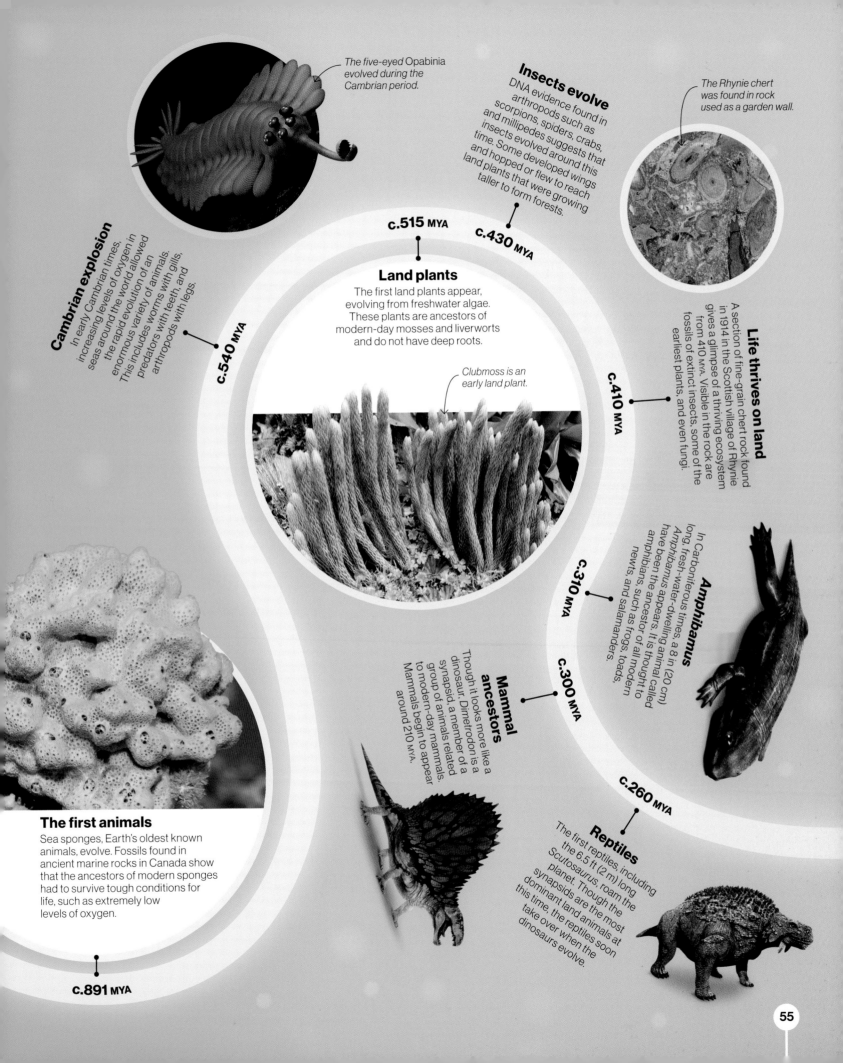

The five-eyed Opabinia evolved during the Cambrian period.

Insects evolve
DNA evidence found in arthropods such as scorpions, spiders, crabs, and millipedes suggests that insects evolved around this time. Some developed wings and hopped or flew to reach land plants that were growing taller to form forests.

The Rhynie chert was found in rock used as a garden wall.

c.515 MYA

c.430 MYA

Cambrian explosion
In early Cambrian times, increasing levels of oxygen in seas around the world allowed the rapid evolution of an enormous variety of animals. This includes worms with gills, predators with teeth, and arthropods with legs.

Land plants
The first land plants appear, evolving from freshwater algae. These plants are ancestors of modern-day mosses and liverworts and do not have deep roots.

Clubmoss is an early land plant.

c.540 MYA

c.410 MYA

Life thrives on land
A section of fine-grain chert rock found in 1914 in the Scottish village of Rhynie gives a glimpse of a thriving ecosystem from 410 MYA. Visible in the rock are fossils of extinct insects, some of the earliest plants, and even fungi.

c.310 MYA

Amphibamus
In Carboniferous times, a 8 in (20 cm) long, fresh-water-dwelling animal called Amphibamus appears. It is thought to have been the ancestor of all modern amphibians, such as frogs, toads, newts, and salamanders.

c.300 MYA

Mammal ancestors
Though it looks more like a dinosaur, Dimetrodon is a synapsid, a member of a group of animals related to modern-day mammals. Mammals begin to appear around 210 MYA.

The first animals
Sea sponges, Earth's oldest known animals, evolve. Fossils found in ancient marine rocks in Canada show that the ancestors of modern sponges had to survive tough conditions for life, such as extremely low levels of oxygen.

c.260 MYA

Reptiles
The first reptiles, including the 6.5 ft (2 m) long Scutosaurus, roam the planet. Though the synapsids are the most dominant land animals at this time, the reptiles soon take over when the dinosaurs evolve.

c.891 MYA

PLANTS AND FUNGI

From the tiniest fungal spore to the tallest tree, plants and fungi come in all shapes and sizes, and are crucial to life on Earth. Without them, Earth would be a barren rocky planet, just like its neighbors in the solar system. The secret to most plants' success is photosynthesis—the ability to transform light from the sun into food, which they use to grow. Plants use clever and complex strategies to survive. Many rely on the wind and animals to spread far and wide, while others have evolved to tough it out in deserts and other extreme environments.

Single-celled ancestor

Green algae, the ancestors of plants, evolve in water. They are microscopic single cells and can make their own food by using sunlight. No fossils of green algae from this time have yet been found.

Branching out

Green algae begin to form simple strings made of many cells. The oldest known fossil of a multicellular alga is *Proterocladus antiquus*, a tiny branched seaweed that grew to about 0.1 in (3 mm) long.

Moving on to land

True plants appear. Their bodies are more complex than multicellular algae, and they can grow on land. Early plants, such as liverworts, mosses, and hornworts, are still alive today.

Ancient survivors, such as liverworts, give us clues about early plants.

c.1.5 BYA

c.1 BYA

c.500 MYA

Living fossil

The first ginkgo trees appear. Only one species of these gymnosperms survives today. Also known as the maidenhair tree, it's often described as a "living fossil" as it appears to be identical to ginkgos from millions of years ago.

Ginkgo leaves turn bright yellow in fall.

The story of plants

Plants evolved from microscopic algae (simple aquatic organisms) half a billion years ago. Many different types of plants have appeared over their long history, and they have transformed our planet, providing food and oxygen for animals and cooling the climate by removing carbon dioxide from the air. Today, more than 400,000 known plant species cover Earth. Sadly, many species are at serious risk of extinction because of habitat loss and climate change.

c.190 MYA

Unusual flower

The aquatic angiosperm *Archaefructus* has its male and female reproductive organs on its stems rather than in flowers with petals. Beautifully preserved fossils of the entire plant have since been discovered by scientists.

Photosynthesis

Plants make their own food in their leaves by a process called photosynthesis. They use sunlight energy to change the gas carbon dioxide from the air and water from the soil into sugars, which can fuel their growth. A waste product of photosynthesis is the gas oxygen, which animals, including humans, need to breathe.

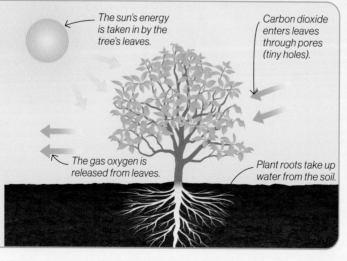

The sun's energy is taken in by the tree's leaves.

Carbon dioxide enters leaves through pores (tiny holes).

The gas oxygen is released from leaves.

Plant roots take up water from the soil.

Archaefructus flowers grew above the plant's leaves to increase the chance of pollination.

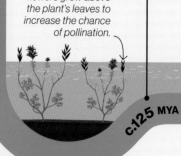

c.125 MYA

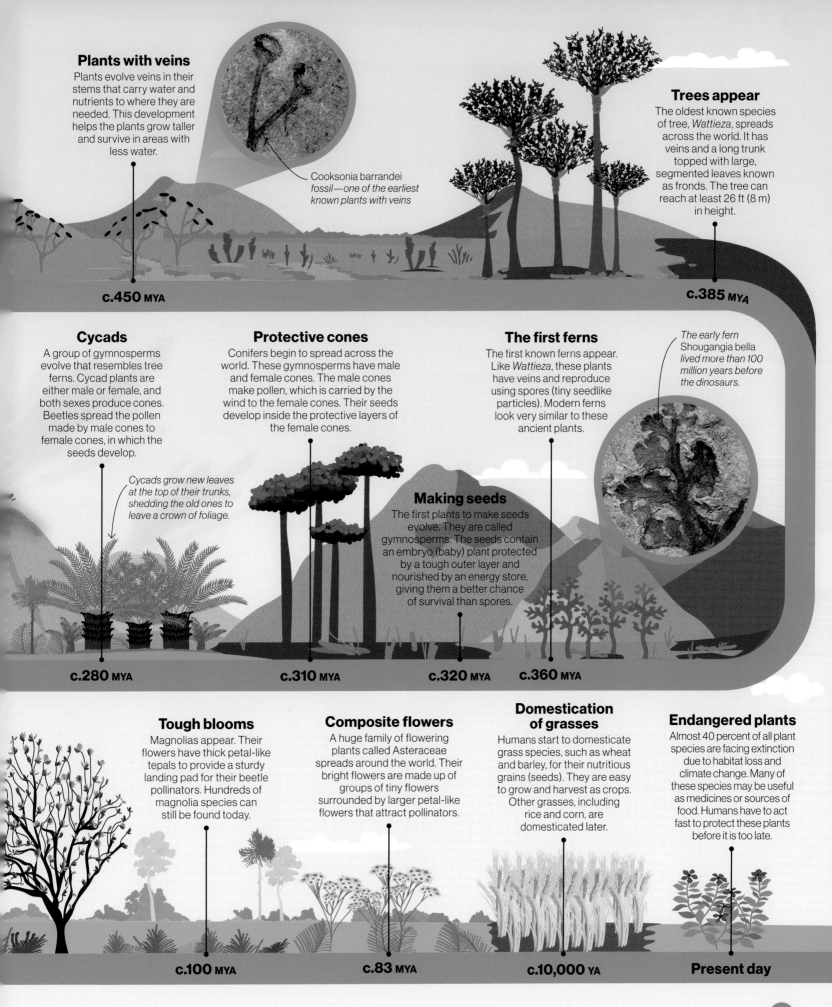

Plants with veins

Plants evolve veins in their stems that carry water and nutrients to where they are needed. This development helps the plants grow taller and survive in areas with less water.

Cooksonia barrandei fossil—one of the earliest known plants with veins

Trees appear

The oldest known species of tree, *Wattieza*, spreads across the world. It has veins and a long trunk topped with large, segmented leaves known as fronds. The tree can reach at least 26 ft (8 m) in height.

c.450 MYA

c.385 MYA

Cycads

A group of gymnosperms evolve that resembles tree ferns. Cycad plants are either male or female, and both sexes produce cones. Beetles spread the pollen made by male cones to female cones, in which the seeds develop.

Cycads grow new leaves at the top of their trunks, shedding the old ones to leave a crown of foliage.

Protective cones

Conifers begin to spread across the world. These gymnosperms have male and female cones. The male cones make pollen, which is carried by the wind to the female cones. Their seeds develop inside the protective layers of the female cones.

The first ferns

The first known ferns appear. Like *Wattieza*, these plants have veins and reproduce using spores (tiny seedlike particles). Modern ferns look very similar to these ancient plants.

The early fern Shougangia bella lived more than 100 million years before the dinosaurs.

Making seeds

The first plants to make seeds evolve. They are called gymnosperms. The seeds contain an embryo (baby) plant protected by a tough outer layer and nourished by an energy store, giving them a better chance of survival than spores.

c.280 MYA

c.310 MYA

c.320 MYA

c.360 MYA

Tough blooms

Magnolias appear. Their flowers have thick petal-like tepals to provide a sturdy landing pad for their beetle pollinators. Hundreds of magnolia species can still be found today.

Composite flowers

A huge family of flowering plants called Asteraceae spreads around the world. Their bright flowers are made up of groups of tiny flowers surrounded by larger petal-like flowers that attract pollinators.

Domestication of grasses

Humans start to domesticate grass species, such as wheat and barley, for their nutritious grains (seeds). They are easy to grow and harvest as crops. Other grasses, including rice and corn, are domesticated later.

Endangered plants

Almost 40 percent of all plant species are facing extinction due to habitat loss and climate change. Many of these species may be useful as medicines or sources of food. Humans have to act fast to protect these plants before it is too late.

c.100 MYA

c.83 MYA

c.10,000 YA

Present day

Seed growth

Fertilized plants produce seeds, which carry tiny, young plants (plant embryos) inside them. Often the seeds need to travel far away from the parent plant to avoid competing for light and nutrients. Seeds may be shaped differently, but they all germinate in the same way— they settle their roots first and grow upward toward sunlight.

Horse chestnut seeds
The shiny brown seeds start to sprout after their spiny casings split open and release them.

Peach pit
A peach tree will take three to four years to mature from its large, woody pit.

Coffee beans
These round seeds need plenty of heat to grow and produce bean-filled berries.

From seed to plant

Although seeds come in many shapes and sizes, they all contain a tiny, young plant called a plant embryo, which lies dormant (inactive), until the right conditions allow it to sprout and grow into a plant—a process called germination. To germinate, all seeds need water, warmth, and oxygen. Each seed takes its own time to germinate. A soybean takes eight days to make its first true leaves.

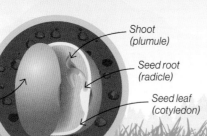

Shoot (plumule)

Seed root (radicle)

Seed coat

Seed leaf (cotyledon)

The seed coat breaks apart as the leaves inside expand.

Day 1

Inside the seed is a plant embryo (a tiny, young plant).

Day 2

The seed root comes out before the leaves.

Day 3

Roots anchor the seedling into the soil.

Day 4

Germination
The dry soybean seed lies dormant, waiting for the ideal moment to germinate (sprout). When conditions are right, it soaks up water from the soil and swells. The seed comes to life, as the cells inside its embryo begin to grow and divide.

First root
The seed root, also known as the radicle, breaks out of the seed coat, using energy stored inside the seed. It bursts out at the small hole through which water entered the seed. The plumule (shoot) will eventually grow upwards from the same hole.

Growing root
The seed root detects gravity and sinks deeper into the soil to find water and nutrients to feed the plumule inside the seed. Root tips are full of starch particles, which fall to the bottom of the root cells to indicate which way is up.

Young shoot
The seed root turns into a true root, sending out side roots to search for more water and nutrients. The seed coat surrounding the seed splits apart and a young shoot emerges and grows upward until it breaks out of the soil.

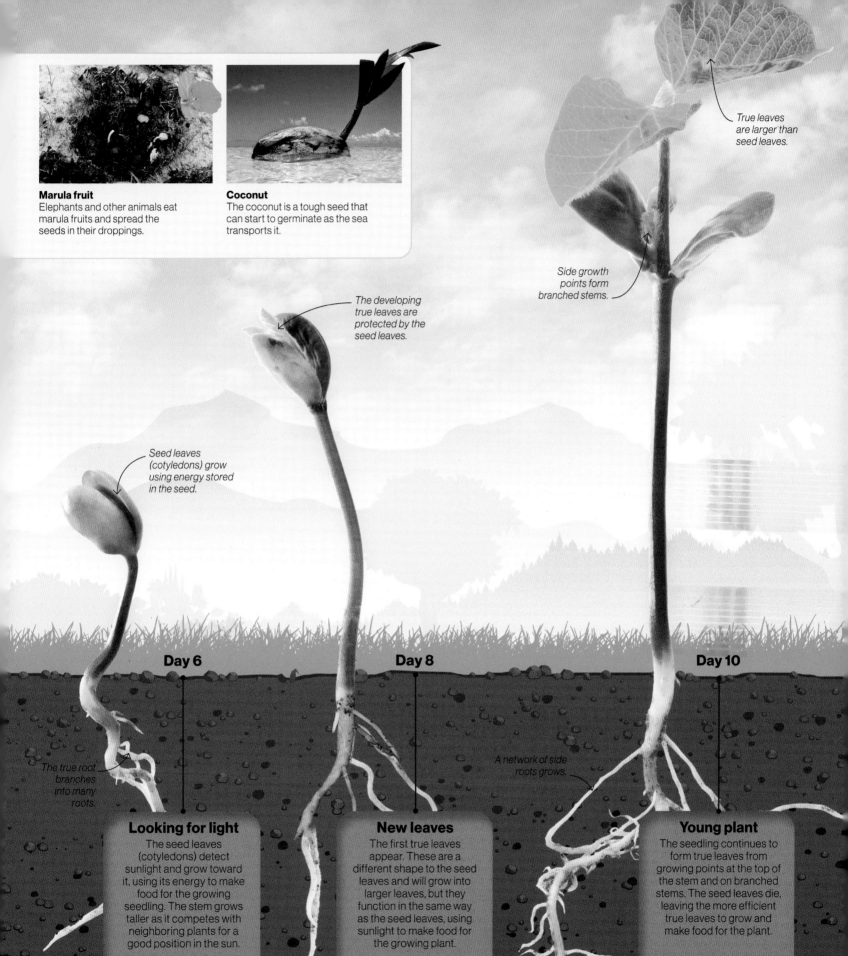

Marula fruit
Elephants and other animals eat marula fruits and spread the seeds in their droppings.

Coconut
The coconut is a tough seed that can start to germinate as the sea transports it.

True leaves are larger than seed leaves.

The developing true leaves are protected by the seed leaves.

Side growth points form branched stems.

Seed leaves (cotyledons) grow using energy stored in the seed.

Day 6

Day 8

Day 10

The true root branches into many roots.

A network of side roots grows.

Looking for light
The seed leaves (cotyledons) detect sunlight and grow toward it, using its energy to make food for the growing seedling. The stem grows taller as it competes with neighboring plants for a good position in the sun.

New leaves
The first true leaves appear. These are a different shape to the seed leaves and will grow into larger leaves, but they function in the same way as the seed leaves, using sunlight to make food for the growing plant.

Young plant
The seedling continues to form true leaves from growing points at the top of the stem and on branched stems. The seed leaves die, leaving the more efficient true leaves to grow and make food for the plant.

Fast forest

A forest can take decades to grow—unless it is a bamboo forest, that is. Bamboo prefers tropical and temperate climates and is the fastest-growing plant on Earth. It can add 3 ft (1 m) in a day to its length—that is more than four times the height of this page. It reaches such impressive heights because it has a hollow core and does not waste energy, growing most of its leaves only once it's tall.

Short but sweet

Unlike long-lived plants such as trees, annual plants such as the sweet pea plant germinate, grow, flower, and die within one year. While trees prefer to scatter their seeds in new areas, annuals often drop their seeds so that they land nearby—if the parent survived in that area, the offspring will probably be able to do the same next year, once the parent plant has died.

Each flower has five petals, typical of a member of the pea family.

Flower buds have pale green petals, which change to vibrant pink, purple, red, or white before opening.

Each leaf has a tendril for climbing.

Each seedling has two seed leaves for photosynthesis.

The seed root anchors the plant into the ground and collects nutrients and water.

March–April	April	May–August	June–September

Seed germination
Round seeds stay in the soil over winter and usually germinate in early spring, when the weather begins to warm up. Each seed contains a baby plant with two seed leaves and a seed root. The seedling shoot grows quickly upward to begin collecting sunlight as soon as it emerges from the soil.

Seedling
As climbing plants, sweet pea seedlings twirl around in search of something to hold on to. When they find some support, such as another plant, they latch on using tendrils and quickly grow to a height of about 6.5 ft (2 m). Climbing and latching on to things means they do not waste energy making sturdier stems.

Flower buds
The aim of all annual plants is to flower quickly so they can produce the next generation of seeds. Rapid growth means the sweet pea is ready to start flowering about three months after germination, with buds forming from May or June and continuing throughout the summer.

Flower blooming
The sweet scent of sweet pea flowers fills the air in the summer, attracting many species of bee pollinators. No one flower lasts more than a few days, but the plant can keep flowering for many weeks if its dead flowers are removed.

Different ways of flowering

Landing pad
Some pea-family flowers have fused petals called a keel, making a landing pad for bees. When pushed down, the keel reveals parts that coat the bee in pollen, which the bee takes to other flowers.

Fake mushroom
The plant *Aspidistra elatior* has unusual purple rosette flowers that appear at soil level. These are pollinated by fungus gnats, which mistake them for mushrooms.

Long tongue
Christmas orchid flowers have a long tube that contains nectar. The orchid is pollinated by hawk moths, which have tongues up to 12 in (30 cm) long.

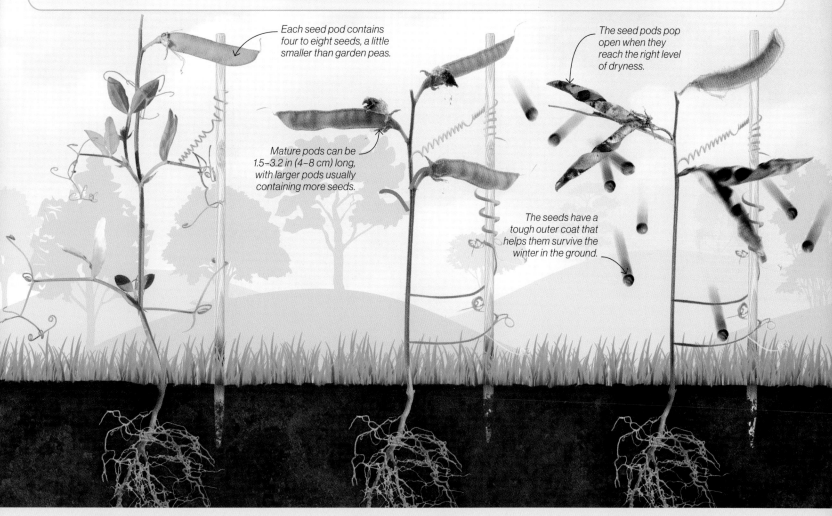

Each seed pod contains four to eight seeds, a little smaller than garden peas.

The seed pods pop open when they reach the right level of dryness.

Mature pods can be 1.5–3.2 in (4–8 cm) long, with larger pods usually containing more seeds.

The seeds have a tough outer coat that helps them survive the winter in the ground.

June–September

Seed pods
Pollinated flowers quickly produce seed pods, which contain the seeds of the next generation of plants. A ripe seed pod tells the plant that flowering has been successful and can now finish, but if the pods are removed, then the plant will continue to flower and produce seed pods.

August–October

Ripening pods
Sweet pea pods ripen (become ready for the next stage) in about three to six weeks, swelling as the seeds grow, before drying and turning brown and brittle. The parent plant dies at the end of the growing season. This is important, as it gives the offspring a place to grow the following year.

Autumn–March

Exploding pods
The inside of the seed pod dries faster than the outside, building tension along the pod wall. Eventually, it explodes along its length, scattering the seeds in many directions so the next generation of seedlings do not have to fight each other for light, water, and nutrients. The remains of the dead plant will rot away over the winter, returning its nutrients to the soil. The seeds lie dormant in the soil until the following spring.

The bat puts its tongue into the bell-shaped flower to drink the nectar.

The flower's position means that the bat must approach from directly beneath it. When the bat feeds on the flower, pollen falls and sticks to the bat's throat.

Underwood's long-tongued bat

Nighttime pollinators

The majority of plants are pollinated by insects. To attract them, these plants tend to have colorful flowers that open in the daytime. A small number of plants, such as *Merinthopodium neuranthum* shown here, have evolved to rely on bats—nocturnal animals that are unable to see colors—to pollinate them. The flowers of bat-pollinated plants tend to be bell-shaped and pale and flower at night. Bats can transport a lot of pollen in one go and can also travel farther than insects, which helps pollinate plants over a wide area.

Day 1

Seeds

Although seeds have been bred out of some orange varieties, oranges naturally contain seeds. Inside every seed is a baby plant (embryo) and the food it needs to fuel its growth. A seed needs weeks of warmth and water to germinate.

From seed to fruit

To protect and spread their seeds, plants produce fruits. Fruits tend to be brightly colored and tasty to make them irresistible to the animals that eat them. They develop from flowers that have been pollinated (the process that fertilizes the flower's seed to create a baby plant). It takes many years for these orange trees to bear fruits.

Cherry flower to fruit

Like oranges, cherries grow from flowers. When the stigma (the female part) of one flower receives pollen from the anther (the male part) of another flower, pollination occurs and a baby plant (known as an embryo) grows inside the flower's seed. The ovary that surrounds the seed turns into the edible flesh of the fruit.

CHERRY FLOWER

White or pink petals attract insects.

Stigma (the female part of the flower) is sticky to collect pollen from other flowers brought by insects.

The anthers (the male parts of a flower) make pollen.

The ovary holds the seed and will turn into the fruit's flesh.

The seed contains the baby plant.

CHERRY FRUIT

Skin of cherry

A woody shell has formed around the seed to protect it.

The ovary has grown into the fruit's edible flesh.

The seed has grown in size.

2 months after flowering

Fruits appear

After a pollinated flower has withered away, its fertilized ovary (a part of the female reproductive organ) remains on the tree's branch and grows into a fruit. After two months, the fruit is around 1.4 in (3.5 cm) in diameter. It is hard, green, and not yet sweet enough to attract animals to eat it. Inside, new seeds are starting to form.

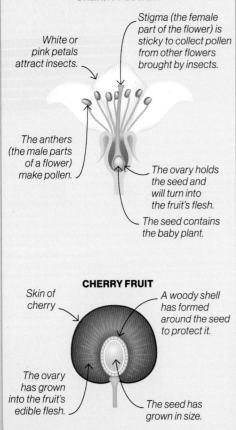

Large green fruits

The fruits, known as oranges, grow to maximum size and their seeds continue to develop. The oranges are slightly sweeter, but that is overpowered by an acidic taste that puts off fruit-eating animals. The tree needs constant water. If there is not enough water the tree sheds its fruits to keep itself alive.

5 months after flowering

Seedling

Weeks 2–8

The seed leaves provide nourishment and fuel for the shoot's growth until the plant's true leaves appear. Once the leaves peek through the soil, the shoot becomes a seedling. Orange leaves are evergreen and need lots of sunlight to grow the seedling up to 5 ft (1.5 m) in the first year.

Sapling

Years 1–3

Once the seedling grows taller than 3 ft (1 m), it is called a sapling. It continues to grow taller over time. It also develops more treelike features—ts gray bark protects green shoots and develops sharp thorns.

Flower blossom

About a decade after germination, the sapling matures into an adult tree and starts to grow flowers. The flowers attract insects that get covered in its sticky pollen. The insects then carry this pollen to other flowers to pollinate them.

The white flowers have a sweet scent to attract bees—the orange tree's main pollinator.

10–15 years later

Changing color

In cool climates, oranges behave like tree leaves in fall and turn orange because they lose their chlorophyll (the pigment that makes them green). In tropical climates, high temperatures at all times mean oranges (and leaves) remain green because they keep their chlorophyll.

6 months after flowering

Ripe fruits

When an orange ripens, its skin turns waxy for peeling away from the sweetened fruit inside—the perfect treat for many birds and mammals. When the animal eventually excretes the orange's hardy seeds, they will grow far from the parent tree so they are not competing for light and water.

7 months after flowering

Fall–Winter

Dormant bud

A strawberry plant's flower buds start to form in the fall. Then, along with the rest of the plant, the buds become dormant (inactive) over winter, when the temperature falls.

A bud is a tiny, developing plant growth.

Sepal

Spring Days 1–10

Day 11

Growing bud

In spring, the buds start to open as the days get longer and warmer. Green, leaflike sepals protect the bud as it grows. Inside, the parts of the flower are developing, causing the bud to enlarge.

Pollen grains

As the bud continues to grow, the male parts of the developing flower, known as stamens, start to produce pollen. Pollen is a fine yellow powder that carries the male sex cells of plants from one flower to another, helping plants reproduce.

Pollen

Receptacle (this will become the red part of the strawberry)

Day 16

Growing flower

The carpels (the female parts of flowers) are now mature. After flowers open, the sticky tips of pistils will catch pollen brought from other flowers by insects.

Day 18

Day 20

Open flower

The strawberry flower's scent attracts many insects, including bees, hoverflies, and butterflies. By transporting pollen between flowers, the insects help fertilize the flower.

Flower dies

Once the flower has been pollinated, the stamens and flower petals die. The carpels begin to produce seeds, and the base of the flower—the receptacle—starts to swell. The receptacle will eventually form the sweet, edible part of the strawberry.

How strawberries grow

Strawberries are red, heart-shaped fruits, with a juicy texture and sweet taste. You might think the fruit is the red fleshy part (which is known as the receptacle), but actually it is the tiny, brown seeds covering the strawberry's surface that form the fruit. On a single strawberry, there can be up to 400 of these little seeds. The small plant produces strawberries during the warm months of summer.

Day 25

Small green strawberry
The receptacle continues expanding. Embedded in it are developing seeds. The sepals, the protective casing that originally covered the flower bud, are still attached to the strawberry.

Day 30

Large green strawberry
Chlorophyll, the green pigment in the strawberry, collects energy from sunlight and uses it to make energy to fuel its growth. The seeds on the outside of the strawberry continue to grow.

Day 33

Small pale-green strawberry
The chlorophyll starts to break down and the strawberry appears paler in color. If you ate it now, the strawberry would taste tart and feel hard in texture.

Day 35

Large pale-green strawberry
As the strawberry nears its final size, it becomes sweeter. The seeds are almost at their final size too. But it still has not turned its distinctive red color.

Day 37

Turning red
The strawberry starts to produce a red pigment called anthocyanin. The strawberry changes color from pale green to red, starting at the tip. It now tastes much sweeter.

Day 44

Ripe red strawberry
A ripe strawberry is bright red in color and tastes sweet to attract animals. When an animal eats the strawberry, it spreads the seeds in its droppings.

Mold growth

If a piece of fruit is left in a warm, damp environment for a few days, it will soon be covered with a dusty-colored fuzz. This fuzz is mold, a type of fungus (a spore-producing organism that feeds on plant or animal matter). The mold may look unappetizing—and you definitely should not eat it—but it plays a very important role in the natural environment. Mold breaks down dead and decaying plants and animals, helping to recycle their nutrients.

Types of mold

There are many thousands of types of mold. Some species can be used to make medicines or foods such as cheese, but others can be harmful if left to grow out of control. Molds can also be a problem for farmers—certain species spread quickly and can destroy entire fields of crops.

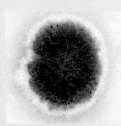

Penicillium
One type of mold, penicillium, kills bacteria. It is used to produce penicillin, an antibiotic medicine, which has saved millions of lives.

Black mold
This robust dark green or black sootlike mold can grow in many different environments. It is often found growing on foods such as onions.

Black bread mold
Growing quickly indoors, this mold loves foods such as bread or fruit. It is white at first, then turns black once the spores develop.

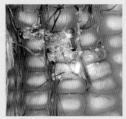

Corn mold
This fungus contaminates corn cobs with toxins that can be dangerous for humans and animals to eat. It spreads quickly through farmers' crops.

The thin skin of a strawberry provides little protection against mold spores floating in the air.

Day 1

Fresh fruit
Microscopic mold spores (the tiny reproductive cells of mold) are carried in the air. They germinate when they land on a moist food source, such as this fresh strawberry and start to establish a colony. The spores enter the strawberry through its thin skin, often where it has been bruised or damaged.

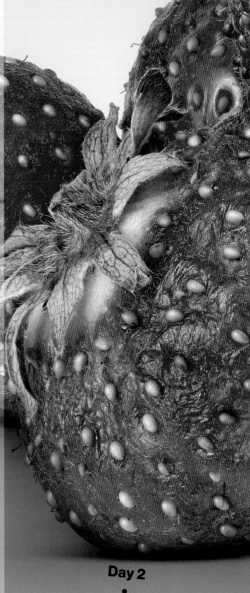

The strawberry's skin is starting to collapse inward.

Day 2

First signs of mold
As the strawberry's skin weakens, it becomes easier for more mold spores to get inside. The fruit begins to feel soft and look wet and unappetizing.

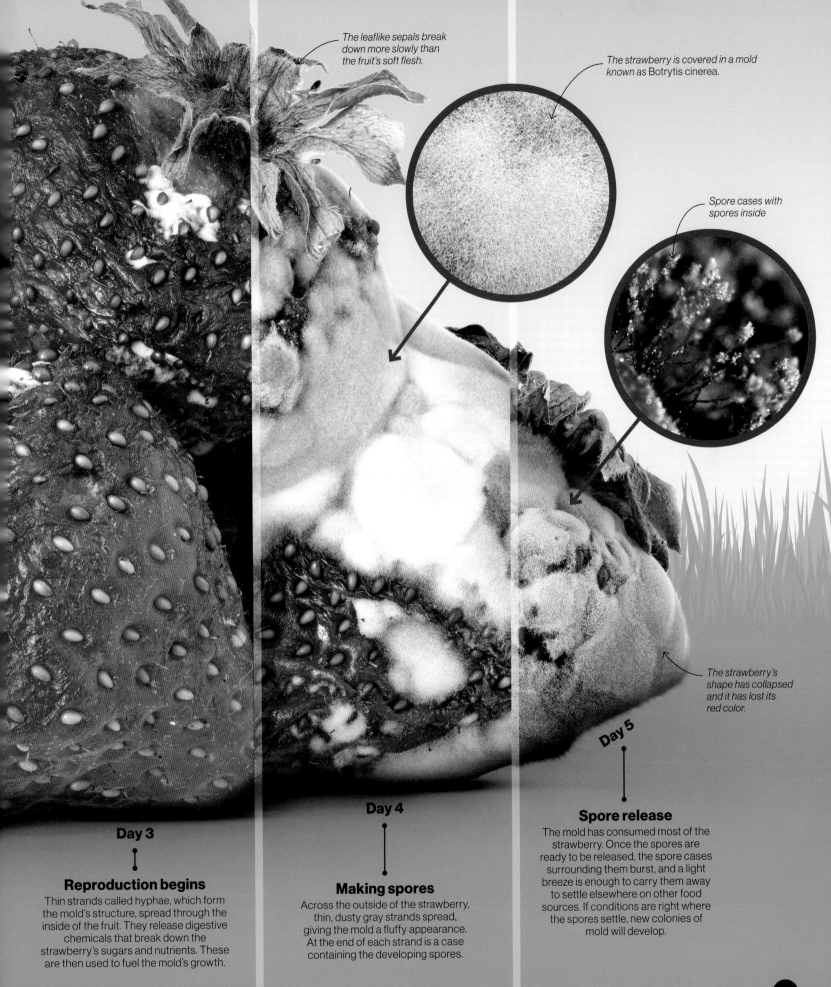

The leaflike sepals break down more slowly than the fruit's soft flesh.

The strawberry is covered in a mold known as Botrytis cinerea.

Spore cases with spores inside

The strawberry's shape has collapsed and it has lost its red color.

Day 5

Day 4

Day 3

Reproduction begins

Thin strands called hyphae, which form the mold's structure, spread through the inside of the fruit. They release digestive chemicals that break down the strawberry's sugars and nutrients. These are then used to fuel the mold's growth.

Making spores

Across the outside of the strawberry, thin, dusty gray strands spread, giving the mold a fluffy appearance. At the end of each strand is a case containing the developing spores.

Spore release

The mold has consumed most of the strawberry. Once the spores are ready to be released, the spore cases surrounding them burst, and a light breeze is enough to carry them away to settle elsewhere on other food sources. If conditions are right where the spores settle, new colonies of mold will develop.

73

Day 1

Seed germinates

Many creatures, including monkeys, bats, and birds, eat the sweet pulp inside cacao pods and discard the bitter seeds. The seeds begin to germinate as soon as they land on the forest floor.

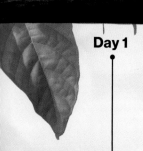

Day 10

Seedling emerges

Young cacao seedlings grow in the shade of other trees, where they shelter from strong sunlight and winds. They often grow alongside rubber, banana, or palm trees. The seedlings need regular rainfall and rich, well-drained soils to flourish.

Years 4–5

Tree matures

A mature tree is about 26 ft (8 m) tall, with leaves up to 20 in (50 cm) long. At about 4–5 years old, the tree begins to flower and produce some pods.

Years 8–10

Full flowering

Cacao trees reach peak productivity around 8–10 years old, and they then flower throughout the year. Unlike most plants, the flowers emerge directly from the trunk and branches of the tree, rather than on new shoots.

1 month after flowering

Pollination

Each flower is 0.78 in (2 cm) and is cream or pale pink in color. They take 30 days to develop and are pollinated by flies. Of the 100,000 flowers produced each year, only 0.1 percent will mature into a cacao pod.

The gall midge carries pollen between cacao flowers as it seeks out sweet, sticky nectar.

Cacao to chocolate

For thousands of years, people have cultivated the cacao tree for its seeds—cacao beans. The Aztec people who lived in present-day Mexico considered them so valuable that they used them as a form of currency. Cacao trees grow in tropical climates, including parts of South America, Asia, and Africa. Although the beans taste bitter when harvested, they can be turned into one of the most popular sweet treats of all—chocolate!

Bean to bar

Cacao pods are harvested by hand; farmers use a machete or knife to slice them from the tree. The cacao beans are removed and left in the sun to ferment for a week before they are dried. The beans are then roasted and deshelled before being ground up and melted into cocoa mass. This can be mixed with sugar and milk, then molded into chocolate bars or other chocolate-flavored foods.

Pods ripen

Cacao pods ripen over a few months, changing color from green to yellow, orange, or red. The mature pods are around 10 in (25 cm) long, and each contain around 20–40 seeds.

4–5 months after flowering

Time to harvest

Not all orange and red pods are ripe, so farmers check the flesh underneath the skin—if the flesh is yellow, the pod is ready to pick. The trees constantly make fruits, so harvesting happens throughout the year.

6 months after flowering

The tightly packed seeds are surrounded by a sweet white pulp, which many animals love to eat.

White bloom
The 2.5 in (6 cm) white flower opens at dawn. Cotton flowers can pollinate themselves, but pollination by bees and butterflies produces much more cotton. Either way, the flowers are pollinated within hours and they close at dusk.

Pollinated flower
The closed flower turns pink the day after pollination, then a deep purple-red the next. Cotton fiber development has already begun at the base of the flower, which will become the cotton boll.

Days 22–23

The bud already contains petals, and male and female parts, ready for flowering.

Bud develops
The young bud grows, forming what is known as a "match-head square." It is surrounded by a pyramid of three leaflike structures—called bracts—for protection. Here, two bracts have been removed so the bud can be seen.

Ready to flower
The bud is reaching full size and is now shaped like a candle flame, as it starts to emerge from the bracts. Over the next few days, it grows rapidly in preparation for flowering.

Day 21

Day 16

Day 6

First flower buds
After around 35 days of cotton plant growth, tiny triangular flower buds appear. These are approximately 0.1 in (3 mm) long. Each plant will flower for 4–6 weeks.

Day 1

Cotton life cycle

Cotton thread is made from fluffy fibers surrounding cotton plant seeds. Each seed pod (called a boll) contains two types of cotton fibers: long fibers (known as staples) are twisted together into threads and used to make clothing and toys, while the shorter fibers (called linters) are woven into lower-quality fabrics such as bandages, or used to make paper.

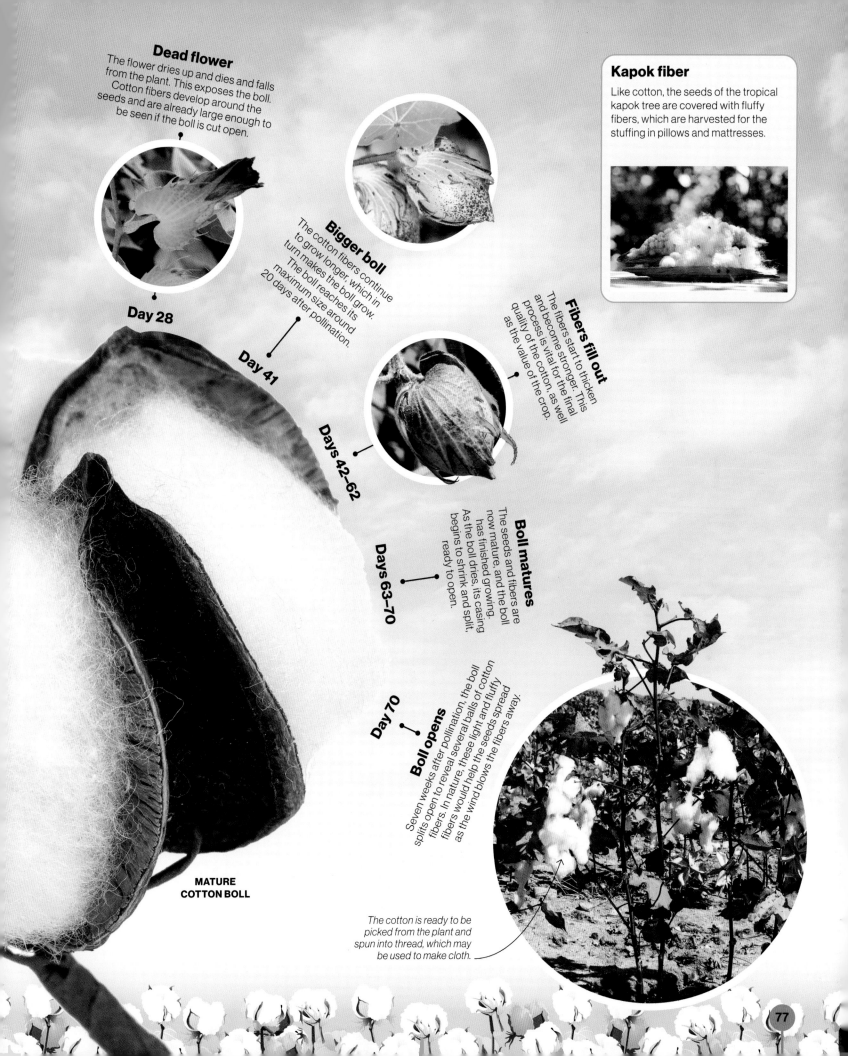

Dead flower

The flower dries up and dies and falls from the plant. This exposes the boll. Cotton fibers develop around the seeds and are already large enough to be seen if the boll is cut open.

Day 28

Bigger boll

The cotton fibers continue to grow longer, which in turn makes the boll grow. The boll reaches its maximum size around 20 days after pollination.

Day 41

Days 42–62

Fibers fill out

The fibers start to thicken and become stronger. This process is vital for the final quality of the cotton, as well as the value of the crop.

Days 63–70

Boll matures

The seeds and fibers are now mature, and the boll has finished growing. As the boll dries, its casing begins to shrink and split, ready to open.

Day 70

Boll opens

Seven weeks after pollination, the boll splits open to reveal several balls of cotton fibers. In nature, these light and fluffy fibers would help the seeds spread as the wind blows the fibers away.

MATURE COTTON BOLL

The cotton is ready to be picked from the plant and spun into thread, which may be used to make cloth.

Kapok fiber

Like cotton, the seeds of the tropical kapok tree are covered with fluffy fibers, which are harvested for the stuffing in pillows and mattresses.

10 days
Boerhavia repens

Water is scarce in the Sahara Desert in northern Africa, so some plants, such as *Boerhavia repens*, take advantage of any rainfall by germinating and flowering within days. Their seeds can survive for years in the dry soil.

6 weeks
Arabidopsis thaliana

A short life cycle, small size, and ease of growth have led to scientists around the world using *Arabidopsis thaliana* to study crops and plant health. We know more about it than almost any other plant.

Up to 1 year
Sunflower

Sunflowers are annual plants. Their seeds germinate in spring as the weather gets warmer. They then flower through summer, and set seed again in fall, dying to make room for the next generation.

2,500 years
Baobab tree

Many baobabs survive for 1,000 to 2,500 years, but changing rainfall patterns as a result of climate change are causing many of these ancient trees in Africa to die prematurely.

2,300 years
Sacred fig

Jaya Sri Maha Bodhi was planted in 288 BCE, making it the oldest known human-planted tree in the world. It is very sacred to Buddhist people, who travel for long distances to visit the tree.

2,000+ years
Jōmon Sugi

This ancient tree grows in a remote location on the Japanese island of Yakushima. Other conifer trees of the same species, *Cryptomeria*, were introduced to China over 1,000 years ago, with some surviving to this day.

3,500 years
Ginkgo biloba

Unlike most plants, ginkgo trees do not start to age or become weaker once they reach maturity. They are unusually resistant to disease throughout their long lives.

4,500 years
Posidonia australis

In 2022, scientists were shocked to discover that a vast seagrass bed off the coast of Australia, covering 77 sq miles (200 sq km), was all one plant that used a network of roots to spread and grow for thousands of years.

5,000+ years
Bristlecone pine

A bristlecone pine named Methuselah is the oldest single tree in the world. Harsh conditions high in the White Mountains of California mean it grows slowly and forms very hard wood, which protects it from pests and disease.

2 years
Foxglove

As biennial plants, foxgloves grow a spiral of leaves in their first year and rest over winter. They then produce a tall stem with many bell-shaped flowers in their second year before dying.

5 years
Kangaroo paw

This unusual southwestern Australian perennial plant flowers in spring and summer, after which the leaves die back to a stemlike root called a rhizome that acts as a food store over the cooler winter months.

50+ years
Hydrangea

Like most perennials, hydrangeas usually die from drought, damage, or infections rather than old age. Under ideal conditions, these bushes can live for over 50 years, growing weaker over time.

2,000 years
Welwitschia mirabilis

This plant produces only two leaves, which split into ribbons during strong winds. Rain is scarce in the Namib Desert in southern Africa, so *Welwitschia mirabilis* grows very slowly.

300 years
Holly tree

Many trees, such as this holly, are long-lived perennials. Although they grow more slowly than annuals, they produce strong branches that can be replaced if damaged, helping them survive storms or pest invasions.

150 years
Ashikaga's wisteria tree

The oldest wisteria tree, at Ashikaga Flower Park in Japan, draws big crowds to see its 80,000 purple blossoms.

9,550 years
Old Tjikko

This ancient Norway spruce in the Fulufjället Mountains of Sweden started to grow at the end of the last ice age. It is the root system of Old Tjikko, rather than the visible tree, that is thought to be around 9,550 years old.

Plant life spans

Plants can live for a few weeks or thousands of years, depending on which plant group they are in. Annuals grow, flower, and die in the same year, often germinating (sprouting) in spring and dying in late summer. Biennials focus on leaf growth in their first year, then flower and die in their second. Perennials grow for decades, or even centuries, often dying from infections, drought, or a lack of nutrients rather than old age.

Year in a forest

Thousands of species of animals, plants, and fungi live in the beech forests of Europe. In spring and summer, there is plenty of food and the forest is full of life. In fall, when the days cool and shorten, the trees shed their leaves. By winter, food is scarce and some animals have to search far and wide to find enough, while others hibernate to survive until spring.

White-tailed eagles build huge nests in beech forests near lakes and coasts.

In spring, beech leaves sprout from buds that were inactive through winter.

Tawny owls nest in tree holes and hunt for mice at night.

By summer, beech leaves are darker and thicker.

Beech flowers
These flowers open in April, and the pollen they make is blown away by the wind.

Slipper orchid
This orchid, a type of flower, pairs up with a fungus to exchange nutrients.

Brown bear
After hibernating all winter, hungry bears search for plentiful roots, berries, insects, fish, and other animals to eat in summer.

Fallow deer
These deer live in forests but may get into nearby fields to eat crops.

The forest awakens
Spring begins, and soft new leaves and small pompom-like flowers break out of buds on beech tree branches. Spring flowers such as bluebells and wild garlic bloom, covering the forest floor.

Wild garlic blooms early in spring.

Maximum growth
Lots of sunlight and warm weather mean plants can grow quickly in summer if there is enough water. Herbivores gorge on colorful berries, leaves, and tubers (nutritious underground stems), while carnivores can easily find prey.

Flowers such as red campion bloom in summer, attracting insect pollinators.

SPRING

SUMMER

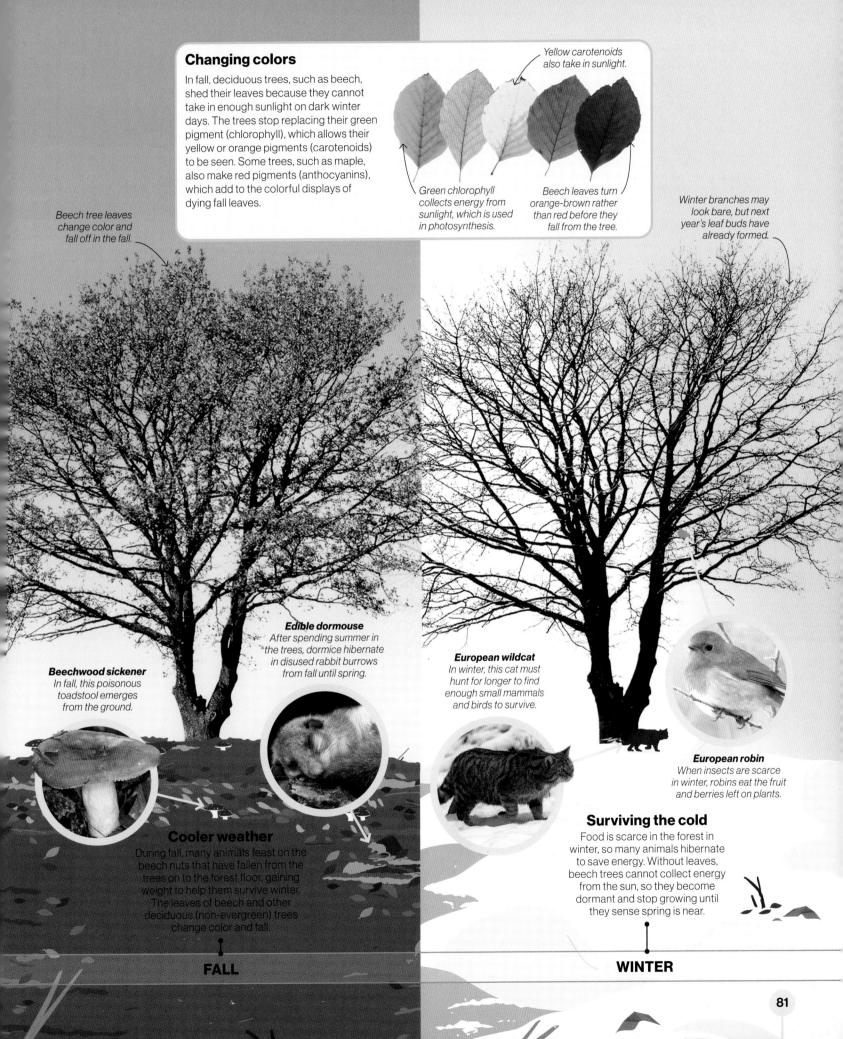

Changing colors

In fall, deciduous trees, such as beech, shed their leaves because they cannot take in enough sunlight on dark winter days. The trees stop replacing their green pigment (chlorophyll), which allows their yellow or orange pigments (carotenoids) to be seen. Some trees, such as maple, also make red pigments (anthocyanins), which add to the colorful displays of dying fall leaves.

Yellow carotenoids also take in sunlight.

Green chlorophyll collects energy from sunlight, which is used in photosynthesis.

Beech leaves turn orange-brown rather than red before they fall from the tree.

Beech tree leaves change color and fall off in the fall.

Winter branches may look bare, but next year's leaf buds have already formed.

Beechwood sickener
In fall, this poisonous toadstool emerges from the ground.

Edible dormouse
After spending summer in the trees, dormice hibernate in disused rabbit burrows from fall until spring.

European wildcat
In winter, this cat must hunt for longer to find enough small mammals and birds to survive.

European robin
When insects are scarce in winter, robins eat the fruit and berries left on plants.

Cooler weather

During fall, many animals feast on the beech nuts that have fallen from the trees on to the forest floor, gaining weight to help them survive winter. The leaves of beech and other deciduous (non-evergreen) trees change color and fall.

Surviving the cold

Food is scarce in the forest in winter, so many animals hibernate to save energy. Without leaves, beech trees cannot collect energy from the sun, so they become dormant and stop growing until they sense spring is near.

FALL

WINTER

Quaking aspens

The fall colors of quaking aspen trees in the Wasatch Mountains of Utah are an impressive sight—but you can also identify the trees by their sound! Their flat, broad leaves pick up even a gentle breeze and cause the whole tree to gently tremble and quake, hence their name. The trees here are all part of a single organism known as Pando—each tree starts life as a shoot from Pando's shared root system, and all are genetically identical clones. Individual trees may live for hundreds of years, but the root system they sprout from is many tens of thousands of years old.

Life of an oak tree

The common oak grows across Europe, North America, northern Africa, and western Asia. Its distinctive leaves and acorn fruit make it one of the most recognizable trees. Throughout its life span of up to 2,000 years, the oak tree provides a home for a huge variety of animals, fungi, and even other plants. The tree is often featured in folklore and myths, and its wood was once widely used for constructing buildings and ships.

Making acorns

In spring, the wind blows pollen from one oak's male flowers (found in long, dangling strips known as catkins) to the tiny pink female flowers hidden between another oak's leaves. After pollination, the female flowers produce acorns. These nuts might one day grow into new oak trees, but they are also a favorite food of animals such as jays, squirrels, and badgers.

Male flowers
Each green bump along these dangling catkins is a pollen-making male flower.

A single jay can bury as many as 3,000 acorns a month.

Oak galls

Galls are growths on oak trees caused by gall wasps, which lay their eggs in developing oak leaves. After hatching, the larvae (grubs) release chemicals that cause the oak to grow the galls. The larvae live inside them, eating away at the gall tissue.

Inside the acorn's tough shell is a seed.

| Fall | Spring | 2 months | 10 years | 50 years |

Acorn falls
Some of the acorns that fall from an oak tree to the ground are collected and buried by small mammals, such as squirrels, and jays (a type of bird) ready for when food is scarce during winter. Occasionally, the animals forget where they left them.

Germination
In spring, the seed inside the acorn takes in water and germinates (sprouts). A root grows down into the soil, and then the first leaves emerge about a week later.

Seedling
The soft, young leaves of the oak seedling absorb sunlight, providing the energy that the young tree will use to grow 12–20 in (30–50 cm) each year. The rounded lobes of oak leaves make the plants easy to recognize.

Sapling
Each year, the young oak tree adds more wood to its trunk. When the trunk reaches 1 in (2.5 cm) in diameter at about 4.5 ft (1.4 m) above the ground, the young tree is known as a sapling. At this size, it is not yet able to make acorns.

Acorns grow
The oak tree continues growing steadily. It now starts to produce flowers and crops of acorns. Over its long lifetime, the tree will make millions of acorns, each with the potential to grow into a new tree.

Young acorns
Growing acorns are protected by scaly cups that will eventually cover only the top of the nut.

Acorns in late summer
The acorns are still green in summer. By fall, they will harden, turn brown, and then fall off.

Oak trees can grow up to 130 ft (40 m) in height.

Branches die due to damage or drought.

During a mast year, an oak tree can produce up to 10,000 acorns.

An oak tree's girth (circumference) may reach more than 20 ft (6 m) in old age.

150 years

700 years

1,000 years or more

Prime of life
The large tree is now mature and produces acorns each year. Every 5 to 10 years, the tree channels extra energy into a bumper crop of acorns—this is known as a mast year. With so many acorns, there is a good chance that many will escape being eaten and grow into new trees.

Old age
The tree reaches old age. The dead and decaying wood in its trunk is eaten away by fungi, leaving a hollow surrounded by bark-covered living wood. Many animals take advantage of the protective hollow. Birds and bats roost here. Hedgehogs hibernate and snakes lay their eggs inside in the leaf litter (dead plant material).

Death
The ancient oak tree begins to die. Its hollow trunk, weakened by disease, can no longer support its heavy branches. Some oaks may live as long as 2,000 years. The Major Oak, the largest common oak in the UK, is about 1,000 years old and weighs 23 tons.

Life and death of leaves

Found in temperate climates, deciduous trees shed their leaves every year and, by doing so, symbolize the changing of the seasons. The first green leaves of spring are a welcome change from the bare branches of winter. Dense leaves provide shade in the summer sun, while the colors of fall leaves signal winter is almost here once more.

Inside a bud

Deciduous trees make their new leaves before fall using energy from their summer growth period. To survive over winter, the leaves are protected at the center of buds surrounded by modified thickened leaves called scales.

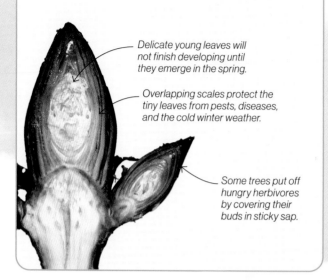

Delicate young leaves will not finish developing until they emerge in the spring.

Overlapping scales protect the tiny leaves from pests, diseases, and the cold winter weather.

Some trees put off hungry herbivores by covering their buds in sticky sap.

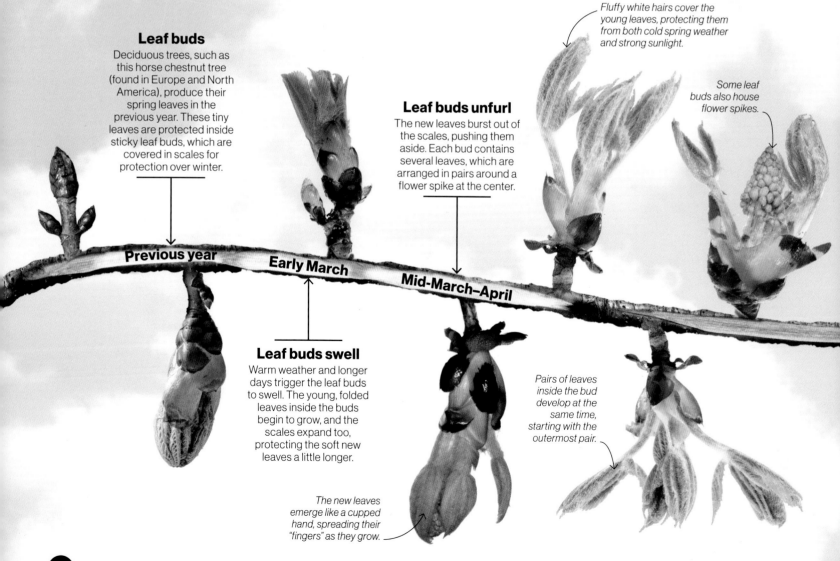

Leaf buds

Deciduous trees, such as this horse chestnut tree (found in Europe and North America), produce their spring leaves in the previous year. These tiny leaves are protected inside sticky leaf buds, which are covered in scales for protection over winter.

Leaf buds unfurl

The new leaves burst out of the scales, pushing them aside. Each bud contains several leaves, which are arranged in pairs around a flower spike at the center.

Fluffy white hairs cover the young leaves, protecting them from both cold spring weather and strong sunlight.

Some leaf buds also house flower spikes.

Leaf buds swell

Warm weather and longer days trigger the leaf buds to swell. The young, folded leaves inside the buds begin to grow, and the scales expand too, protecting the soft new leaves a little longer.

Pairs of leaves inside the bud develop at the same time, starting with the outermost pair.

The new leaves emerge like a cupped hand, spreading their "fingers" as they grow.

Previous year

Early March

Mid-March–April

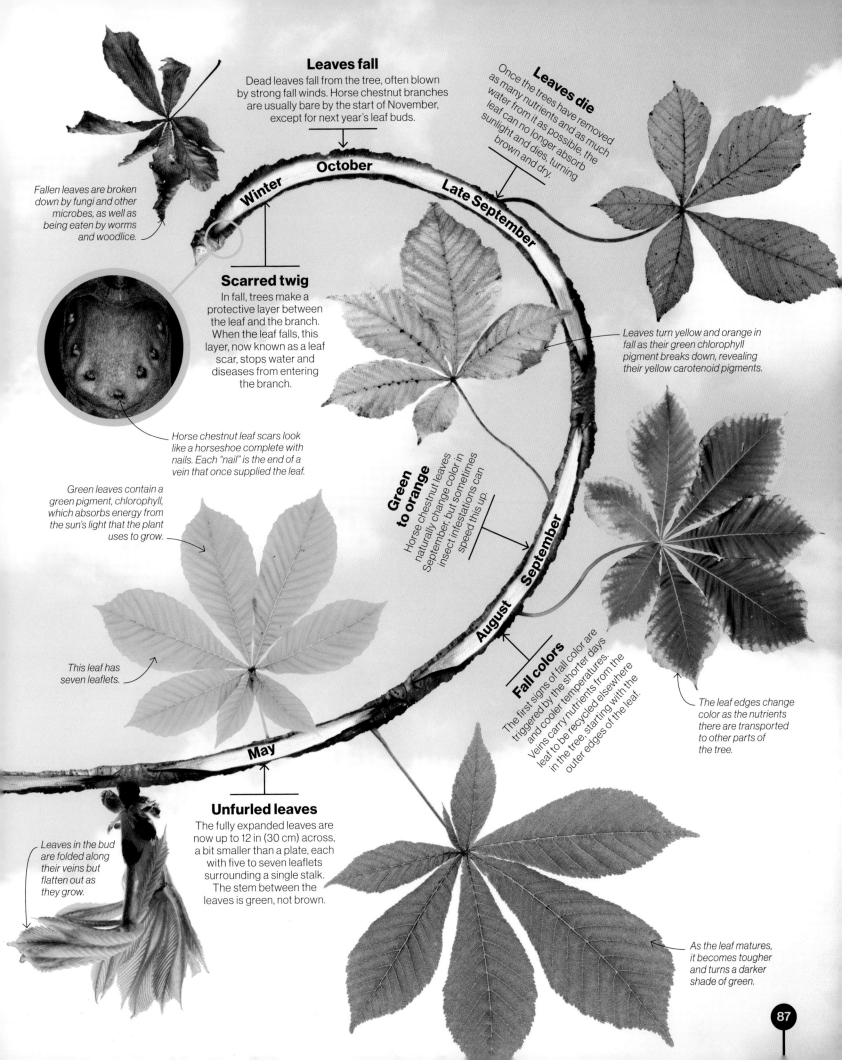

Leaves fall
Dead leaves fall from the tree, often blown by strong fall winds. Horse chestnut branches are usually bare by the start of November, except for next year's leaf buds.

Leaves die
Once the trees have removed as many nutrients and as much water from it as possible the leaf can no longer absorb sunlight and dies, turning brown and dry.

October

Winter

Late September

Fallen leaves are broken down by fungi and other microbes, as well as being eaten by worms and woodlice.

Scarred twig
In fall, trees make a protective layer between the leaf and the branch. When the leaf falls, this layer, now known as a leaf scar, stops water and diseases from entering the branch.

Leaves turn yellow and orange in fall as their green chlorophyll pigment breaks down, revealing their yellow carotenoid pigments.

Horse chestnut leaf scars look like a horseshoe complete with nails. Each "nail" is the end of a vein that once supplied the leaf.

Green leaves contain a green pigment, chlorophyll, which absorbs energy from the sun's light that the plant uses to grow.

Green to orange
Horse chestnut leaves naturally change color in September, but sometimes insect infestations can speed this up.

September

August

This leaf has seven leaflets.

Fall colors
The first signs of fall color are triggered by the shorter days and cooler temperatures. Veins carry nutrients from the leaf to be recycled elsewhere in the tree, starting with the outer edges of the leaf.

The leaf edges change color as the nutrients there are transported to other parts of the tree.

May

Unfurled leaves
The fully expanded leaves are now up to 12 in (30 cm) across, a bit smaller than a plate, each with five to seven leaflets surrounding a single stalk. The stem between the leaves is green, not brown.

Leaves in the bud are folded along their veins but flatten out as they grow.

As the leaf matures, it becomes tougher and turns a darker shade of green.

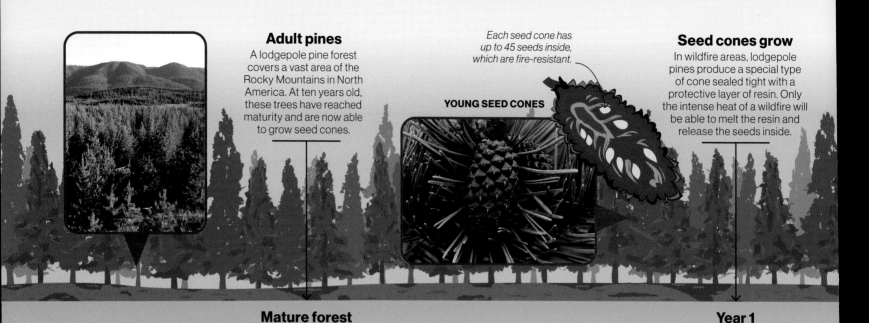

Adult pines
A lodgepole pine forest covers a vast area of the Rocky Mountains in North America. At ten years old, these trees have reached maturity and are now able to grow seed cones.

Each seed cone has up to 45 seeds inside, which are fire-resistant.

YOUNG SEED CONES

Seed cones grow
In wildfire areas, lodgepole pines produce a special type of cone sealed tight with a protective layer of resin. Only the intense heat of a wildfire will be able to melt the resin and release the seeds inside.

Mature forest

Year 1

Fire in nature

Wildfires have occurred naturally for millions of years, destroying much of the wildlife in their path, but some plants and trees have evolved over time to use wildfires to their advantage. Some lodgepole pine trees found in the Rocky Mountains, which stretch along the west coast of North America from Canada to New Mexico, produce seed cones that need the heat of fire to open them.

Wildfires in full force
Wildfires can last anywhere from a few weeks to a few months. They end when they run out of fuel—in other words when there is nothing left to burn, when it rains, or when they are put out by firefighters.

**A few weeks to
a few months**

Burning on purpose
Wildfires can be destructive, but they are also vital for fire-adapted plants and trees that depend on them for spreading their seeds. Park rangers light small, controlled fires in Yellowstone National Park, US to give these species a chance at reproducing. In the process, the fire burns dry wood that could lead to uncontrolled, dangerous blazes.

Recovery begins
After the wildfire, the forest floor is charred (burnt) and empty. The lodgepole pine cones were unsealed by the blaze and have released their seeds. They soon begin to sprout without the shadow of other plants to cover them. The nutrient-rich ash helps them to grow quickly.

**LODGEPOLE PINE
SEEDLINGS**

Days and weeks after wildfire ends

Mature seed cone
After two years, the cone is mature. Because they will not release their seeds until the next wildfire, the cones are held on the tree for many years.

MATURE SEED CONE

Each sealed scale protects one or two seeds from hungry animals looking for food to eat.

Year 2

The golden eagle uses the fire as an opportunity to hunt.

The bushy-tailed woodrat comes out of its burrow to escape the fire but draws the watchful eye of the golden eagle.

Wildfires begin
Wildfires typically happen once every 100–300 years in the region, but in dry conditions they may take place more often. They are caused by the summer heat when there is little moisture in the forest. The lodgepole pine trees die, but their seeds survive.

Moose will flee a fire and sometimes avoid it by standing in a lake or stream.

Once every 100–300 years

Recovery continues
The young lodgepole pines grow up to 0.5 m (20 in) in just a few years. Other plant species are slowly returning, often when their seeds are carried into the area by the wind or by animals, such as moose.

Young forest
Ten years after a wildfire, the now-mature lodgepole pine trees start to produce young seed cones. Climate change is making wildfires more frequent, but for now, the seed cones can still mature for many years before a wildfire occurs.

2–3 years after wildfire

10 years and beyond

Desert survivor

Life in a hot desert is hard. The extreme heat and very low rainfall would quickly kill most plants, but some have evolved to survive here. Leaves are a major site of water loss, so cacti, like this saguaro, have replaced their leaves with protective spines. Most succulents have a wide, shallow root system, but the saguaro is an exception. Long roots let them access water deep underground. Their stems take on the job of photosynthesis and also store precious water to help the plant survive many months without rain.

Soaking up water

Many desert plants are succulent, meaning they store water in their thick leaves and stems. After rainfall, shallow roots stretching out just under the soil collect the water before it evaporates. In saguaro cacti, this water is moved into the stem, which stretches to store as much as possible.

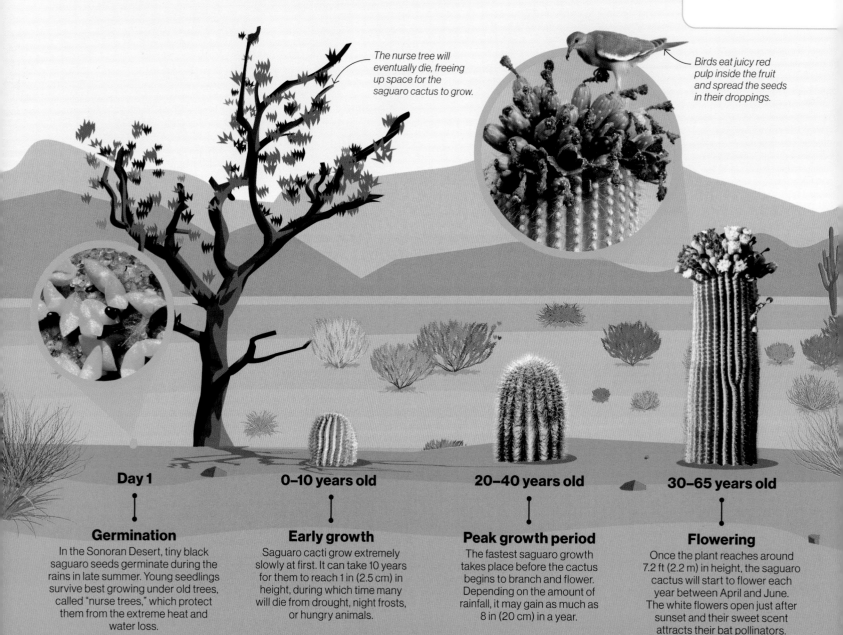

The nurse tree will eventually die, freeing up space for the saguaro cactus to grow.

Birds eat juicy red pulp inside the fruit and spread the seeds in their droppings.

Day 1

Germination
In the Sonoran Desert, tiny black saguaro seeds germinate during the rains in late summer. Young seedlings survive best growing under old trees, called "nurse trees," which protect them from the extreme heat and water loss.

0–10 years old

Early growth
Saguaro cacti grow extremely slowly at first. It can take 10 years for them to reach 1 in (2.5 cm) in height, during which time many will die from drought, night frosts, or hungry animals.

20–40 years old

Peak growth period
The fastest saguaro growth takes place before the cactus begins to branch and flower. Depending on the amount of rainfall, it may gain as much as 8 in (20 cm) in a year.

30–65 years old

Flowering
Once the plant reaches around 7.2 ft (2.2 m) in height, the saguaro cactus will start to flower each year between April and June. The white flowers open just after sunset and their sweet scent attracts their bat pollinators.

The stem folds in pleats like an accordion when it is low on water.

After rain, the pleats unfold and flatten to allow the stem to expand.

Many animals make their homes on or in saguaro stems and arms.

Sharp spines line the water-filled stems of the cacti, protecting them from hungry or thirsty animals.

50–70 years old

First arm

It takes over half a century for a saguaro to form its characteristic arms. Flowers form at the tops of the main stem and each arm, so more arms mean more flowers, more seeds, and possibly more seedlings.

70–150 years old

Prime of life

The cactus continues to grow taller and make more arms—as many as 78 arms have been reported on a single cactus! The main stem often reaches 42.6 ft (13 m) in height, with the tallest measured stem being more than 75.5 ft (23 m) tall.

150–300 years old

Death

Most saguaros live for around 150 to 175 years, although the oldest known individual, called "Old Granddaddy," was around 300 years old when it died. By the time they die, many saguaros will have produced an estimated 40 million seeds.

Flowering desert

This sea of purple flowers is a strange sight, given that it covers the usually parched ground of the Atacama Desert in Chile. Hardy wildflower seeds may lie dormant in the soil for five years or more, before suddenly springing into bloom days after a rainfall. This particular flower, *Cistanthe grandiflora*, is just one of 200 species that grow in the Atacama after the rains come.

Cistanthe grandiflora

Giant of the water

In the slow-moving waters of the Amazon River basin in South America lurks the Amazonian giant water lily (*Victoria amazonica*), one of the world's largest water lilies. Its enormous leaves can grow up to 9.8 ft (3 m) wide in a week, dominating the water's surface and starving other plants of space and sunlight.

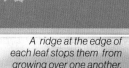

Sharp spines cover the underside of each leaf, protecting them from hungry, nibbling fish.

A ridge at the edge of each leaf stops them from growing over one another.

The leaf bud swings around in circles, pushing other plants out of the way.

Days 1–2

Seed germination
A giant water lily seed will germinate (sprout) in soil only on the riverbed. It starts to grow strong roots to anchor itself in the mud.

Day 10

Leaf bud clears path
The tightly coiled leaf bud grows toward the water's surface on a thick stalk, which can grow up to about 26 ft (8 m) long. Each bud is covered with thick, sharp spines, which help it clear space for itself by pushing other plants out of its path.

Week 2

Unfurling leaf
The leaf bud unfurls (opens) on the water's surface, expanding by more than 8 in (20 cm) a day. As the bud expands, it pushes other plants out of the way, crushing and piercing them with its spiky underside. Within a week, the bud has finished unfurling, forming a single huge leaf.

Month 4

Mature plant
A mature giant water lily plant produces up to 10 leaves each month. Each leaf measures up to 9.8 ft (3 m) across—as wide as a trampoline. Soon, the water lily's leaves completely cover the water's surface, blocking sunlight from reaching the plants beneath.

Pollination

The scarab beetle enters the giant lily's flower to feed. The flower closes overnight with the beetle trapped inside. It gets covered in pollen from the stamen (male part of the flower). When the flower reopens the next day and the beetle flies away to feed on another flower, it transfers the first flower's pollen on to the stigma (female part) of the second.

The beetle is trapped inside the flower overnight.

An aerial view of multiple giant water lily leaves shows how they cover the water's surface.

Month 5

+ 1 day

+ 2 days

Month 8

Flower growth

Several months after sprouting, the giant water lily is ready to flower. Each flower it produces has white petals and is held on a thick stalk that is anchored to the riverbed by the plant's strong roots. The beautiful flowers attract scarab beetles to pollinate the plant.

Locked inside

When a flower is fully developed, it opens at sunset with a strong, fruity scent that attracts nearby beetles. The flowers close overnight, and inside each one is a trapped beetle, which remains there until the flower reopens the next day. While trapped inside, the beetle pollinates the flower.

Dying flower

Now pollinated, the once-white, short-lived flower turns dark pink. It loses its sweet scent and so it is no longer attractive to beetles. The flower slowly sinks down into the water. It will develop into a fruit over the next 2–3 months.

Ripe fruit

When ripe, the fruit rots underwater, releasing hundreds of seeds. Each seed is washed away by the water. Some may get lodged in the riverbed, where they will eventually germinate and grow into more Amazonian giant water lilies ready to dominate the water.

Salty survivors

Found on the shoreline between the land and the sea are mangroves—trees that have the unique ability to live with their roots submerged in salty water. Mangrove forests protect shorelines from wind and waves and prevent sand and soil from rivers being lost to the sea. They also provide shelter to a huge variety of different species such as fish, crabs, and crocodiles. Mangroves can be found along the saltwater coasts of tropical and subtropical countries, including Panama, where this photograph was taken.

From seed to domination

Plants and trees in dense rainforests must compete for space and sunlight to survive, some growing much taller than others to catch the best rays. Strangler fig trees, such as the Florida strangler fig, have developed an unusual way of beating the competition. They build thick roots around another victim tree, known as a "host," steal its light and nutrients, and eventually kill their hosts.

Black howler monkeys may drop or throw the strangler fig seeds, or disperse them in their droppings.

Figs are green at first, turning yellow and then red as they ripen.

The strangler fig seedling is wedged in position high up in the branches of the host tree by its growing network of roots.

Seed distribution
Animals, such as monkeys and birds, eat the fruit of the strangler fig and disperse the seeds in their droppings, which sometimes land in the crook of a branch of a nearby host tree.

Seedling
The strangler fig seed germinates (sprouts) in between the branches of the host tree. Some of the strangler fig's roots extend outward along the bark to search for water and nutrients, while others grow downward to the ground at about 16.5 ft (5 m) every year.

More and more growing strangler fig roots surround the trunk of the host tree.

Roots grow
Above the ground, the hanging roots divide into many thin roots to take up as much water and nutrients from the soil as possible. The roots thicken once they reach the soil, and many more new roots travel down.

Day 1

Years 0–1

Year 1

Fig pollination

The fruit of the Florida strangler fig is pollinated by a single species of fig wasp, known as *Pegoscapus mexicanus*, which tunnels its way into the fig and lays its eggs inside the fruit. Each of the many hundreds of species of fig trees is pollinated by one or very few species of wasps, with the wasp and fig totally reliant on each other for survival. This special relationship is called mutualism.

1 The pollen-covered female wasp enters the fig to lay eggs, pollinating the flowers at the same time.

2 Pollinated flowers produce seeds, while the wasp larvae grow.

3 The wingless male wasps hatch inside the fig first. They search for females to mate with, then digs escape tunnels for the females.

4 The females grow to maturity and exit the fig, collecting pollen as they pass the flower.

Gaps in the network of roots provide homes for insects and other small animals.

Roots fuse together

The strangler fig roots fuse together to make a strong net around the trunk of the host tree. These roots become thicker over time, and are eventually able to support the full weight of the fig.

Years 1–5

Host tree dies

The strangler fig tree has now blocked all sunlight to the host tree and is literally strangling it by stealing its water and nutrients. Unable to survive, the host tree dies and decays, leaving the strangler fig's hollow, lattice trunk.

Years 10–200

No escape!

Attracted by the promise of sweet, tasty nectar, an unsuspecting wasp lands on a Venus flytrap. Suddenly, the hinged leaves spring shut, imprisoning the wasp, which makes a change from its normal diet of flies, spiders, ants, and beetles. This carnivorous plant "eats" its prey by releasing digestive juices that dissolve the wasp, creating an insect soup full of nutrients that can then be absorbed. Catching insects allows the plant to obtain vital nutrients that it cannot get from the soil.

When the tiny trigger hairs are touched by an insect twice, the hinged leaves snap shut.

The bright red leaves, and the smell of nectar, attract insects.

Interlocking teeth form a cage to trap the prey. If the insect wriggles, the cage gets tighter.

Digestive juices secreted inside the hinged leaves take about two weeks to break down the insect's body.

Touch-sensitive trigger hairs

Stinking flower

In the Sumatran rainforest, something stinks. The flower spike of the corpse flower releases a stench as bad as rotting meat or fish. The flower spike, known as an inflorescence, is huge. In fact, at 9.8 ft (3 m) tall, it is the tallest unbranched flower in the world. The smell attracts flies and beetles, which pollinate its many hundreds of flowers that lie at the base of the spike.

The flower spike is almost twice the height of an adult.

Month 1

Month 2

Day 1 of blooming

The corm

For 4–5 years the plant sends up a single giant leaf without producing a flower. Over this time, part of the stem, called a corm, grows underground. It is a food store and each year it grows bigger and bigger.

Flower bud

When the corm reaches 44 lbs (20 kg), it has built up enough energy to send up a flower spike. This spike, or inflorescence, is hidden in a petal-like wrapping, called a spathe.

Fast growth

The flower spike grows very quickly, gaining 6 in (15 cm) each day. When it has reached a height of about 9.8 ft (3 m), the top of the spike starts to poke out of the spathe.

Flower unfurls

The spathe unfurls outward to reveal a purple petal-like skirt that can stretch to 5 ft (1.5 m) wide. The base of the spike is now revealed, which holds hundreds of male and female flowers. The spike begins to smell like rotting meat, giving the plant its name: "corpse flower."

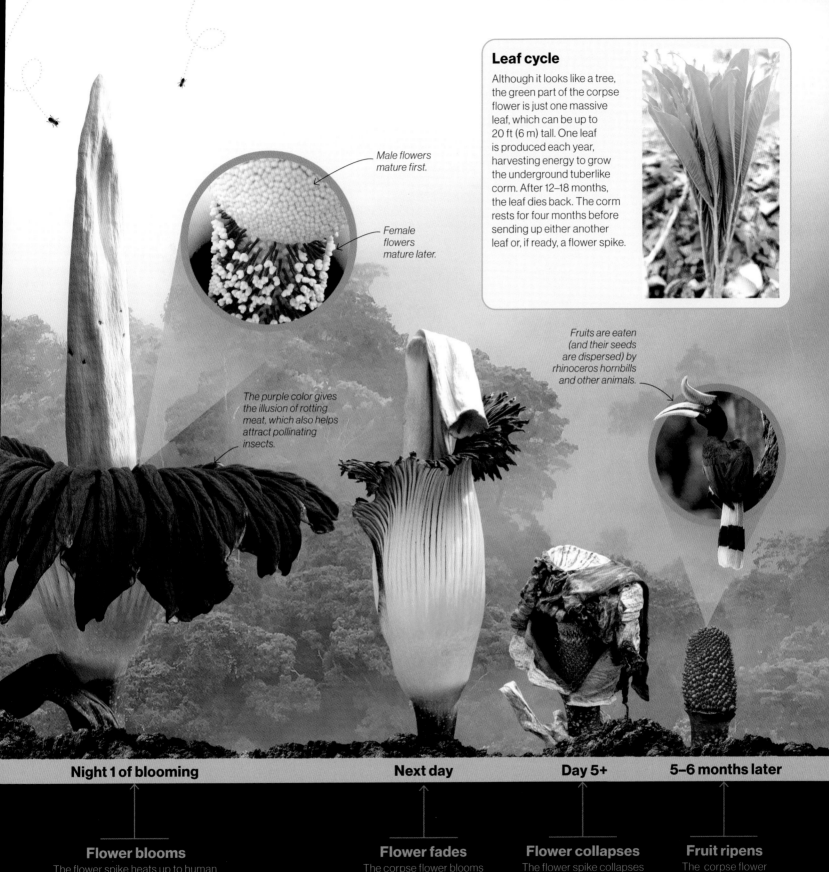

Leaf cycle

Although it looks like a tree, the green part of the corpse flower is just one massive leaf, which can be up to 20 ft (6 m) tall. One leaf is produced each year, harvesting energy to grow the underground tuberlike corm. After 12–18 months, the leaf dies back. The corm rests for four months before sending up either another leaf or, if ready, a flower spike.

Male flowers mature first.

Female flowers mature later.

The purple color gives the illusion of rotting meat, which also helps attract pollinating insects.

Fruits are eaten (and their seeds are dispersed) by rhinoceros hornbills and other animals.

Night 1 of blooming

Next day

Day 5+

5–6 months later

Flower blooms

The flower spike heats up to human body temperature. This helps it release its revolting smell. The stench can travel to just under half a mile (1 km) away, attracting pollinators, such as beetles and flies. The insects crawl inside and pick up pollen when they brush against

Flower fades

The corpse flower blooms (and smells) for just 24–36 hours before starting to shrivel. The pollinated female flowers begin their slow development into fruits.

Flower collapses

The flower spike collapses within a week of flowering, although its thick green stalk remains. The round fruits start to grow from the pollinated flowers. By the time the fruits are ripe in five or six months' time, the flower tissues will

Fruit ripens

The corpse flower makes hundreds of red fruits, each containing one or two seeds. After flowering, the corm rests for a few months before making new leaves or sending up a new

The gills create structure for the cap and produce the spores.

Spores released

Millions of spores are released by tiny reproductive cells called basidia on the gills. The spores fall or are carried away by wind until they settle on the soil, in water, or on plants.

Adult mushroom

As the mushroom matures, the bright red cap becomes more plate-shaped. On its underside are hundreds of thin flaps called gills. These delicate structures produce the mushroom's spores.

Weeks 2–3

About day 7

Days 1–7

Life of mushrooms

Mushrooms are not plants, but members of another kingdom of life, called fungi. They are the fruiting bodies of fungi, like apples on an apple tree. Most of the fungus they grow from is hidden underground, often near tree roots, or inside dead wood, and is made up of threadlike structures called hyphae. These fuse together to form a network—a mycelium—from which mushrooms absorb water and nutrients and eventually grow. When a mushroom, such as this bright red fly agaric, is ripe, it reproduces by releasing millions of tiny particles called spores.

Getting redder

Although the cap increases in size, the white scales do not grow. As the caps surface area gets bigger, it becomes more red. It also changes shape as it grows.

The top of a mushroom is called a cap.

Some spores may be carried away by wind.

Spores settle
The mushroom's tiny seedlike spores have fallen and been scattered by the wind. Many settle on hard, dry surfaces without food or water, and these will probably die. However, those that fall on damp soil may survive.

Dying mushroom
The bright red of the cap starts to fade. Having completed its task to release spores and reproduce, the mushroom collapses and rots. As it decays, it returns nutrients to the soil.

Within days

Around week 3

Days to years later

Days to years later

Day 1 of new mushroom

Hyphae grow
If conditions such as the ground temperature and rainfall are favorable for it to reproduce, thin, threadlike structures called hyphae grow from the fallen spores. This underground network of hyphae is known as mycelium.

Primordia form
The hyphae grow and in places knots may fuse together to form primordia—with the stem, cap, and gills of a young mushroom. Most do not develop further, but some will become an adult mushroom. The fungus directs energy to these primordia.

Small white scales
When the fruiting body of the mushroom first becomes visible, it is covered with small white scales. These are the remains of a protective veil that shields the young mushroom as it develops into an adult.

Different mushrooms
Mushrooms grow in an amazing variety of colors and shapes. They may be white, yellow, brown, orange, red, purple, or blue. Some have flat caps, while others are shaped like a bird's nest. Some look like balls, or are shaped like cages and stars. Certain mushrooms are poisonous.

Bird's nest mushroom

Blue pinkgill

Bridal veil mushroom

Underground communication
A complex underground network of roots, fungi, and bacteria—sometimes called the wood-wide web—helps to connect plants and fungi. They can exchange information via these networks, share nutrients, and move minerals such as carbon, nitrogen, and phosphorus to the plants that are most in need of them.

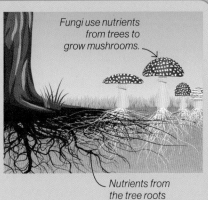

Fungi use nutrients from trees to grow mushrooms.

Nutrients from the tree roots pass to the fungi.

How logs rot

From the moment a branch or an entire tree falls on to the forest floor, it begins to rot. This process can take many years, depending on the log's size, the type of tree it is from, and the living organisms in the forest that can help break it down. The large Douglas fir log shown here takes about 115 years to almost completely decay into soil in a North American forest, whereas dead wood in the warmer, more humid Amazon rainforest in South America can take just 30 years.

How living trees decay

Tree branches usually begin to break down long before they snap off and fall to the ground. Damaged branches can be infected by fungi or bacteria, which start to destroy living tissues, weakening the tree. The fungus shown here causes a disease of conifer trees called red ring rot. It is the most common wood-decay fungus in North America.

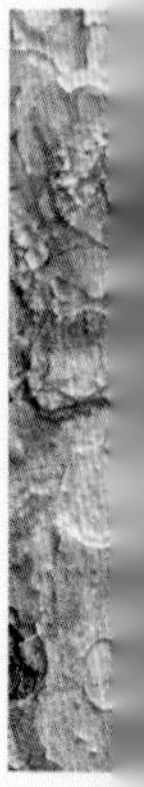

Branch falls

Once a branch of a Douglas fir tree has died, weakened by disease or perhaps a drought, a strong gust of wind can cause it to snap and fall to the forest floor.

Huge banana slugs roam the forest floor, searching for fungi or dead plants to eat.

Day 1

Insect homes

Insects make holes in the log, often to lay their eggs in a safe place. While they remove little of the wood themselves, these holes are gateways for fungi to enter and decompose (decay) the wood.

When adult white-spotted sawyer beetles emerge from the log, they switch their diet from wood to conifer needles.

Year 1

Bear claws

A bear uses its sharp claws to tear into the log to get at the larvae, ants, and other invertebrates hidden inside. Again, the damage gives fungi and other decomposers entry points, speeding up the log's decay.

Small predators, such as this crab spider, explore the log when hunting.

Year 2

White-spotted sawyer beetle larvae (grubs) chew their way through the log, for 1 to 2 years.

Black bears have an amazing sense of smell and can sniff out larvae hidden in logs.

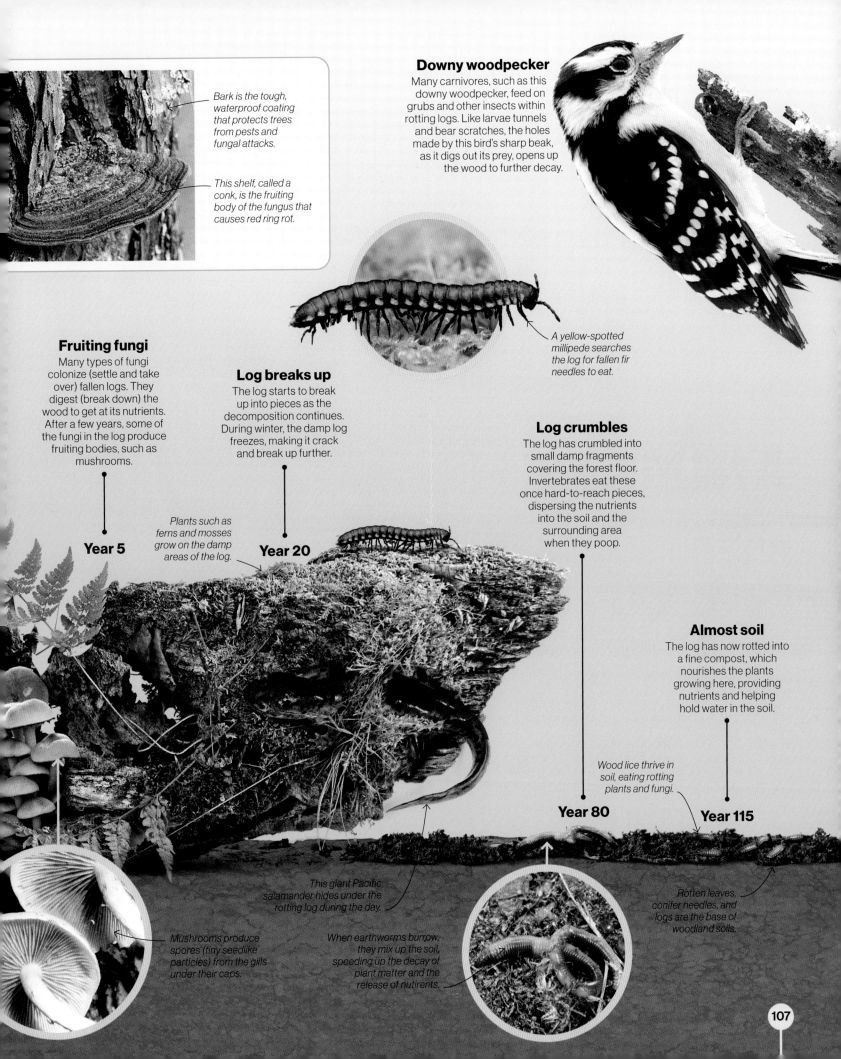

Bark is the tough, waterproof coating that protects trees from pests and fungal attacks.

This shelf, called a conk, is the fruiting body of the fungus that causes red ring rot.

Downy woodpecker

Many carnivores, such as this downy woodpecker, feed on grubs and other insects within rotting logs. Like larvae tunnels and bear scratches, the holes made by this bird's sharp beak, as it digs out its prey, opens up the wood to further decay.

A yellow-spotted millipede searches the log for fallen fir needles to eat.

Fruiting fungi

Many types of fungi colonize (settle and take over) fallen logs. They digest (break down) the wood to get at its nutrients. After a few years, some of the fungi in the log produce fruiting bodies, such as mushrooms.

Log breaks up

The log starts to break up into pieces as the decomposition continues. During winter, the damp log freezes, making it crack and break up further.

Log crumbles

The log has crumbled into small damp fragments covering the forest floor. Invertebrates eat these once hard-to-reach pieces, dispersing the nutrients into the soil and the surrounding area when they poop.

Year 5

Plants such as ferns and mosses grow on the damp areas of the log.

Year 20

Almost soil

The log has now rotted into a fine compost, which nourishes the plants growing here, providing nutrients and helping hold water in the soil.

Wood lice thrive in soil, eating rotting plants and fungi.

Year 80

Year 115

This giant Pacific salamander hides under the rotting log during the day.

Rotten leaves, conifer needles, and logs are the base of woodland soils.

Mushrooms produce spores (tiny seedlike particles) from the gills under their caps.

When earthworms burrow, they mix up the soil, speeding up the decay of plant matter and the release of nutrients.

ANIMALS

With an estimated 7.7 million species worldwide today that we know about, animals are the most diverse form of life. That figure is even higher if you include extinct and not-yet-discovered species. Animals have developed amazing ways to live in almost every habitat on Earth. Some have superpowers, such as the ability to regrow limbs or change color or texture to hide in their surroundings. Others are able to withstand extreme temperatures or endure punishing migrations to find food or a mate. The story of the animal world becomes ever more fascinating with each discovery humans make.

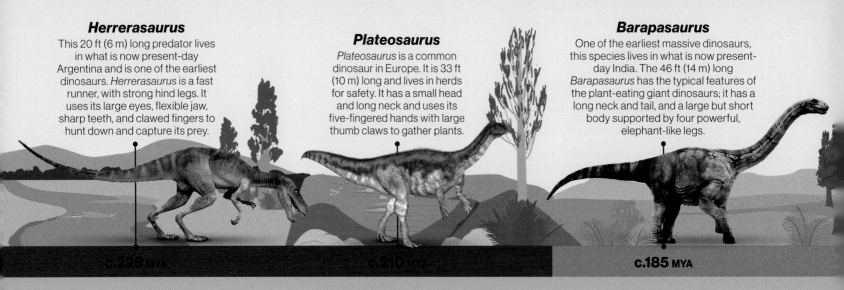

Herrerasaurus

This 20 ft (6 m) long predator lives in what is now present-day Argentina and is one of the earliest dinosaurs. *Herrerasaurus* is a fast runner, with strong hind legs. It uses its large eyes, flexible jaw, sharp teeth, and clawed fingers to hunt down and capture its prey.

c.228 MYA

Plateosaurus

Plateosaurus is a common dinosaur in Europe. It is 33 ft (10 m) long and lives in herds for safety. It has a small head and long neck and uses its five-fingered hands with large thumb claws to gather plants.

c.210 MYA

Barapasaurus

One of the earliest massive dinosaurs, this species lives in what is now present-day India. The 46 ft (14 m) long *Barapasaurus* has the typical features of the plant-eating giant dinosaurs; it has a long neck and tail, and a large but short body supported by four powerful, elephant-like legs.

c.185 MYA

What is a dinosaur?

Dinosaurs were a group of reptiles that emerged during the Triassic era. The name comes from the Greek for "fearfully great lizard," but dinosaurs are not actually lizards. They all lived on land and laid eggs, and many had long tails that helped them balance. All dinosaurs walked with their legs underneath their bodies, which is a key difference from modern reptiles such as lizards and crocodiles.

Lizard
Modern lizards sprawl, with their knees and elbows held at right angles to their bodies.

Crocodile
These reptiles stand with their knees and elbows slightly bent.

Dinosaur
With their limbs tucked underneath their bodies, dinosaurs had an upright stance.

Rise of the dinosaurs

The first dinosaurs evolved around 240 MYA, just 12 million years after a huge extinction event that wiped out more than 70 percent of life on land. Dinosaurs in the early Triassic era were small, darting about to find food and safety. They became much larger and more diverse in the later Triassic and through the Jurassic and Cretaceous periods. This ability to adapt is how they ruled the planet for millions of years.

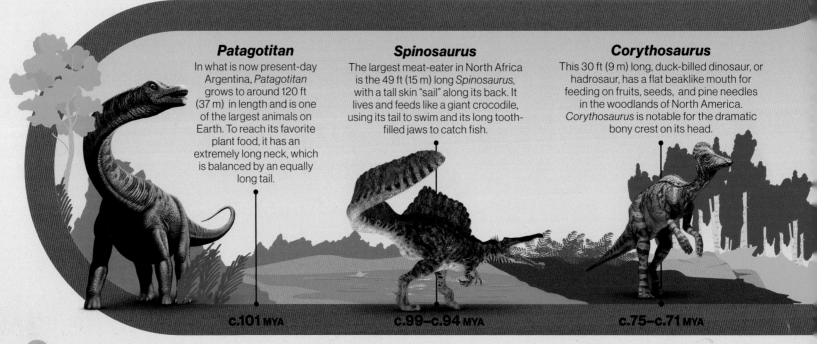

Patagotitan

In what is now present-day Argentina, *Patagotitan* grows to around 120 ft (37 m) in length and is one of the largest animals on Earth. To reach its favorite plant food, it has an extremely long neck, which is balanced by an equally long tail.

c.101 MYA

Spinosaurus

The largest meat-eater in North Africa is the 49 ft (15 m) long *Spinosaurus*, with a tall skin "sail" along its back. It lives and feeds like a giant crocodile, using its tail to swim and its long tooth-filled jaws to catch fish.

c.99–c.94 MYA

Corythosaurus

This 30 ft (9 m) long, duck-billed dinosaur, or hadrosaur, has a flat beaklike mouth for feeding on fruits, seeds, and pine needles in the woodlands of North America. *Corythosaurus* is notable for the dramatic bony crest on its head.

c.75–c.71 MYA

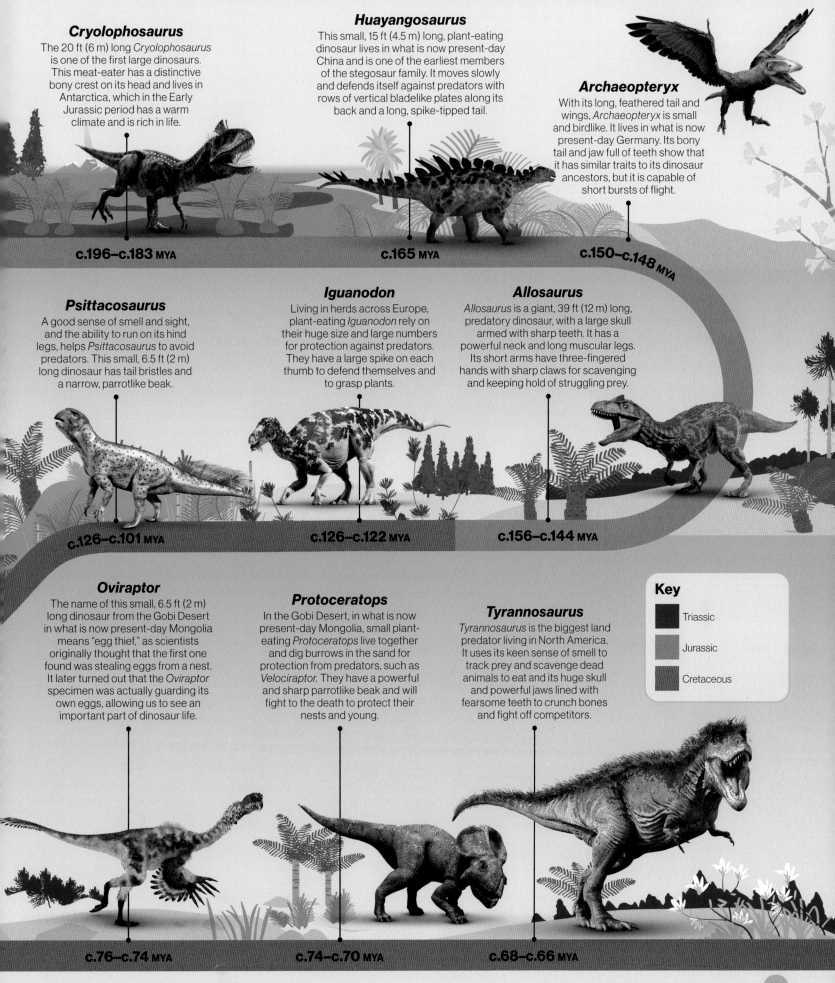

Cryolophosaurus

The 20 ft (6 m) long *Cryolophosaurus* is one of the first large dinosaurs. This meat-eater has a distinctive bony crest on its head and lives in Antarctica, which in the Early Jurassic period has a warm climate and is rich in life.

c.196–c.183 MYA

Huayangosaurus

This small, 15 ft (4.5 m) long, plant-eating dinosaur lives in what is now present-day China and is one of the earliest members of the stegosaur family. It moves slowly and defends itself against predators with rows of vertical bladelike plates along its back and a long, spike-tipped tail.

c.165 MYA

Archaeopteryx

With its long, feathered tail and wings, *Archaeopteryx* is small and birdlike. It lives in what is now present-day Germany. Its bony tail and jaw full of teeth show that it has similar traits to its dinosaur ancestors, but it is capable of short bursts of flight.

c.150–c.148 MYA

Psittacosaurus

A good sense of smell and sight, and the ability to run on its hind legs, helps *Psittacosaurus* to avoid predators. This small, 6.5 ft (2 m) long dinosaur has tail bristles and a narrow, parrotlike beak.

c.126–c.101 MYA

Iguanodon

Living in herds across Europe, plant-eating *Iguanodon* rely on their huge size and large numbers for protection against predators. They have a large spike on each thumb to defend themselves and to grasp plants.

c.126–c.122 MYA

Allosaurus

Allosaurus is a giant, 39 ft (12 m) long, predatory dinosaur, with a large skull armed with sharp teeth. It has a powerful neck and long muscular legs. Its short arms have three-fingered hands with sharp claws for scavenging and keeping hold of struggling prey.

c.156–c.144 MYA

Oviraptor

The name of this small, 6.5 ft (2 m) long dinosaur from the Gobi Desert in what is now present-day Mongolia means "egg thief," as scientists originally thought that the first one found was stealing eggs from a nest. It later turned out that the *Oviraptor* specimen was actually guarding its own eggs, allowing us to see an important part of dinosaur life.

c.76–c.74 MYA

Protoceratops

In the Gobi Desert, in what is now present-day Mongolia, small plant-eating *Protoceratops* live together and dig burrows in the sand for protection from predators, such as *Velociraptor*. They have a powerful and sharp parrotlike beak and will fight to the death to protect their nests and young.

c.74–c.70 MYA

Tyrannosaurus

Tyrannosaurus is the biggest land predator living in North America. It uses its keen sense of smell to track prey and scavenge dead animals to eat and its huge skull and powerful jaws lined with fearsome teeth to crunch bones and fight off competitors.

c.68–c.66 MYA

Key

- Triassic
- Jurassic
- Cretaceous

Evolution of flight

Throughout Earth's history, only four groups of animals have independently evolved to fly: insects, birds (including avian dinosaurs), bats, and extinct reptiles called pterosaurs. Flying is a special way of moving—animals that fly use their wings to flap, creating a "lift" force that stops them from falling and pushes them up and up, higher into the air.

Pterosaurs
The name of these reptiles means "winged lizard." Pterosaurs evolve from small reptiles that climb in trees. They become extinct at the same time as their non-avian dinosaur relatives, about 66 million years ago.

Clawed wing
The crow-size bird *Confuciusornis* is a strong flyer with short, square wings. It has three clawed fingers sticking out of each wing. These are perhaps used for climbing through trees or for fighting.

Flying dinosaurs
Like a dinosaur, *Archaeopteryx* has teeth and a bony tail, but it can also fly for short distances. The discovery of feathered fossils of *Archaeopteryx* is one of the first finds that make paleontologists think that birds evolved from dinosaurs.

First fliers
Mazothairos is a species of insect that is one of the earliest known flying animals. They have simple flight muscles, with four wings that are probably held flat like those of a dragonfly, and an extra pair of small winglets behind the head.

Early insects
Some fossil experts have spotted features in *Rhyniella praecursor*—one of the earliest insects—that later evolve for flight. *Rhyniella* can leap into the air when threatened.

Flying fish
The first flying fish evolve in Triassic times. They can only glide, using their powerful tails to make long leaps above the water. They do this to avoid being snapped up by bigger fish below the surface.

| c.360 MYA | c.330 MYA | c.240 MYA | c.225 MYA | c.147 MYA | c.127 MYA |

Origins of flight

Today's birds are the descendants of small feathered dinosaurs that found a way to fly. Dinosaurs evolved feathers for staying warm, for camouflage, or possibly for displaying to each other. There are different theories about how these animals became able to take to the skies.

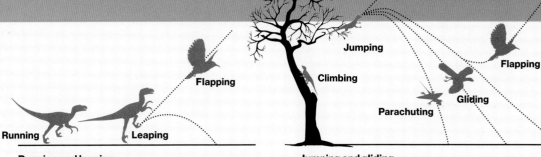

Running   Leaping   Flapping

Jumping   Climbing   Flapping   Gliding   Parachuting

Running and leaping
Flight may have evolved from fast, feathered dinosaurs running and leaping, with no gliding stage in between.

Jumping and gliding
It is possible that feathered dinosaurs used clawed fingers on their wings to climb trees. At the top, they could jump and glide down to safety, or possibly flap up even higher.

Glider
Microraptor, a distant cousin of *Archaeopteryx*, is a dinosaur with four feathery wings, one on each arm and leg. Experts think the wings are too small for flying. Instead, *Microraptor* probably uses them to glide from branch to branch.

Bats
Bats are the only mammals that can fly. They have wings made from flexible skin that is stretched over very long finger bones. Unlike birds, most bats fly during the night.

Peregrine falcon
Evolving from other falcons around this time, this medium-size bird of prey is the fastest flyer of all time. It hunts other flying birds in midair, knocking them out of the sky with a high-speed dive that can reach 200 mph (320 km/h).

Controlled flight
Eoalulavis is one of the first birds with an "alula": a flexible thumb bone in the middle of the wing. The alula smooths out the airflow above the wings at low speeds and is used by today's birds to have more control over their flight.

Parachute glider
This Australian marsupial evolves a furry flap of skin called a patagium, like a parachute, to allow it to glide down from trees. Several other tree-dwelling mammal species, such as flying squirrels, evolve to do this in other parts of the world.

Gliding lizard
There are many kinds of "flying lizard." Instead of using its arms or legs as wings, this forest reptile's wide, gliding wings are made from long rib bones that grow sideways from the body.

c.125 MYA   **c.122 MYA**   **c.115 MYA**   **c.52 MYA**   **c.5 MYA**   **c.2.1 MYA**

Fall of the dinosaurs

Dinosaurs were the dominant land animals for about 165 million years. Massive plant-eaters such as *Edmontosaurus*, horned *Triceratops*, and tiny *Microceratus* grazed on grass and trees, while meat-eaters such as *Tyrannosaurus* hunted them. The skies were filled with flying reptiles called pterosaurs, and giant reptiles, including mosasaurs and plesiosaurs, ruled the oceans. Then, one day at the end of the Cretaceous Period, about 66 million years ago, an enormous meteorite crashed into Earth, wiping out more than half of all life, including almost all of the dinosaurs.

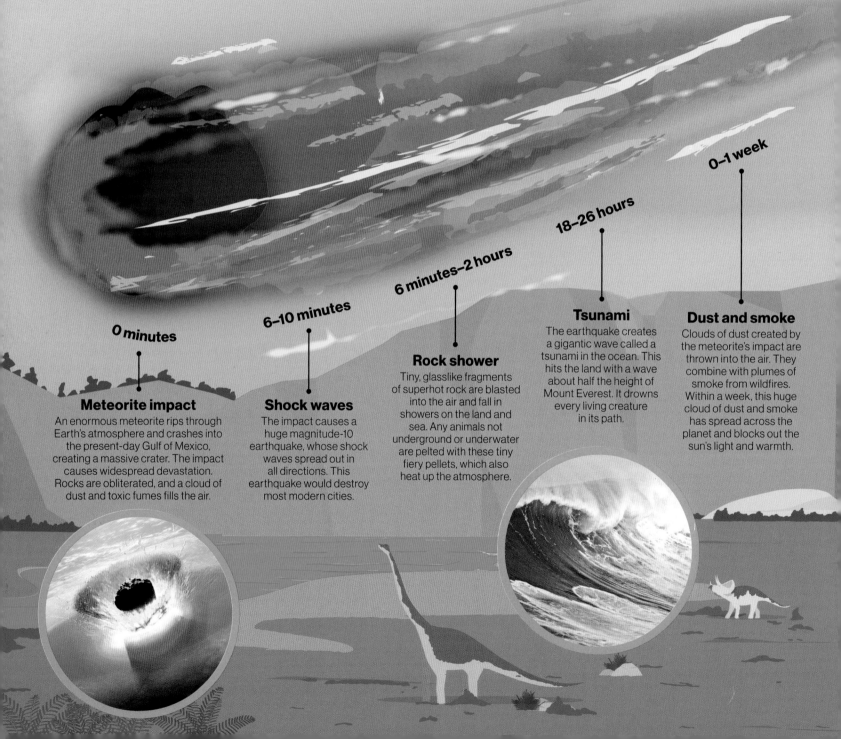

0 minutes

Meteorite impact

An enormous meteorite rips through Earth's atmosphere and crashes into the present-day Gulf of Mexico, creating a massive crater. The impact causes widespread devastation. Rocks are obliterated, and a cloud of dust and toxic fumes fills the air.

6–10 minutes

Shock waves

The impact causes a huge magnitude-10 earthquake, whose shock waves spread out in all directions. This earthquake would destroy most modern cities.

6 minutes–2 hours

Rock shower

Tiny, glasslike fragments of superhot rock are blasted into the air and fall in showers on the land and sea. Any animals not underground or underwater are pelted with these tiny fiery pellets, which also heat up the atmosphere.

18–26 hours

Tsunami

The earthquake creates a gigantic wave called a tsunami in the ocean. This hits the land with a wave about half the height of Mount Everest. It drowns every living creature in its path.

0–1 week

Dust and smoke

Clouds of dust created by the meteorite's impact are thrown into the air. They combine with plumes of smoke from wildfires. Within a week, this huge cloud of dust and smoke has spread across the planet and blocks out the sun's light and warmth.

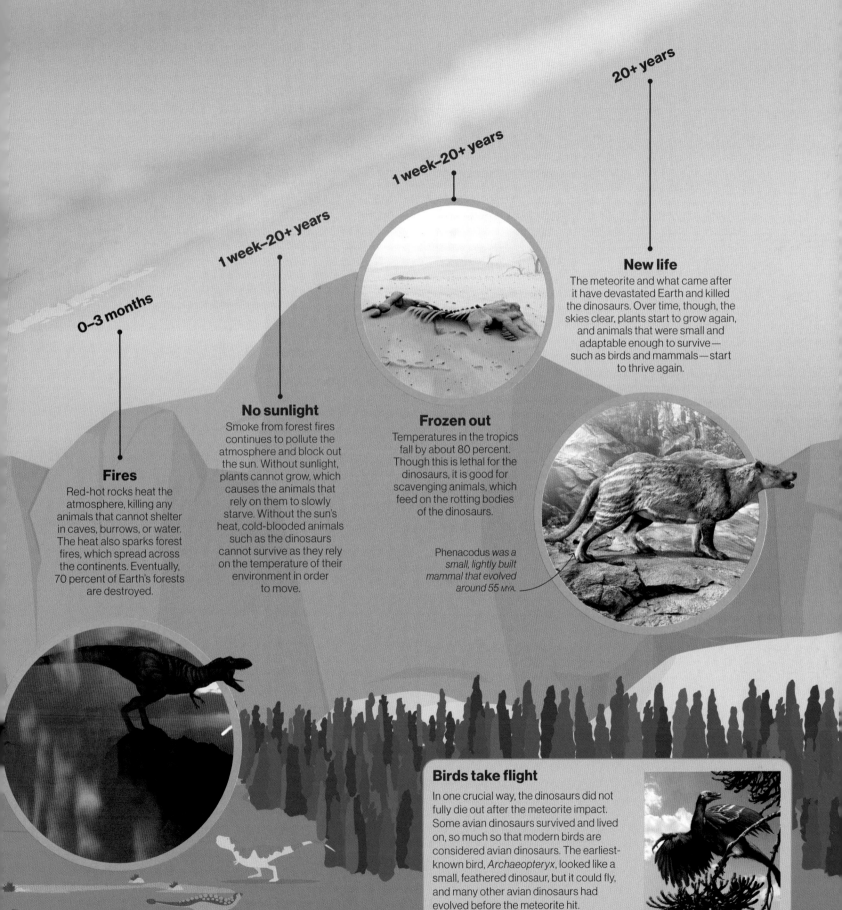

0–3 months

Fires

Red-hot rocks heat the atmosphere, killing any animals that cannot shelter in caves, burrows, or water. The heat also sparks forest fires, which spread across the continents. Eventually, 70 percent of Earth's forests are destroyed.

1 week–20+ years

No sunlight

Smoke from forest fires continues to pollute the atmosphere and block out the sun. Without sunlight, plants cannot grow, which causes the animals that rely on them to slowly starve. Without the sun's heat, cold-blooded animals such as the dinosaurs cannot survive as they rely on the temperature of their environment in order to move.

1 week–20+ years

Frozen out

Temperatures in the tropics fall by about 80 percent. Though this is lethal for the dinosaurs, it is good for scavenging animals, which feed on the rotting bodies of the dinosaurs.

Phenacodus was a small, lightly built mammal that evolved around 55 MYA.

20+ years

New life

The meteorite and what came after it have devastated Earth and killed the dinosaurs. Over time, though, the skies clear, plants start to grow again, and animals that were small and adaptable enough to survive—such as birds and mammals—start to thrive again.

Birds take flight

In one crucial way, the dinosaurs did not fully die out after the meteorite impact. Some avian dinosaurs survived and lived on, so much so that modern birds are considered avian dinosaurs. The earliest-known bird, *Archaeopteryx*, looked like a small, feathered dinosaur, but it could fly, and many other avian dinosaurs had evolved before the meteorite hit.

Death and decay

As soon as an animal or plant dies, its body becomes food for other organisms. Over the following days and months, the soft flesh is eaten by scavengers, or it starts to decay. If the animal or plant dies in or near water and is covered by sand or mud (sediment) before it decays completely, the process of fossilization begins.

Start

Burial

Over thousands of years, the remains of dead plants and animals that sink to the bottom of seas, rivers, lakes, and swamps are buried in layer after layer of soft sediment. Sometimes this happens because water levels rise and cover areas that once were dry land.

Up to thousands of years

The dead animal will soon start to be covered in layers of sediment.

The soft parts of the animal have decayed or been eaten, but the hard parts remain and these are what get turned to stone.

The layers of sediment are compressed by other layers above and harden into solid rock.

How fossils form

Fossils are the remains of animals, plants, and other traces of life preserved in rocks. There are a few ways that this can happen, but the most common way is shown above—when sand and mud cover an organism soon after it dies and begin to turn it to stone. Usually, only the hard parts, such as shells, bones, teeth, and wood, are tough enough to survive the destructive process of fossilization.

Fossilization

The soft layers of sediment build up over millions of years and are compressed (squashed down) to form hard rock. The fossil may be flattened by physical pressure, dissolved, or replaced by minerals in the water. The hard body parts—bones and shells—of animals buried in the rock eventually turn to stone.

Types of fossils

Many fossils form by being turned to stone, but there are other kinds:

Body fossils
These are the hard parts of the original plant or animal—usually wood, bone, teeth, or shell—preserved in their original form, after the flesh has been eaten or decayed.

Trace fossils
Animals leave traces behind, such as footprints, burrows, eggs, and dung (shown here), all of which can be preserved as fossils.

Casts and molds
If the body fossil dissolves after the sediment has turned to rock, it leaves a space, called a mold, in the shape of the fossil. A cast that looks like the fossil can form if the mold is filled with minerals.

Millions of years

In cold environments, animals may be frozen in ice. This method of fossilization often preserves softer body parts, such as fur and skin.

Finding fossils

Millions of years later, movements in Earth's crust, or the work of wind and water erosion, may bring the layers that contain fossils to the surface. Fossils are very fragile, and digging them out without damaging them is hard work.

Hundreds of millions of years

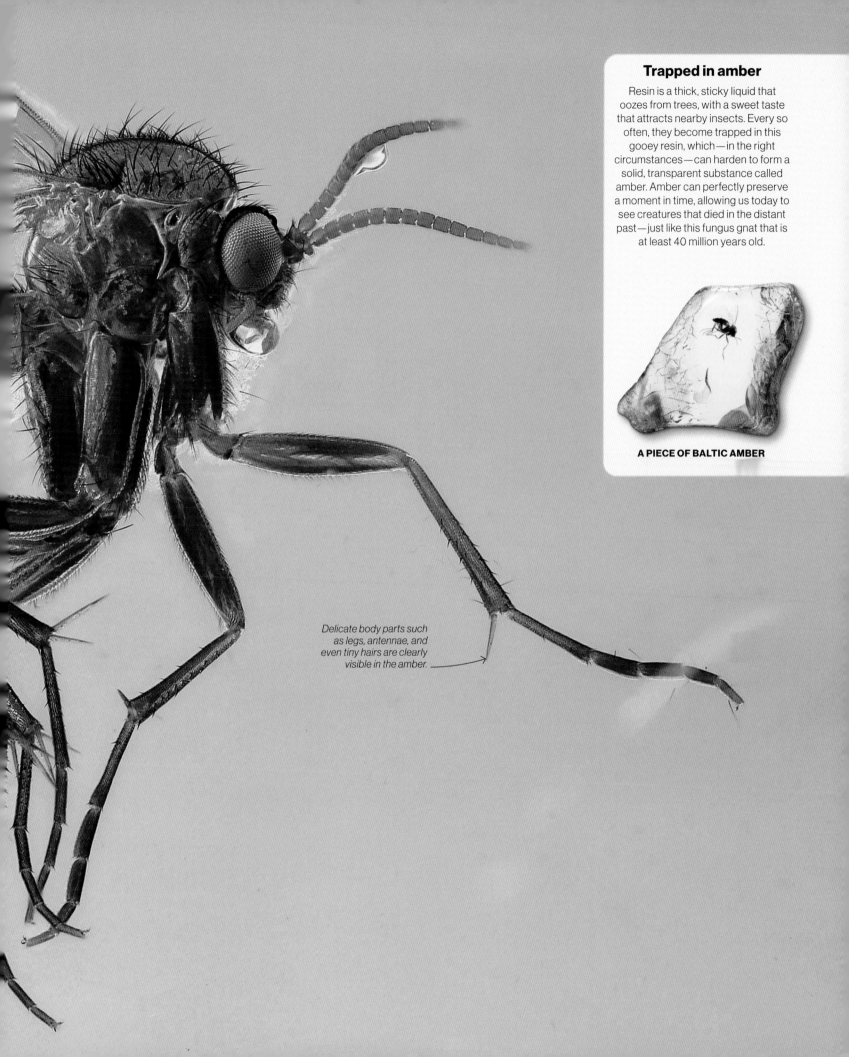

Trapped in amber

Resin is a thick, sticky liquid that oozes from trees, with a sweet taste that attracts nearby insects. Every so often, they become trapped in this gooey resin, which—in the right circumstances—can harden to form a solid, transparent substance called amber. Amber can perfectly preserve a moment in time, allowing us today to see creatures that died in the distant past—just like this fungus gnat that is at least 40 million years old.

A PIECE OF BALTIC AMBER

Delicate body parts such as legs, antennae, and even tiny hairs are clearly visible in the amber.

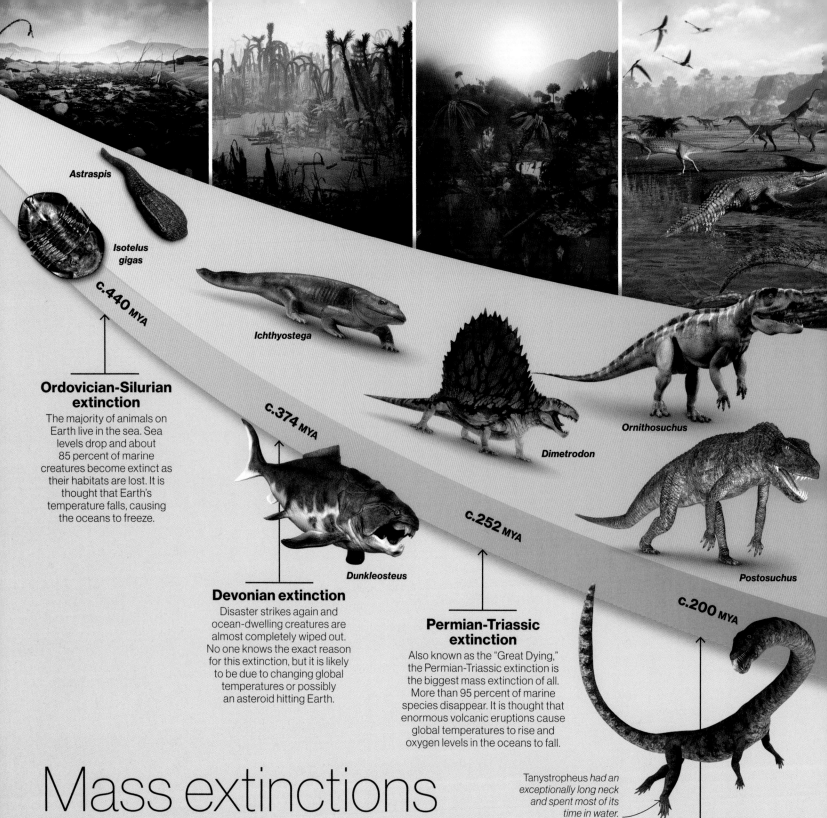

Astraspis

Isotelus gigas

c.440 MYA

Ichthyostega

Ordovician-Silurian extinction

The majority of animals on Earth live in the sea. Sea levels drop and about 85 percent of marine creatures become extinct as their habitats are lost. It is thought that Earth's temperature falls, causing the oceans to freeze.

c.374 MYA

Dunkleosteus

Devonian extinction

Disaster strikes again and ocean-dwelling creatures are almost completely wiped out. No one knows the exact reason for this extinction, but it is likely to be due to changing global temperatures or possibly an asteroid hitting Earth.

Dimetrodon

Ornithosuchus

c.252 MYA

Permian-Triassic extinction

Also known as the "Great Dying," the Permian-Triassic extinction is the biggest mass extinction of all. More than 95 percent of marine species disappear. It is thought that enormous volcanic eruptions cause global temperatures to rise and oxygen levels in the oceans to fall.

Postosuchus

c.200 MYA

Mass extinctions

Tanystropheus *had an exceptionally long neck and spent most of its time in water.*

Triassic-Jurassic extinction

The Triassic-Jurassic extinction is probably the result of gigantic volcanoes spewing lava and gases into the air, causing global warming. The gases reduce the oxygen levels in the atmosphere and oceans. Around 80 percent of all species on Earth die out.

Of all the animal species that have ever lived on Earth, an estimated 98 percent are now extinct. Most of these species were wiped out during catastrophic events, such as volcanic disruption of Earth's climate. However, more recently an enormous number are at risk of extinction because of human activities. When a huge number of species dies over a short period of time, it is called a mass extinction.

Compsognathus

Tyrannosaurus rex

Utahraptor

Caspian tiger (1970s)

Great auk (1844)

Dodo (Late 17th century)

Cuban red macaw (1860s)

c.66 MYA

11,700 YA–Present day

Metriorhynchus looked like a crocodile but had a tail fluke and feet like flippers for swimming.

Cretaceous-Tertiary extinction

A massive asteroid 7.5 miles (12 km) wide hits Earth. Dust, fumes, and debris fill the air, blocking out sunlight and causing temperatures to fall. The after-effects of this impact kill more than half of all life on Earth, including all non-avian dinosaurs.

Steller's sea cow lived in Arctic waters—humans had hunted them to extinction by 1768.

Holocene extinction

As humans now dominate Earth, the existence of other animal and plant species is increasingly threatened. The Caspian tiger and the dodo are just two examples of creatures now extinct due to human activities. Rising temperatures, pollution, and habitat loss put more than a million species at risk of extinction.

Like rodents

The multituberculates—a group of rodentlike animals—are the most widely spread group of mammals on Earth. Some are the size of modern-day beavers, but others are as small as mice.

c.65 MYA

First penguin

Waimanu is as large as an emperor penguin. And, like modern penguins, it is probably flightless, with wings suited for propelling it quickly through water and a long bill ideal for grasping fish.

c.62 MYA

After the dinosaurs

Between the end of the age of dinosaurs and the appearance of modern-day animals, prehistoric mammals, birds, and other reptiles had an opportunity to flourish. Many new species evolved, including some of the largest creatures ever to have existed.

Big bird

With a long neck, long powerful legs, and a massive bill, *Gastornis* is thought to have fed on tough vegetation. The largest known of these flightless birds grew to 6.5 ft (2 m) tall—taller than most humans.

c.52–56 MYA

Unlike on modern bats, each toe had claws.

Fossils indicate that Palaeophis may have grown to 39 ft (12 m) long.

Earliest bat

About 10 in (25 cm) long and with a wingspan twice that distance, *Onychonycteris* is capable of flight. We do not know whether it used echolocation (using echoes to figure out where it is), like modern bats, or sight to find its way around.

Ancient snake

Though similar to modern-day snakes, *Palaeophis* must have been aquatic creatures, since the fossils have been found in ancient-ocean sediment in Europe, North America, and Africa.

c.48–56 MYA

c.52.5 MYA

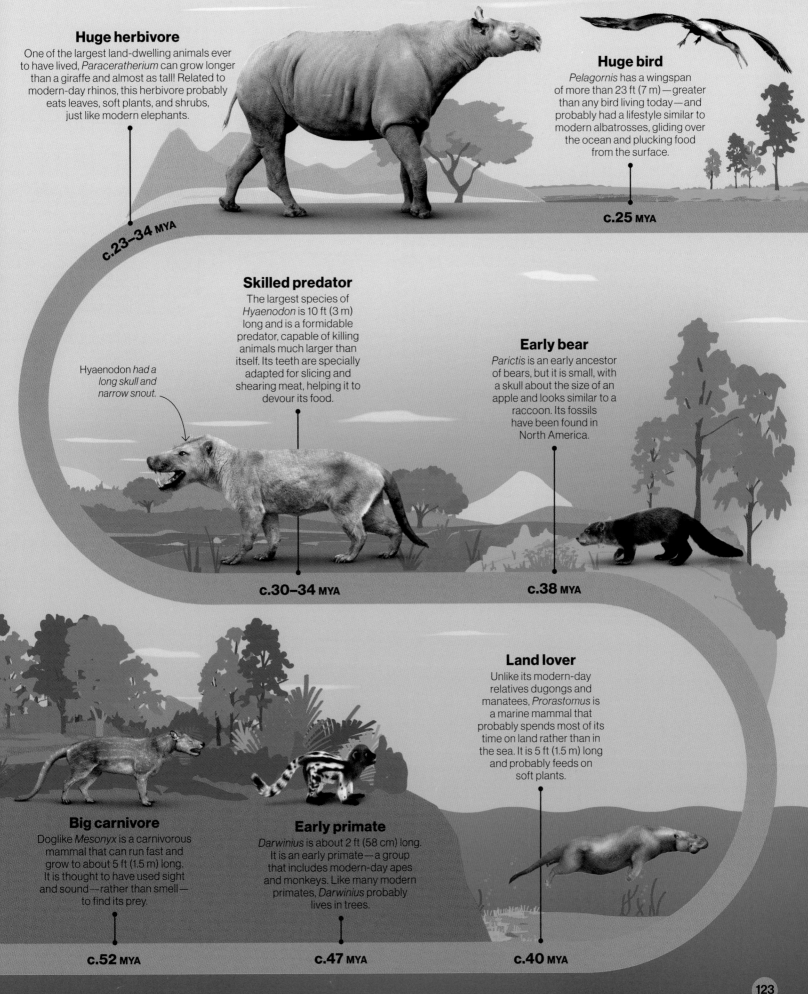

Huge herbivore

One of the largest land-dwelling animals ever to have lived, *Paraceratherium* can grow longer than a giraffe and almost as tall! Related to modern-day rhinos, this herbivore probably eats leaves, soft plants, and shrubs, just like modern elephants.

c.23–34 MYA

Huge bird

Pelagornis has a wingspan of more than 23 ft (7 m)—greater than any bird living today—and probably had a lifestyle similar to modern albatrosses, gliding over the ocean and plucking food from the surface.

c.25 MYA

Skilled predator

The largest species of *Hyaenodon* is 10 ft (3 m) long and is a formidable predator, capable of killing animals much larger than itself. Its teeth are specially adapted for slicing and shearing meat, helping it to devour its food.

Hyaenodon had a long skull and narrow snout.

c.30–34 MYA

Early bear

Parictis is an early ancestor of bears, but it is small, with a skull about the size of an apple and looks similar to a raccoon. Its fossils have been found in North America.

c.38 MYA

Land lover

Unlike its modern-day relatives dugongs and manatees, *Prorastomus* is a marine mammal that probably spends most of its time on land rather than in the sea. It is 5 ft (1.5 m) long and probably feeds on soft plants.

Big carnivore

Doglike *Mesonyx* is a carnivorous mammal that can run fast and grow to about 5 ft (1.5 m) long. It is thought to have used sight and sound—rather than smell—to find its prey.

c.52 MYA

Early primate

Darwinius is about 2 ft (58 cm) long. It is an early primate—a group that includes modern-day apes and monkeys. Like many modern primates, *Darwinius* probably lives in trees.

c.47 MYA

c.40 MYA

Pakicetus

Wolf-sized with the long, sharp teeth of a meat-eater, *Pakicetus* has—like *Indohyus*—hoofed feet, heavy bones, and whalelike ear bones. It is at home on land and in freshwater pools, and feeds on fish and other small animals.

Indohyus

The small, deerlike *Indohyus* has an inner ear structure that shows it may be an early ancestor of the whales. Living by lakes and rivers, it has dense bones that give it enough weight to wade underwater, perhaps to avoid predators or find food.

c.50 MYA

c.47 MYA

c.47 MYA

c.45 MYA

Its large webbed feet helped propel it through the water.

The flipperlike feet were perfect for paddling in shallow waters where there was lots of food.

Rodhocetus

The back legs of the 8 ft (2.5 m) long *Rodhocetus* are longer than its front legs, and it has large, webbed feet. Although this fish eater is well equipped for life in the open sea, it can still move on land.

Ambulocetus

Nearly 13 ft (4 m) long, *Ambulocetus* has short legs, webbed feet, and a muscular tail. This powerful predator hunts like a crocodile and is more at home in shallow salty coastal waters than on land.

Whale evolution

Whales are warm-blooded, air-breathing mammals that live in water. But 50 million years ago, the ancestors of whales were not swimming in seas—they were living on land and walking on four legs. These hoofed animals, distantly related to hippos, gradually started feeding in the water. Slowly, their bodies started changing, and eventually they left dry land forever.

c.43– c.37 MYA

Dorudon

Growing to 16 ft (5 m) long, *Dorudon* has tiny hind flippers and lives entirely in water. It still has the sharp, daggerlike teeth of its mammal ancestors and can hear underwater, which helps it to catch fish. It is now hairless.

Dorudon's *flippers replaced the hind legs of its ancestors.*

It had small flippers instead of front legs.

c.34 MYA

Odontocetes

Odontocetes are one of two groups of whales still living today. This group includes dolphins, sperm whales, and porpoises. All are intelligent predators. To hunt and communicate, they use echolocation—the ability to find prey through the creation and reflection of sound waves.

Its nostrils were between the snout and the top of the head.

Over millions of years, the flippers became longer and more powerful.

c.34 MYA

Mysticetes

The other group of living whales are the mysticetes, or baleen whales. These feed by sieving masses of tiny creatures from the seawater through bristly baleen plates in their mouths. They include the blue whale, the largest animal that has ever lived.

Unlike their ancestors, whales (and dolphins too) have no hair—they are kept warm instead by a thick layer of fat under their skin known as blubber.

Blowhole evolution

Whales are mammals, so they must always return to the surface for air. Blowholes on the top of their heads are like giant nostrils to help them breathe. With each stage of evolution, whales have become ever better adapted to life in water. Over many millions of years, their nostrils have shifted backward, from the end of the snout to the top of the head, to become a blowhole.

c.56–47.8 MYA
Phosphatherium

At 24 in (60 cm) long, this mammal is tiny compared to its descendants and it has no trunk. It probably lives near rivers, eating plants that grow along the bank.

c.41–28 MYA
Barytherium

With a name meaning "heavy beast," this is the first big proboscidean, at about 10 ft (3 m) long. It has a short, flexible snout, and eight small tusks inside its mouth that it uses like scissors to cut through plant stems.

c.36–35 MYA
Palaeomastodon

This early elephant has a short flexible trunk, and its tusks are shaped for scooping plants out of water. It stands at a maximum of 6 ft (1.8 m) tall, and weighs 2 tons.

c.7–5 MYA
Primelephas

Although its name means "first elephant," it is thought to be more closely related to woolly mammoths than today's elephants. Its four tusks (two above, and two below its mouth) are suited for digging or scraping.

c.37–30 MYA
Phiomia

Phiomia is one of the first relatives to develop a trunk—although it is quite short, like a snout. The upper tusks are used for scraping off bark and perhaps also for fighting.

c.23–5 MYA
Gomphotherium

This species has four tusks, which are 6.5 ft (2 m) long. It uses them to dig out food, such as roots, from dry soil as Earth is warming at this time.

A huge jaw helped with grinding up tough plants.

Elephant evolution

Elephants are the largest land animals on Earth. They are the last of the proboscideans, a line of large animals that had a long, flexible proboscis—more commonly known as a trunk—that they used to grab food and water. Despite this, the very earliest elephant ancestors were not particularly big, and some did not even have a trunk—these features evolved over time.

c.7–0.13 MYA
Anancus

This giant has two huge straight tusks, which can grow up to 10 ft (3 m) long. *Anancus* is a similar size to modern elephants, but it is not a direct ancestor. It is a descendant of *Gomphotherium*.

c.5 MYA–11,000 YA
American mastodon

During the Ice Age, this species develops a thick, hairy coat to survive the cold temperatures. It is a distant cousin of today's elephants, with curved tusks used for pulling down branches.

c.2.6 MYA–4,000 YA
Woolly mammoth

Another Ice Age tusker, the woolly mammoth has a thick double coat of fur to keep it warm. Woolly mammoths are found across North America, Europe, and northern Asia, and survive long enough to be hunted by early humans.

Present day Asian elephant

The second largest land animal living today, this elephant lives in the forests of southern and eastern Asia, where it eats grass, leaves, and twigs. It forms small family groups led by a female.

Present day African bush elephant

Standing 11.5 ft (3.5 m) tall and weighing 6 tons, the African bush elephant is the biggest land animal around today. Older males tend to live alone, while females and their offspring stay in large family groups.

The top layer of fur had a blanket of long hairs.

The tusks were probably used for fighting.

The tip of the trunk has two flexible "fingers," which elephants use for grabbing and holding things.

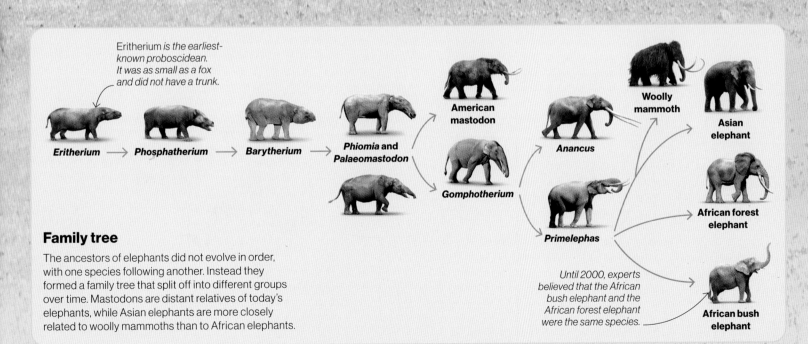

Eritherium is the earliest-known proboscidean. It was as small as a fox and did not have a trunk.

Eritherium → **Phosphatherium** → **Barytherium** → **Phiomia and Palaeomastodon**

American mastodon

Gomphotherium

Anancus

Primelephas

Woolly mammoth

Asian elephant

African forest elephant

Until 2000, experts believed that the African bush elephant and the African forest elephant were the same species.

African bush elephant

Family tree

The ancestors of elephants did not evolve in order, with one species following another. Instead they formed a family tree that split off into different groups over time. Mastodons are distant relatives of today's elephants, while Asian elephants are more closely related to woolly mammoths than to African elephants.

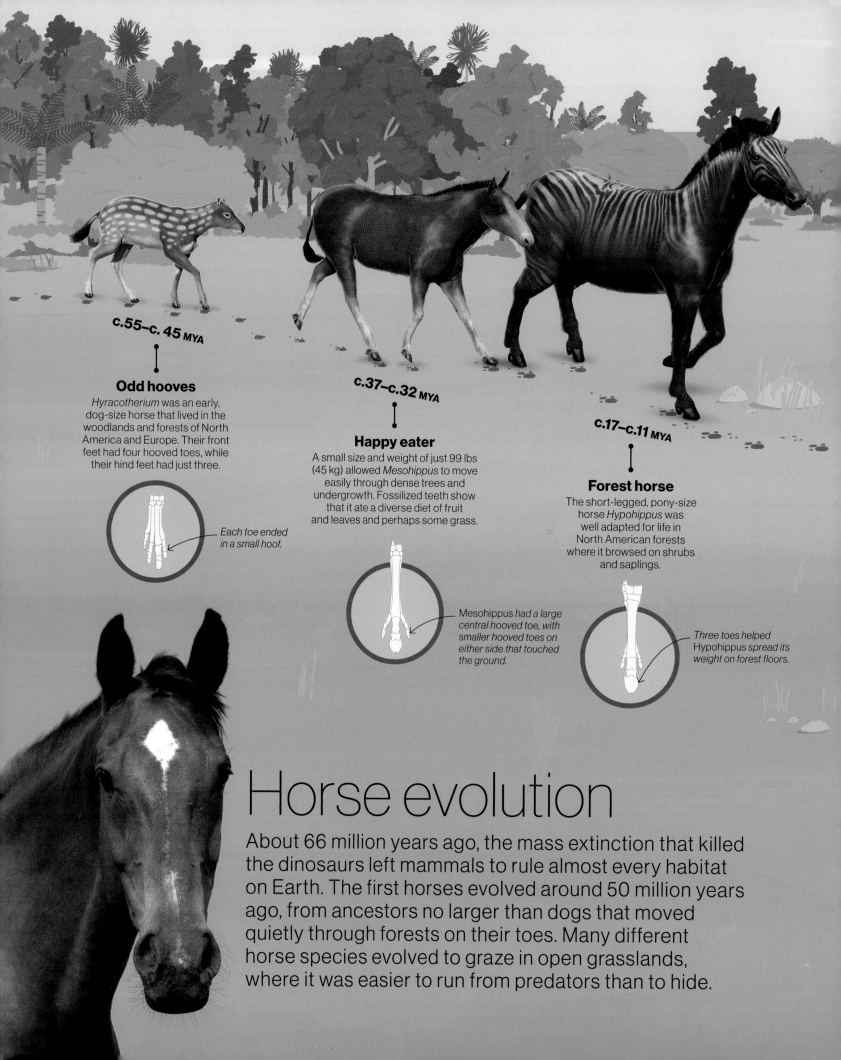

Odd hooves

Hyracotherium was an early, dog-size horse that lived in the woodlands and forests of North America and Europe. Their front feet had four hooved toes, while their hind feet had just three.

c.55–c. 45 MYA

Each toe ended in a small hoof.

Happy eater

A small size and weight of just 99 lbs (45 kg) allowed *Mesohippus* to move easily through dense trees and undergrowth. Fossilized teeth show that it ate a diverse diet of fruit and leaves and perhaps some grass.

c.37–c.32 MYA

Mesohippus had a large central hooved toe, with smaller hooved toes on either side that touched the ground.

Forest horse

The short-legged, pony-size horse *Hypohippus* was well adapted for life in North American forests where it browsed on shrubs and saplings.

c.17–c.11 MYA

Three toes helped Hypohippus spread its weight on forest floors.

Horse evolution

About 66 million years ago, the mass extinction that killed the dinosaurs left mammals to rule almost every habitat on Earth. The first horses evolved around 50 million years ago, from ancestors no larger than dogs that moved quietly through forests on their toes. Many different horse species evolved to graze in open grasslands, where it was easier to run from predators than to hide.

A coat of hair helps horses regulate their body temperature.

c.13–c.5 MYA

Standing horse

Dinohippus weighed around 440 lbs (200 kg) but was small compared to modern horses. It was the first horse with legs adapted to save energy by standing still over long periods.

Some Dinohippus *fossils show one toe, while others have three.*

c.12–c.1 MYA

Across continents

More than 60 *Hipparion* species spread from North America across Asia to Europe, making it one of the most widespread horses. A single hooved toe supported its weight.

Hipparion had traces of other toes, but they did not reach the ground.

c.5 MYA–Present day

Modern horses

All today's horses, donkeys, and zebras are members of the genus (group) *Equus*. The species *Equus caballus* is the sole surviving member of the horse family, though there are many different kinds.

A modern horse's single hooved toe is an adaptation for fast, long running.

Browsers to grazers

As the global climate became drier over the last 50 million years, horses' teeth adapted for grazing on tough grasses. Their cheek teeth have sharp ridges for grinding and grow constantly to prevent them from being totally worn down.

A horse's front teeth are strong with deep roots for tearing leaves off plants.

Today

Homo sapiens
(c.300,000 YA–Present day)
Where found: evolved in Africa, now worldwide
Homo sapiens is the most successful human species. They use their physical and social skills to adapt to most environments on Earth.

YOU ARE HERE

Denisovans
(c.200,000–50,000 YA)
Where found: Europe and Asia
Little is known about the Denisovans; they are known mostly from DNA remains in a few teeth and bones.

Homo heidelbergensis
(c.700,000–200,000 YA)
Where found: Europe; possibly Asia; East and South Africa
With brains as big as that of *Homo sapiens*, and muscular bodies, this species makes complex tools (such as spears), hunts large animals, builds shelters, and uses fire.

1 MYA

Homo erectus
(c.1.89 MYA–110,000 YA)
Where found: North, East, and South Africa; West Asia (Dmanisi, Georgia); East Asia (China and Indonesia)
This species has a similar hairless body and build to *Homo sapiens* with long legs that allow it to travel long distances. *Homo erectus* ("upright man") uses stone handaxes. They spread out of Africa and into Asia.

Homo habilis
(c.2.4–1.4 MYA)
Where found: East and South Africa
The chimp-sized *Homo habilis* ("handy man") is thought to be one of the first hominin species to make stone tools. Its diet includes meat cut from dead animals using these tools.

2 MYA

Australopithecus africanus
(c.3.3–2.1 MYA)
Where found: South Africa
Australopithecus africanus is one of 10 known *Australopithecus* species. It is the first early hominin to be discovered (in 1924) and firmly locates ancient hominin evolution in Africa. It has a small brain but can walk upright.

Australopithecus afarensis
(c.3.85–2.95 MYA)
Where found: East Africa (Ethiopia, Kenya, and Tanzania)
The remains of over 300 individuals are believed to be the best-known early humanlike species. The species has a slightly bigger brain than chimpanzees, and can walk upright and make simple tools. It still spends time living in trees.

3 MYA

Human evolution

4 MYA

The story of how humans evolved is more than 7 million years long, and more than 20 extinct human relatives have been discovered. Modern humans, known as *Homo sapiens*, originated in Africa from where early hominins—our ancestors—started to leave their home in the trees to walk upright on two legs. As hominins evolved, they settled all over the world.

5 MYA

6 MYA

Ancient roots

We learn a lot about our early ancestors from fossils. Hominins can be grouped by the features they share, and different groups contain several species. Our modern *Homo* group evolved from the most ancient and apelike *Ardipithecus* group.

Homo
Around 2.4 million years ago, the *Homo* species appeared in Africa and over time spread worldwide. All in the group later became extinct, apart from *Homo sapiens*.

Paranthropus
Several African species—the *Paranthropus* species—had strongly built skulls, and massive jaws and teeth for chewing tough plants.

Ardipithecus
The first group of African apes to evolve some humanlike features, such as walking upright on two feet, was still very chimplike.

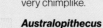
Australopithecus
The best known of the African hominin species, *Australopithecus* had long arms for tree-climbing and legs for walking upright. This species probably ate fruit.

Homo neanderthalensis
(c.400,000–40,000 YA)
Where found: Europe and southwestern to central Asia
The skilled Neanderthal species have large brains and are powerfully built hunters. They make tools and weapons, live in small family groups across Europe and Asia, and breed with *Homo sapiens* before eventually dying out.

Homo floresiensis
(c.100,000–50,000 YA)
Where found: Asia (Indonesia)
This tiny species, nicknamed "hobbit," combines a small body and brain with the ability to make stone tools and hunt. *Homo floresiensis* fossils have been found only on the Indonesian island of Flores.

Australopithecus/ Paranthropus robustus
(c.1.8–1.2 MYA)
Where found: South Africa
Remains of this heavily built, robust species are discovered in South Africa (in 1938). It may use tools made from bone to dig for tough plant roots, which it chews with powerful jaws and large teeth.

Paranthropus boisei
(c.2.3–1.2 MYA)
Where found: East Africa (Ethiopia, Kenya, Tanzania, and Malawi)
Paranthropus boisei is recognizable by its powerful jaws and large teeth. It has strong facial muscles and bones for chewing. Males are much taller and heavier than females.

Ardipithecus ramidus
(c.4.5–4.32 MYA)
Where found: East Africa (Middle Awash and Gona, Ethiopia)
Fossils show that this apelike species lives in woodland and can walk upright and climb trees. Males and females are of similar size and eat a mixed diet of fruit, nuts, leaves, and possibly small mammals.

Sahelanthropus tchadensis
(c.7–6 MYA)
Where found: West–Central Africa (Chad)
One of the earliest chimplike species, this plant-eater has similar canine teeth to *Homo sapiens* and can walk upright on two feet.

30 days
Mosquito
From egg to wriggling larva and then adult, mosquitoes mature in 7–10 days. Male mosquitoes live for only a week or so as adults, whereas females can live for up to a month.

5 months
Turquoise killifish
North Africa's killifish live in seasonal puddles that form during the rainy season. Within 14 days of hatching from eggs, they are adults, seeking mates and laying their own eggs before the puddle dries up.

1 year and 30 minutes
Mayfly
One species of mayfly in the southeastern United States spends about a year as larvae in streams. In spring, the adults emerge and live just long enough (5–30 minutes) to mate and for the females to lay eggs.

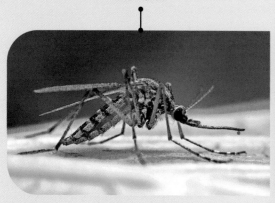

200+ years
Bowhead whale
This Arctic-dwelling whale is one of the world's longest-living mammals. It has the biggest mouth—one-third of its body length—in the animal kingdom. Life in cold water may explain why it lives so long.

150+ years
Galapagos giant tortoise
This long-lived reptile makes its home on the Galapagos Islands. Giant tortoises can weigh up to 880 lbs (400 kg)—about as heavy as a horse—and famously reach great ages of 150 years or more.

100+ years
Atlantic lobster
Lobsters found on the Atlantic coast of North America are thought to live for 100 years or more. Unlike many other animals, lobsters continue to grow until the day they die.

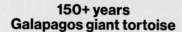

400+ years
Greenland shark
The giant Greenland shark swims slowly through the icy waters of the North Atlantic and Arctic oceans. Its metabolism is very slow, slowing down the speed at which it ages.

500+ years
Ocean quahog clam
The number of growth rings on an ocean quahog clam's outer shell show how old it is. These clams live in the North Atlantic and are harvested for food. They are known to live for more than 500 years.

4,000+ years
Black coral
Corals are colonies made up of tiny living animals, called polyps. Scientists have discovered ancient black corals deep beneath the sea. One colony in Hawaii is thought to be over 4,000 years old.

14 years
Cheetah

These speedy predators live for an average of 14 years in the wild but can last up to 20 years in captivity. Males do not live as long because they often get injured defending their territories.

25 years
Hellbender

America's largest salamander, the hellbender, is thought to live up to 25 years in fast-flowing rivers and streams in the eastern United States. It is an ambush predator, meaning it spends much of its time sitting still, waiting for prey to swim by.

30 years
Burmese python

This powerful python is commonly found near villages, and even cities, in Southeast Asia, India, and China, searching for prey. It reaches lengths of up to 22 ft (6.7 m) and can live for up to 30 years in the wild.

50+ years
Albatross

This enormous seabird is the longest living bird species in the wild. With a 12 ft (3.7 m) long wingspan, it can be found flying above the seas of the southern hemisphere. Albatrosses tend to breed later than other birds, at about 10 years old, and typically mate for life.

40 years
Trapdoor spider

These spiders cover the entrance to their burrow with a "trap door," made of soil and silk, and wait to pounce on prey. Some have been found to live more than 40 years, although 5–20 years is thought more common.

35 years
Chimpanzee

Our closest living relatives, chimpanzees live in large family groups of around 30 members. Some have been known to live more than 60 years in the wild.

11,000 years
Sea sponge

It is difficult to identify the age of a sea sponge, but they can have very long lives. One sponge collected from the East China Sea was estimated to be 11,000 years old (give or take a few thousand years).

Animal life spans

Life can be fleeting or long-lasting in the animal kingdom. All animals have a "clock" in their genetic code that determines the maximum length of time they can live. An easier life may extend this time, which is why some—though not all—generally live longer in captivity than in the wild. Early humans rarely lived past the age of 40, but with modern medicine, clean water, and enough food, the average life span is now over 70.

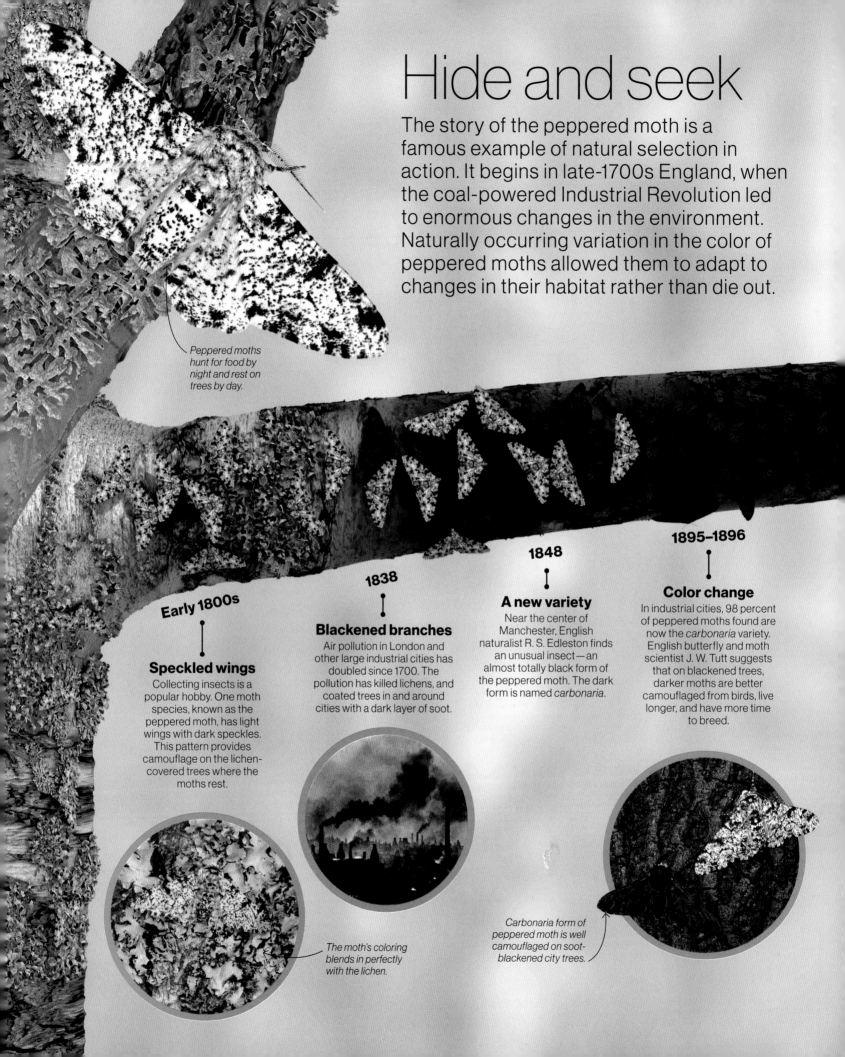

Hide and seek

The story of the peppered moth is a famous example of natural selection in action. It begins in late-1700s England, when the coal-powered Industrial Revolution led to enormous changes in the environment. Naturally occurring variation in the color of peppered moths allowed them to adapt to changes in their habitat rather than die out.

Peppered moths hunt for food by night and rest on trees by day.

Early 1800s

Speckled wings

Collecting insects is a popular hobby. One moth species, known as the peppered moth, has light wings with dark speckles. This pattern provides camouflage on the lichen-covered trees where the moths rest.

The moth's coloring blends in perfectly with the lichen.

1838

Blackened branches

Air pollution in London and other large industrial cities has doubled since 1700. The pollution has killed lichens, and coated trees in and around cities with a dark layer of soot.

1848

A new variety

Near the center of Manchester, English naturalist R. S. Edleston finds an unusual insect—an almost totally black form of the peppered moth. The dark form is named *carbonaria*.

Carbonaria form of peppered moth is well camouflaged on soot-blackened city trees.

1895–1896

Color change

In industrial cities, 98 percent of peppered moths found are now the *carbonaria* variety. English butterfly and moth scientist J. W. Tutt suggests that on blackened trees, darker moths are better camouflaged from birds, live longer, and have more time to breed.

Natural selection

Naturalists Charles Darwin and Alfred Russel Wallace proposed the theory of natural selection in the mid-1800s. They explained how animals that happen to be better suited to their environment are most likely to survive long enough to breed, passing on their helpful features to the next generation. Over time, these features become more common in the population.

Birds find it easy to spot dark-colored moths on healthy, lichen-covered tree branches.

1953–1955
Moth experiments

English insect scientist Bernard Kettlewell carries out experiments to test the theory that peppered moth color change is an example of natural selection. He finds that birds eat more of the light-colored moths, which are easier to spot.

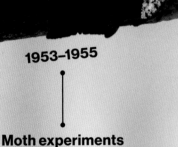

The British Clean Air Act, brought in four years after The Great Smog (a period of severe air pollution) killed more than 4,000 people in London, results in cleaner city air.

1956
Cleaning up the air

New laws are made to reduce air pollution in cities from smoke and soot. Lichens begin to grow back, and trees shed their sooty bark.

1970
Speckled again

Industrial areas continue to get cleaner and greener. Pale peppered moths begin to be spotted more often in places where the air was previously polluted. Many new experiments support Kettlewell's findings that it is the difference in peppered moths' coloring that explains their different survival rate.

1972
Digital support

The first-ever computer simulation of peppered moth adaptation is used to help test Tutt's theory that it is a case of natural selection at work. The results agree with naturalists' early observations of color change in peppered moths.

2001–2009
Selective pressure

English geneticist Mike Majerus carries out experiments involving 4,864 peppered moths. His results show that on unpolluted trees, birds prey more on dark-colored *carbonaria* moths, which are not as well camouflaged, than on the lighter speckled moths.

2016
In the genes

Scientists find the gene responsible for a *carbonaria* peppered moth's color. A different team calculates that the change to this gene happened by chance in 1819, then spread quickly through the moth population due to the advantages it gave in the changing environment.

Life in the fast lane

Mayflies have one of the shortest adult lives in the insect world, but it is packed with action. They begin life underwater at the bottom of a pond or shallow river. The young mayfly, known as a nymph, can spend up to two years living in the water, feeding and growing. Emerging as adults, they have just a day or two to take flight, mate, and reproduce before their brief lives end.

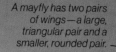

A mayfly has two pairs of wings—a large, triangular pair and a smaller, rounded pair.

Egg laying
Female mayflies can produce thousands of eggs. Some lay their eggs on plants sprouting from the water. Others drop them on to the water's surface, and the eggs sink to the bottom. The mayfly's life is about to begin.

Day 1

Hatching
The newly hatched mayfly is called a nymph. It is very small—about the size of a grain of sand. The nymph has six legs but no wings, and the gills along its back allow it to breathe underwater.

Week 2

Molting
As the nymph grows, its exoskeleton becomes too small, so it sheds and replaces it regularly in a process called molting. A mayfly nymph molts between 14 and 50 times in its life, getting bigger with each stage.

Week 4

Almost fully grown
The mayfly nymph is now about 0.8 in (2 cm) long and almost ready to transform into an adult. It swims up to the water's surface and flies to a nearby stem where it moults again into a subimago – the last stage before it becomes an adult.

Months 11–24

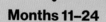

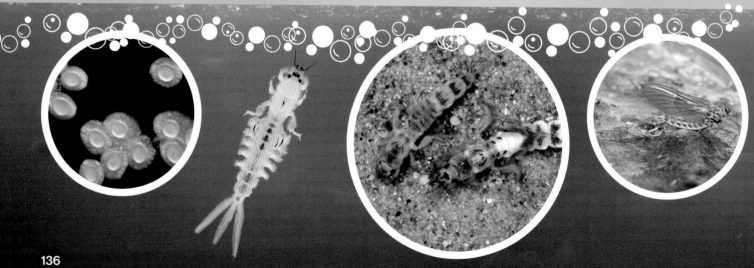

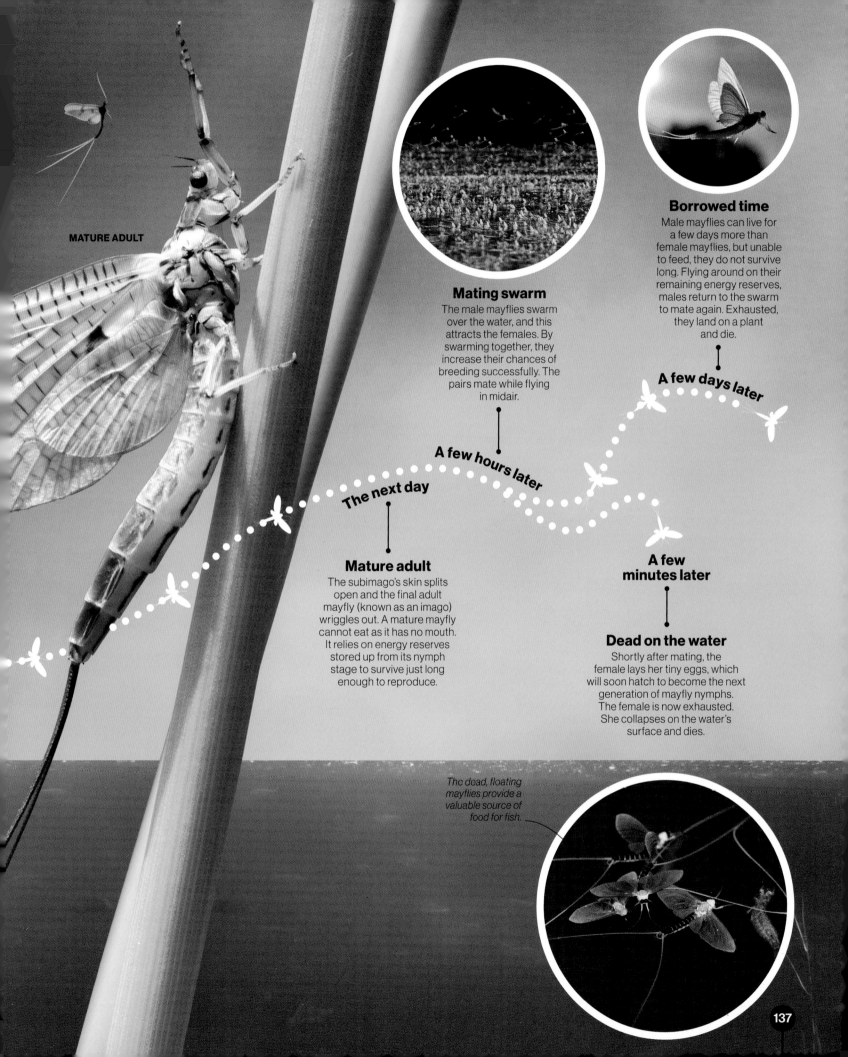

MATURE ADULT

Mating swarm

The male mayflies swarm over the water, and this attracts the females. By swarming together, they increase their chances of breeding successfully. The pairs mate while flying in midair.

Borrowed time

Male mayflies can live for a few days more than female mayflies, but unable to feed, they do not survive long. Flying around on their remaining energy reserves, males return to the swarm to mate again. Exhausted, they land on a plant and die.

A few days later

A few hours later

The next day

Mature adult

The subimago's skin splits open and the final adult mayfly (known as an imago) wriggles out. A mature mayfly cannot eat as it has no mouth. It relies on energy reserves stored up from its nymph stage to survive just long enough to reproduce.

A few minutes later

Dead on the water

Shortly after mating, the female lays her tiny eggs, which will soon hatch to become the next generation of mayfly nymphs. The female is now exhausted. She collapses on the water's surface and dies.

The dead, floating mayflies provide a valuable source of food for fish.

Cicadas in sync

Cicadas are famous for being the world's loudest insects. Like many other insects, they begin their lives as nymphs, gradually changing into adults ready to mate. Most of the 3,000 or so species of cicadas can be spotted in small numbers each year, but the periodical cicadas of eastern North America are different. Once every 13 or 17 years, billions of cicada adults emerge at the same time. Birds can not possibly eat them all, so most survive long enough to breed.

A few minutes later

Final molt

The nymph climbs the first vertical surface it sees and sheds its exoskeleton for the final time. The adult cicada that emerges is fragile and pale at first, but quickly toughens and becomes darker in color.

Each foot has a sharp hook to grasp tree bark.

Nymphs emerge

After 13 or 17 years, and when the soil temperature is a comfortable 64°F (18°C), the nymph crawls out of the soil and into the daylight.

Year 17

Growing bigger

Nymphs molt (shed their exoskeleton) every few years, to allow their body to grow. With each molt, the nymph's body gets closer to its adult form.

The cicada spends almost all of its life in darkness as a nymph.

Week 8 – Year 17

An hour later

Life in the trees

Most cicadas live less than two months as adults. Males sit in the trees, singing loudly to attract females. The sound is made by two patches of thin, drumlike skin known as tymbals on each side of their abdomens. The tymbals vibrate hundreds of times a second, creating a clicking sound.

During their time in the trees, adult cicadas eat very little.

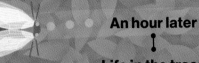

Adult periodical cicadas are about 0.7–1.2 in (2–3 cm) in size, and orange and black, with bulging red eyes.

Weeks 2–6

Weeks 6–8

A group of cicadas hatching at the same time is known as a brood.

Laying eggs

Once they have mated, female cicadas use a sharp part on their abdomens to cut grooves in soft branches or stems in which they lay hundreds of eggs. After mating and laying eggs, adult cicadas die.

Eggs hatch

Newly hatched nymphs crawl or fall to the ground, where they burrow into soft soil. All the periodical cicadas in an area start their life underground at about the same time.

Sucking sap

A periodical cicada nymph spends either 13 or 17 years underground, depending on the species. The nymphs crawl through soil using powerful front legs, feeding on sap from plant roots.

Week 8–Year 17

How do they know?

It is still a mystery how billions of periodical cicadas know that 13 or 17 years have passed, and all emerge at exactly the same time. One theory is that they detect changes in plant sap as the seasons pass.

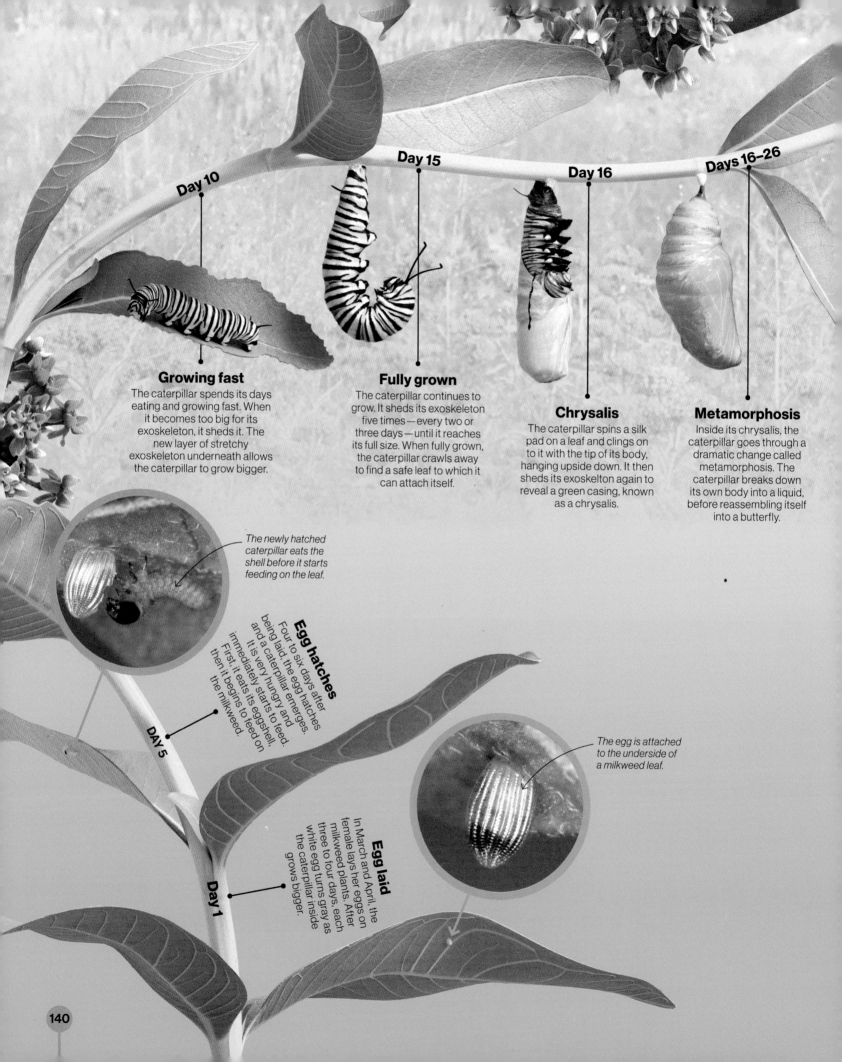

Day 10

Growing fast

The caterpillar spends its days eating and growing fast. When it becomes too big for its exoskeleton, it sheds it. The new layer of stretchy exoskeleton underneath allows the caterpillar to grow bigger.

Day 15

Fully grown

The caterpillar continues to grow. It sheds its exoskeleton five times—every two or three days—until it reaches its full size. When fully grown, the caterpillar crawls away to find a safe leaf to which it can attach itself.

Day 16

Chrysalis

The caterpillar spins a silk pad on a leaf and clings on to it with the tip of its body, hanging upside down. It then sheds its exoskelton again to reveal a green casing, known as a chrysalis.

Days 16–26

Metamorphosis

Inside its chrysalis, the caterpillar goes through a dramatic change called metamorphosis. The caterpillar breaks down its own body into a liquid, before reassembling itself into a butterfly.

The newly hatched caterpillar eats the shell before it starts feeding on the leaf.

DAY 5

Egg hatches

Four to six days after the egg hatches being laid, the egg hatches and a caterpillar emerges. It is very hungry and immediately starts to feed. First it eats its eggshell, then it begins to feed on the milkweed.

The egg is attached to the underside of a milkweed leaf.

Day 1

Egg laid

In March and April, the female lays her eggs on milkweed plants. After three to four days, each white egg turns gray as the caterpillar inside grows bigger.

Almost ready

The chrysalis darkens as the skin of the butterfly's body turns black. The day before the adult butterfly emerges, the orange and black pattern of its wings can be seen.

Chrysalis splits

The chrysalis breaks open near the bottom and an adult butterfly starts to emerge. Its wings are crumpled, wet, and small. By pumping hemolymph (blood) from its body into its wings, they grow bigger. The butterfly must wait for its wings to dry before it can fly.

Adult flies away

An hour later, the butterfly's wings are dry and strong—the butterfly is now ready to fly. It sips nectar from flowers to gain energy. And within days, it finds a mate so it can breed and create the next generation of monarch butterflies.

Monarch butterfly life cycle

Butterflies undergo one of the most dramatic changes in all of the natural world. While many plants and animals start life as a smaller version of their parents, butterflies and moths start life as caterpillars, which look nothing like adult butterflies. A caterpillar has a segmented body that grows rapidly over the course of a few days by shedding its exoskeleton. When it is time, the caterpillar forms a hard outer case called a chrysalis. Inside, its body completely breaks down and is transformed into a butterfly or moth, free to fly away to start its adult life.

Milkweed plant

Monarch migration

In fall, millions of monarch butterflies across North America load up with nectar and begin an incredible migration to the warmer south. Flying for as long as two months, they cover a distance of up to 3,000 miles (4,800 km) to spend winter resting in conifer forests in central Mexico and the coast of California. In spring, the butterflies begin their return journey, taking four to five generations to reach the most northernly parts of their range in southern Canada.

Fungus farmers

There are several dozen species of tropical leaf-cutter ants and all live in very complex societies, also known as colonies. As their name suggests, they are skilled at slicing through leaves, which they then bring back to their nest. They use these leaf fragments to make a kind of compost, upon which a unique fungus grows. The ants feed this fungus to their queen and the young in their colonies.

Day 1

Egg-laying

The queen is the largest ant in the colony, and her only task is to lay eggs. During her lifetime, she may lay between 150 million and 200 million eggs. At this stage, all of the other members of the colony are her daughters.

Day 18

Eggs hatch

The eggs laid by the queen hatch after about 18 days. Not all hatch, though. Worker ants feed some of the eggs to older growing larvae (young ants) and eat some themselves.

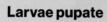

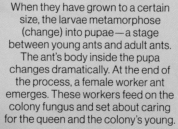

Days 40–50

Larvae pupate

When they have grown to a certain size, the larvae metamorphose (change) into pupae—a stage between young ants and adult ants. The ant's body inside the pupa changes dramatically. At the end of the process, a female worker ant emerges. These workers feed on the colony fungus and set about caring for the queen and the colony's young.

Day 60

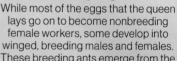

Mating flight

While most of the eggs that the queen lays go on to become nonbreeding female workers, some develop into winged, breeding males and females. These breeding ants emerge from the colony together, fly high, and mate. Each female mates with many males.

Fungus farm workers

Leaf-cutter ant workers are responsible for growing a type of fungus for the larvae to eat. After the leaves have been brought inside the nest, workers chew them into a soft mulch. They then tend to the mulch as the fungus grows on it. The ants farm the fungus by keeping it clean and secreting chemicals that help it to grow. Finding, cutting, and carrying the leaves, and then making the fungus, requires ants to do different jobs.

Minors protect the source of the leaves and the foraging route from any possible disruption.

Mediae cut and transport the bulk of the leaves to the nest.

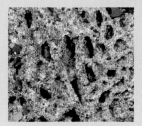
Minims tend to the fungus garden and feed the larvae.

Majors guard the nest against enemies and clear the route to the nest.

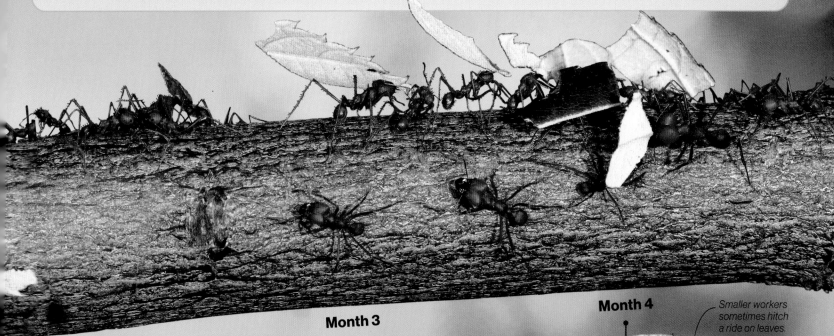

Month 4

Smaller workers sometimes hitch a ride on leaves.

Month 3

Month 2

Once back on the ground, the females lose their wings.

A new brood

A new queen digs a burrow and feeds her first few eggs to the fungus she has brought with her. If successful, the new colony will have a growing fungus store and eggs, larvae, and pupae after about a month. Once workers emerge, they get to work straight away.

A new colony

Fertilized females fly off in search of new nesting sites to set up a new colony with them as queens. Very few will be successful. Each one takes a wad of fungus with them to start their own fungus garden.

A new generation

As the colony grows, several distinct classes of ants emerge that do different tasks. They must work together if the colony is to survive. A colony can contain more than 1,000 chambers and can cover 0.19 sq miles (0.5 sq km)—an area about three-quarters the size of Disneyland, California.

Mouse decay

A dead animal—even one as small as a mouse—provides opportunities for new life. Depending on the conditions, a miniature ecosystem can begin to form in and around the corpse within just a few minutes. Each organism, from microbes such as bacteria to flies and beetles, helps to recycle the nutrients that once formed the building blocks of the mouse's body.

Active decay begins

The decomposing skin splits and the body deflates as the smelly gases inside are released. Fly maggots begin to feed on the mouse's internal organs, and the strong stench of decomposition attracts yet more insects.

Fly larvae hatch

Tiny larvae, known as maggots, hatch from fly eggs. The maggots are not strong enough to eat through the mouse's skin but enter its body through its eyes, ears, mouth, or open wounds.

Corpse bloats

Hydrogen sulfide and methane gases produced by bacteria in the mouse's gut cause its abdomen to bloat. Its skin turns gray or green, and more flies are attracted to the foul-smelling corpse.

Flies lay eggs

As soon as an animal, such as this mouse, dies, microbes already present in the body begin to reproduce unchecked. Nearby blow flies and carrion flies detect the smell of gases released by bacteria, and arrive to lay eggs.

3 days after death

3 days after death

2 days after death

Minutes after death

Conditions such as location, temperature, and moisture levels will affect the speed at which the mouse decays.

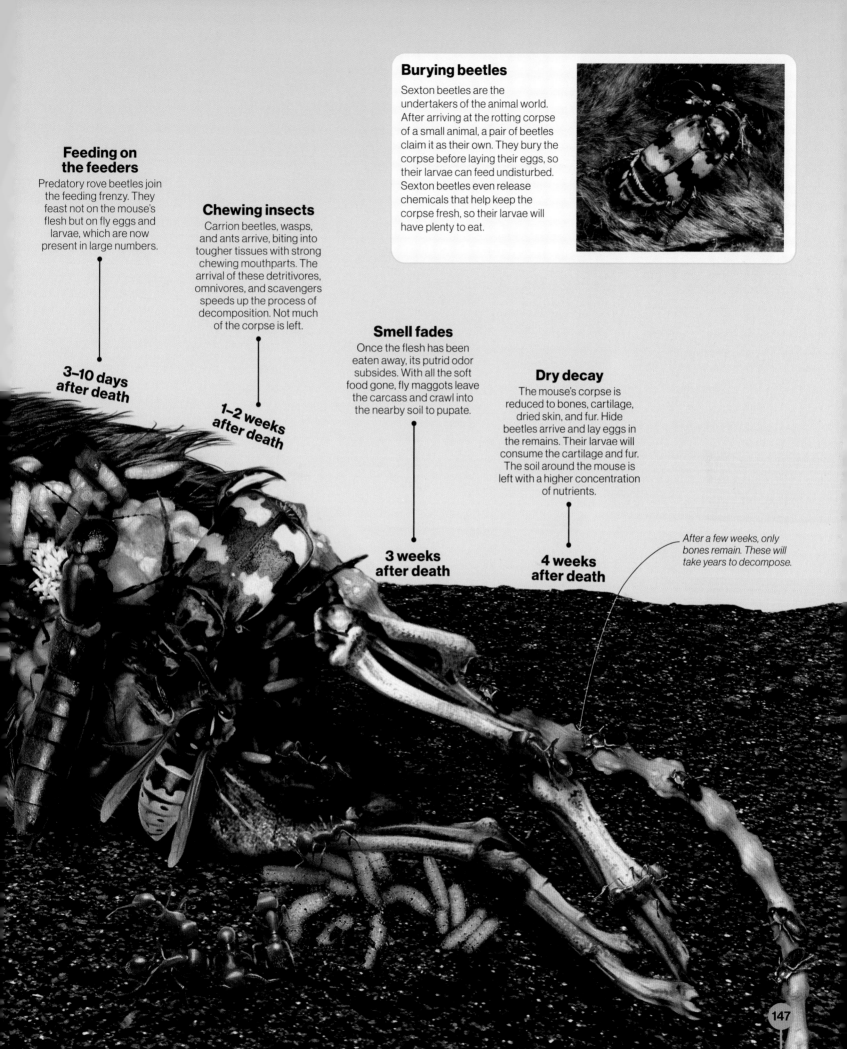

Feeding on the feeders

Predatory rove beetles join the feeding frenzy. They feast not on the mouse's flesh but on fly eggs and larvae, which are now present in large numbers.

3–10 days after death

Chewing insects

Carrion beetles, wasps, and ants arrive, biting into tougher tissues with strong chewing mouthparts. The arrival of these detritivores, omnivores, and scavengers speeds up the process of decomposition. Not much of the corpse is left.

1–2 weeks after death

Burying beetles

Sexton beetles are the undertakers of the animal world. After arriving at the rotting corpse of a small animal, a pair of beetles claim it as their own. They bury the corpse before laying their eggs, so their larvae can feed undisturbed. Sexton beetles even release chemicals that help keep the corpse fresh, so their larvae will have plenty to eat.

Smell fades

Once the flesh has been eaten away, its putrid odor subsides. With all the soft food gone, fly maggots leave the carcass and crawl into the nearby soil to pupate.

3 weeks after death

Dry decay

The mouse's corpse is reduced to bones, cartilage, dried skin, and fur. Hide beetles arrive and lay eggs in the remains. Their larvae will consume the cartilage and fur. The soil around the mouse is left with a higher concentration of nutrients.

4 weeks after death

After a few weeks, only bones remain. These will take years to decompose.

Year in a bee colony

Honey bees work together to ensure the survival of their colony. A single queen rules the colony and lays all the eggs, and most of the other bees are workers, doing different jobs depending on their age. The size of the colony changes with the seasons, becoming smaller in the cold of winter to keep the number of mouths to feed to a minimum and growing its workforce in summer.

Staying cool

The new queen mates midflight with several male bees, called drones, and builds the remaining colony up to over 50,000 bees. Workers go out to look for water and spit it out on the hive to keep it cool.

July

Goodbye drones

The days are getting shorter and there is less food to go around. The colony does not need males during winter, so the drones are expelled from the hive by the workers and not allowed to return. As long as the hive has enough honey to eat and stays disease-free, it will survive the winter.

September

Keeping warm

Inside the hive, workers surround the queen and the younger bees, huddling together and vibrating their wings and abdomens to stay warm in winter. The hive is cozy, thanks to the heat generated by the workers.

January

Early April

Early April

The eggs hatch

The eggs are hatching. To begin with, the larvae are fed royal jelly—a rich, nutrient-packed food that helps the bees to develop. But after three days, all except the developing queens are then fed honey and pollen.

A growing colony

As spring arrives, the days grow longer and flowers bloom. The queen bee lays eggs to more than double the size of the colony from the 20,000 bees that overwintered here. She may lay up to 2,000 eggs each day.

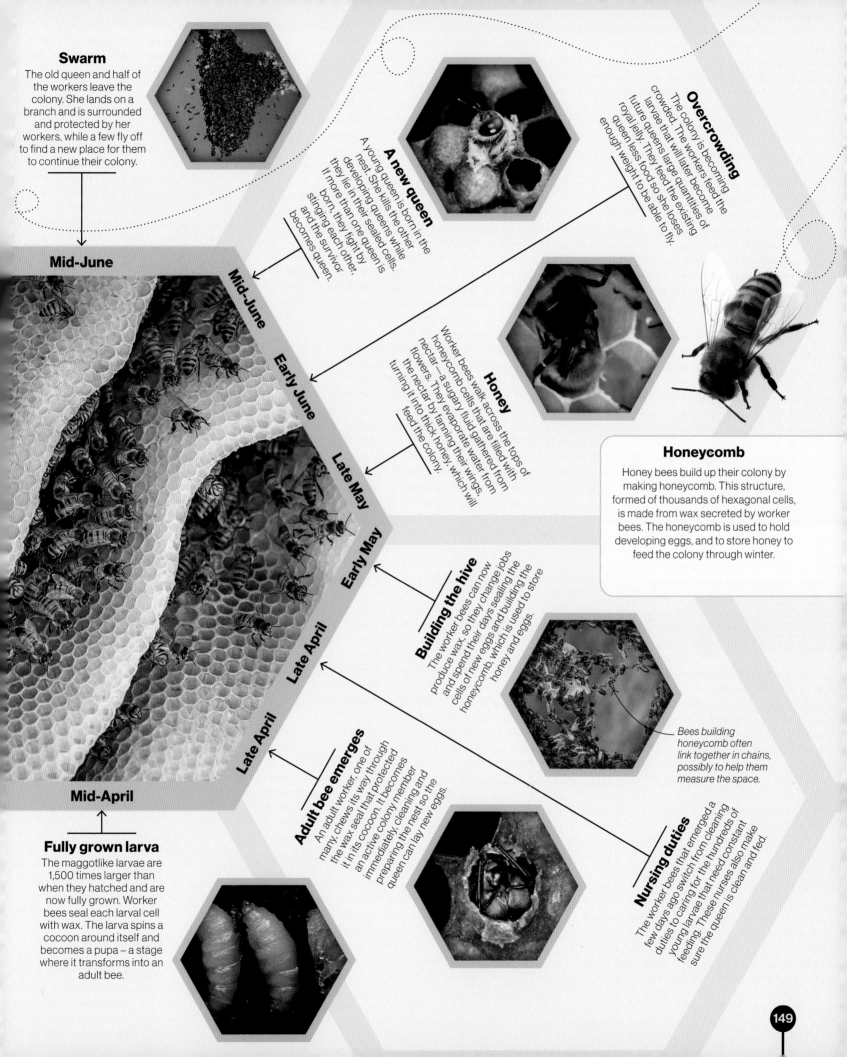

Swarm

The old queen and half of the workers leave the colony. She lands on a branch and is surrounded and protected by her workers, while a few fly off to find a new place for them to continue their colony.

Overcrowding

The colony is becoming crowded. The workers feed the larvae that will later become future queens large quantities of royal jelly. They feed the existing queen less food so she loses enough weight to be able to fly.

A new queen

A young queen is born in the nest. She kills the other developing queens while they lie in their sealed cells. If more than one queen is born, they fight by stinging each other, and the survivor becomes queen.

Honey

Worker bees walk across the tops of honeycomb cells that are filled with nectar—a sugary fluid gathered from flowers. They evaporate water from the nectar by fanning their wings, turning it into thick honey, which will feed the colony.

Honeycomb

Honey bees build up their colony by making honeycomb. This structure, formed of thousands of hexagonal cells, is made from wax secreted by worker bees. The honeycomb is used to hold developing eggs, and to store honey to feed the colony through winter.

Building the hive

The worker bees can now produce wax, so they change jobs and spend their days sealing the cells of new eggs and building the honeycomb, which is used to store honey and eggs.

Bees building honeycomb often link together in chains, possibly to help them measure the space.

Adult bee emerges

An adult worker one of many, chews its way through the wax seal that protected it in its cocoon. It becomes an active colony member immediately, cleaning and preparing the nest so the queen can lay new eggs.

Nursing duties

The worker bees that emerged a few days ago switch from cleaning duties to caring for the hundreds of young larvae that need constant feeding. These nurses also make sure the queen is clean and fed.

Fully grown larva

The maggotlike larvae are 1,500 times larger than when they hatched and are now fully grown. Worker bees seal each larval cell with wax. The larva spins a cocoon around itself and becomes a pupa – a stage where it transforms into an adult bee.

Mid-June

Mid-June

Early June

Late May

Early May

Late April

Late April

Late April

Mid-April

Dining with dung beetles

Large herbivores such as elephants cannot fully digest their tough plant food, so their dung is rich in nutrients. For many insects, including dung beetles, this dung is a complete meal. Dung beetles play a vital role in grassland ecosystems by recycling the nutrients and dispersing plant seeds trapped in dung. There are three types of dung beetles: rollers, which roll dung into a ball and bury it (shown here); tunnelers, which dig down into a pile of dung; and dwellers, which live on top of it.

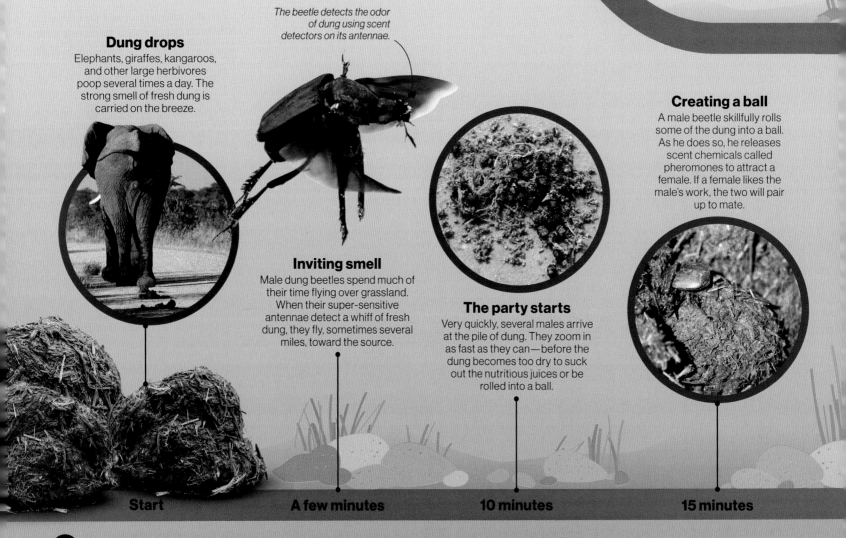

2 weeks–2 months later

Adults emerge
The larvae have transformed into adult dung beetles. They dig their way out of the brood ball and emerge ready to find fresh dung of their own.

Dung drops
Elephants, giraffes, kangaroos, and other large herbivores poop several times a day. The strong smell of fresh dung is carried on the breeze.

The beetle detects the odor of dung using scent detectors on its antennae.

Inviting smell
Male dung beetles spend much of their time flying over grassland. When their super-sensitive antennae detect a whiff of fresh dung, they fly, sometimes several miles, toward the source.

The party starts
Very quickly, several males arrive at the pile of dung. They zoom in as fast as they can—before the dung becomes too dry to suck out the nutritious juices or be rolled into a ball.

Creating a ball
A male beetle skillfully rolls some of the dung into a ball. As he does so, he releases scent chemicals called pheromones to attract a female. If a female likes the male's work, the two will pair up to mate.

Start   **A few minutes**   **10 minutes**   **15 minutes**

Eggs hatch

After a day or two, tiny, cream-colored larvae hatch from the eggs hidden in the dung balls. The larvae gorge themselves on the nutrient-rich dung that surrounds them.

As it grows bigger, a dung beetle larva sheds its exoskeleton several times.

Dung for dinner

Many other insects are attracted to nutrient-rich dung as a source of food, or for egg-laying. Certain butterflies gather on fresh, wet dung to suck out the juices, adding essential nitrogen and sodium to their diets. This behavior is known as "mud-puddling."

Dung gone

The beetles return to the dung pile to collect more dung to bury. With hundreds of beetles working at once, a pile of fresh elephant dung may disappear in just a couple of hours.

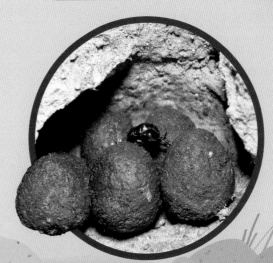

1–2 days later

2 hours later

Rolling the ball

The next challenge is to move the dung ball, which may weigh up to 50 times more than the beetle does. Standing on his front legs, the male walks backward, pushing and stabilizing the ball of dung with his middle and back legs.

Male dung beetles push dung backward, with their heads down.

Digging a tunnel

When they reach a spot where it is easy to burrow, the beetles dig an underground chamber and roll their dung ball inside. The female lays an egg inside the ball of dung, known as a "brood ball."

30 minutes

1 hour later

Ladybug life

There are approximately 6,000 species of this little beetle in different colors and patterns—the seven-spot ladybug (*Coccinella septempunctata*) is the most common. Active in the warmer months, they spend the colder months in a deep sleep known as hibernation.

Safe place

In fall, adult ladybugs search for a place to hibernate, where they can huddle in a group known as a hibernation colony. They might choose a gap under the bark of a tree, nestled among fallen leaves, or inside a cool building.

October

Hunting

For the first few weeks, the larvae drink a sugar-rich liquid, called honeydew, produced by the aphids. As they grow larger, the larvae start to hunt and eat whole aphids, consuming hundreds each day.

The larva is black with colored spots and no wings.

Aphids produce honeydew when eating plant sap—the watery fluid in plants.

Around 4 weeks later

June

Molting

The growing larva's exoskeleton becomes tight, so it sheds its exoskeleton in a process known as molting. Its old exoskeleton splits open and the larva crawls out with a new exoskeleton to fit its bigger body. It molts three more times until it is ready to become an adult.

Stage 1
Stage 2
Stage 3
Stage 4

Pupation

The fully grown larva becomes a pupa (the stage before adulthood). It sticks itself to a leaf or some bark and does not move. Inside, the body is being transformed from the wingless larval form into the adult form.

Emerging

It takes between one and two weeks to complete the pupation stage. The pupal case splits open and the adult emerges. The new adult ladybug has a soft, pale yellow body, which hardens and gradually turns red.

July–August

Around 1–2 weeks later

Deep sleep

The ladybugs sleep through the cold winter when there is nothing for them to eat. They enter a state of suspended animation, where their body slows and their temperature lowers. If disturbed, they will be sluggish and have difficulty flying.

Waking up

The ladybugs wake up hungry after their deep sleep. Around the same time, tiny insects known as aphids hatch from their eggs. Aphids are a favorite food eaten by ladybugs, and this ideal timing means the ladybugs awaken to an aphid feast.

November–February

March–Early April

Hatching

The eggs hatch into larvae (young insects) up to 10 days later. The larva twists out of the egg's shell and eats it before feeding on any unhatched eggs nearby. The now-full larva rests while its exoskeleton dries and hardens.

Laying eggs

The female lays her eggs on the underside of a leaf near plenty of aphids, ensuring food is available when the young ladybugs hatch. The ladybug eggs look like tiny jellybeans and are stuck to the leaf by a form of glue produced by the female.

Mating time

Soon after emerging from hibernation, the male and female ladybugs mate. The males will try to find several mates, but they are now near the end of their life cycle and will soon die.

Between 20–50 eggs are laid by female ladybugs each day.

Up to 10 days later

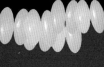

Late May

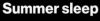

Late April–Early May

The ladybug's wings are protected under the rounded covers known as elytra. These lift up when it flies.

Feeding frenzy

The new adult ladybugs feed for about a month to increase their energy reserves before fall. As temperatures cool, it is a signal that it is time to hibernate. When spring and the warmer weather return, the life cycle will start again.

Summer sleep

Like the ladybug, many animals hibernate through the cold winter, but some species sleep through summer instead. This process is called estivation, and it allows animals to survive long periods without water. During summer, the Australian bogong moth keeps cool inside mountain caves. When fall arrives, it emerges to mate and lay its eggs.

August–September

Relaxed mice

A tiny parasite called *Toxoplasma gondii* uses mice and cats as hosts. It infects mice when they eat food contaminated with parasite cysts (egglike stages), shed in the poop of infected cats. Mice usually avoid anywhere that smells of their predators, such as cats. However, *T. gondii* changes how mice behave, making them much less nervous about danger. The mice are then more likely to be caught and eaten by cats, allowing the parasite to continue its life cycle.

Swollen eye stalks
The sporocyte develops tentacles that spread through the snail's body. Some tentacles penetrate the snail's eye stalks on its head and steadily fill with larvae (young parasites). The larvae move around, making the swollen eye stalks throb with green bands.

Day 365

Days 2–365

Internal invader
The egg develops inside the snail into a branched mass called a sporocyst. This sits in the snail's digestive system, absorbing nutrients. The sporocyst releases chemicals that stop the snail from being able to breed. The snail can then concentrate its energy on nourishing the parasite instead.

Day 1

Becoming infected
An amber snail searches all over its damp, shady habitat for food, including in bird droppings. When it eats an egg of the green-banded brood pouch hidden in the poop, it becomes infected.

154

Heading for sunlight
A snail's eye stalks have eyes at the tips, usually used for helping the snail avoid bright places. However, the parasite now fully in control changes the behavior of the snail, making it head out into the sunlight, where it can easily be seen by predators.

Day 366

Bird food
To a hungry songbird searching for food, the snail's swollen eye stalks look like juicy maggots or caterpillars. The songbird rips off the eye stalks and eats them but leaves the rest of the snail alone.

Day 367

Days 367–409

Inside the bird
Now inside the bird's stomach, the larvae transform into adult parasites. They then head for the cloaca, the bird's rear opening, and cling to the inside using suckers. The worms release eggs, which are mixed into the bird's droppings—ready for the next snail that comes along looking for food.

Zombie snail

The amber snail usually lives a life hidden in the shadows, munching on algae and other microbes among the plants in damp woodlands and beside streams in Europe and North America. However, if the snail is attacked by a wormlike parasite—the green-banded brood pouch—everything changes. When a snail becomes infected, the parasite takes over its body, forcing the snail on a journey straight out of a horror story, with just one way to survive!

Day 367

Infection over
The amber snail is now free of the parasite, and it may even regrow its eye stalks. Without the sporocyst inside it, the snail can restart its reproductive system—and produce more snails for the parasite to attack!

Mind control

The emerald jewel wasp is a skilled assassin. It delivers venom to very specific areas of a cockroach's nervous system, controlling its mind and changing its behaviors— the cockroach becomes zombielike, and ultimately turns into a living food source for the wasp's larvae. Wasps like the emerald jewel wasp are parasitoids—they use other animals as hosts for raising their young.

The wasp's egg sticks to the cockroach's abdomen.

Laying eggs

Once the cockroach is inside the wasp's burrow, the wasp lays one or two small eggs between the cockroach's legs. Then she covers the entrance to her burrow with leaves and other items she can find.

A short while later

Zombie sting

The female wasp makes a second sting into a very specific part of the cockroach's brain and injects venom that stops its nerves from functioning properly. The cockroach becomes slow and unafraid of predators. It grooms itself thoroughly.

The final walk

The wasp chews off half of the cockroach's antennae and drinks the liquid that seeps from the wounds, replenishing her energy. She then leads the zombielike cockroach into her burrow, using the antennae like a leash.

2–3 minutes after first sting

Paralyzing the host

A female jewel wasp stings a cockroach in a nerve center located in the middle of its body. She then injects venom, paralyzing the front legs of the cockroach for 2–3 minutes.

A few seconds later

Start

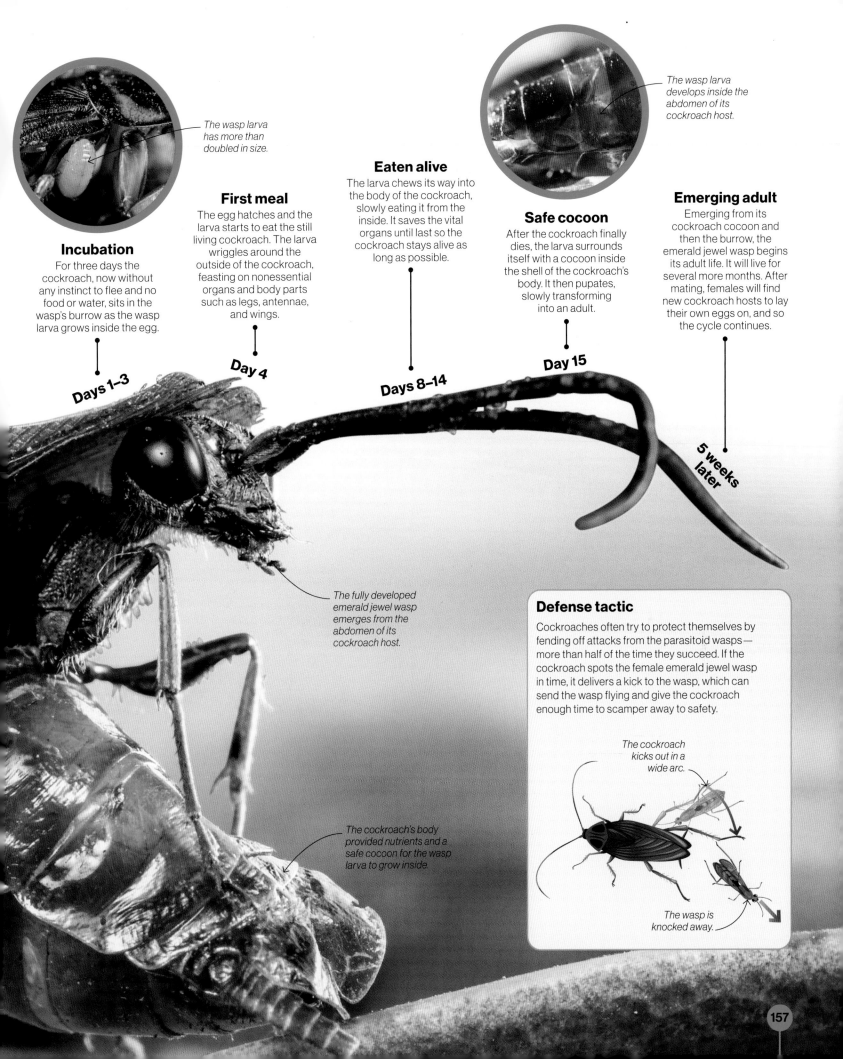

The wasp larva has more than doubled in size.

Incubation

For three days the cockroach, now without any instinct to flee and no food or water, sits in the wasp's burrow as the wasp larva grows inside the egg.

Days 1–3

First meal

The egg hatches and the larva starts to eat the still living cockroach. The larva wriggles around the outside of the cockroach, feasting on nonessential organs and body parts such as legs, antennae, and wings.

Day 4

Eaten alive

The larva chews its way into the body of the cockroach, slowly eating it from the inside. It saves the vital organs until last so the cockroach stays alive as long as possible.

Days 8–14

The wasp larva develops inside the abdomen of its cockroach host.

Safe cocoon

After the cockroach finally dies, the larva surrounds itself with a cocoon inside the shell of the cockroach's body. It then pupates, slowly transforming into an adult.

Day 15

Emerging adult

Emerging from its cockroach cocoon and then the burrow, the emerald jewel wasp begins its adult life. It will live for several more months. After mating, females will find new cockroach hosts to lay their own eggs on, and so the cycle continues.

5 weeks later

The fully developed emerald jewel wasp emerges from the abdomen of its cockroach host.

The cockroach's body provided nutrients and a safe cocoon for the wasp larva to grow inside.

Defense tactic

Cockroaches often try to protect themselves by fending off attacks from the parasitoid wasps—more than half of the time they succeed. If the cockroach spots the female emerald jewel wasp in time, it delivers a kick to the wasp, which can send the wasp flying and give the cockroach enough time to scamper away to safety.

The cockroach kicks out in a wide arc.

The wasp is knocked away.

157

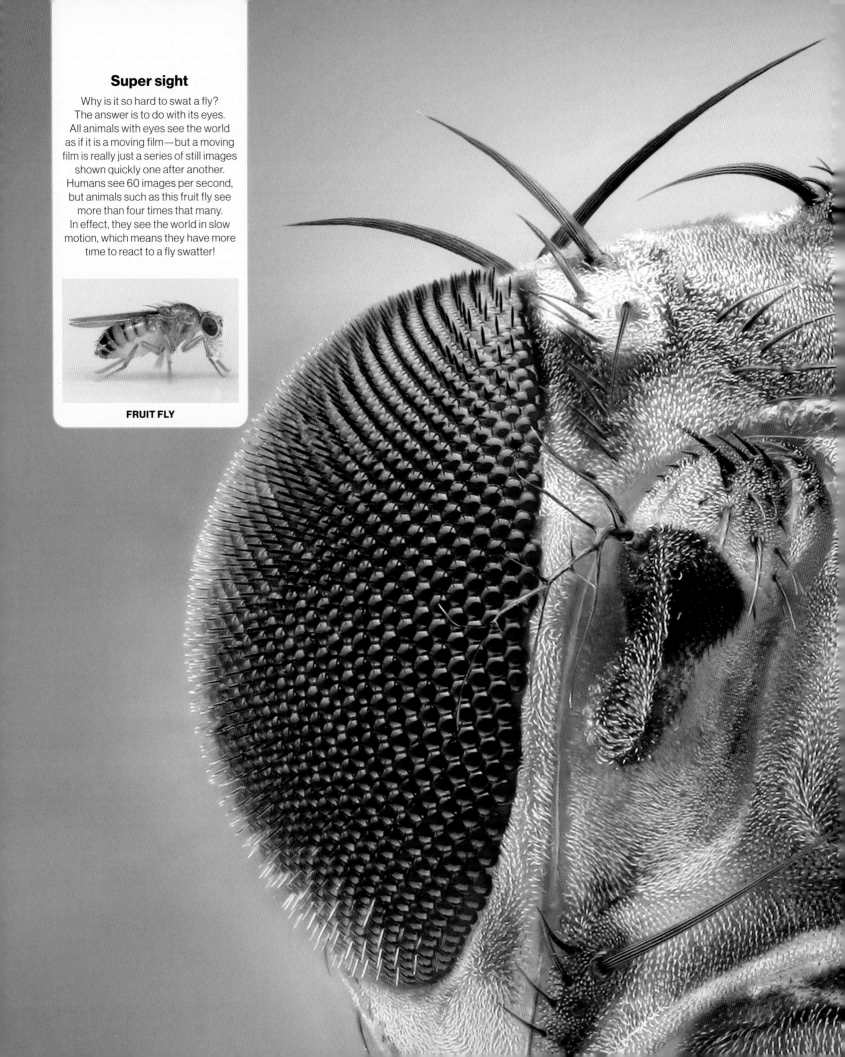

Super sight

Why is it so hard to swat a fly? The answer is to do with its eyes. All animals with eyes see the world as if it is a moving film—but a moving film is really just a series of still images shown quickly one after another. Humans see 60 images per second, but animals such as this fruit fly see more than four times that many. In effect, they see the world in slow motion, which means they have more time to react to a fly swatter!

FRUIT FLY

Cleaning stations

All coral reefs have cleaning stations, where species of shrimp and fish that eat parasites live. Fish and turtles line up to be cleaned. Cleaning stations are usually busy during the day, but there is some nighttime activity too. Although cleaners enter the mouths of predators to clear away parasites, they are never harmed.

Early morning spawning

Fish that live at the bottom of the reef, such as the Hawaiian Sergeant Major, are called demersal fish. They usually spawn early in the morning when there are fewer predators out to eat their eggs.

First light

As the day's first light hits the reef, some corals stretch out their tentacles to expose the tiny algae that live inside them to the sun's rays. This helps the algae produce food by photosynthesis, and the corals get most of their food from the algae.

The eggs attach to the reef with sticky fibers.

Seeing in the dark

The enormous eyes of squirrelfish help them to take in as much low light as possible to spot prey in the dark. Their favorite meals include plankton, worms, and shrimp.

Rainbows at night

Tiny creatures known as comb jellies have come up from deeper waters to feed on free-floating algae. They produce their own light, and their tiny, comblike tentacles can also scatter light, creating a rainbow effect.

03:00
02:00
01:00
00:00
23:00
22:00

04:00   05:00   06:00   07:00

24 hours on the reef

Coral reefs are bursting with life—from the permanent residents that live here to the visitors that pass through in search of food or special services, such as cleaning stations. As the sun sets on the reef, the daytime marine animals hide in the corals to sleep, and the night shift takes over.

21:00   20:00   19:00

Night hunter

A new predator arrives. Having been cautious when the night octopus were around the night sharks, now emerges to hunt. Its long arms reach into the nooks and crevices of the reef, hoping to seize a fish or a crab.

Feeding frenzy

Some young whitetip reef sharks manage to scare a snapper fish out of its night-time hiding place. It tries to escape, but there are too many sharks and it is quickly grabbed and eaten.

Safely asleep

A daisy parrotfish wraps itself in a cocoon made of mucus for the night. This hides its smell from predators and protects it from nibbling parasites while it sleeps. The cocoon takes up to an hour to make.

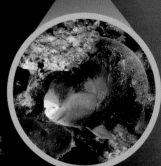

Morning swim

A bigfin reef squid heads for deeper waters after a night hunting prawns, crabs, and fish on the reef. Bigfin squid swim together in large groups for safety to confuse predators, such as tuna.

Coral snack

A sea slug munches on invasive snowflake coral, which grows over black coral and kills it. The slug glides its way to the base of the coral, where it will spend the day avoiding predators.

Midday clean

A green sea turtle stops by the reef to get clean on its way to graze on sea grass beds. Algae-eating fish swarm to its hard shell to have a free meal of algae and the odd parasite.

Taking cover

A giant grouper, weighing 440 lb (200 kg), swims past nocturnal squirrelfish that are in hiding for the day. It is not interested in them, though, as it is on the hunt for a spiny lobster.

Shelf coral is the perfect place for small fish to hide.

Afternoon song

A haunting noise can be heard on the reef. It is the sound of male humpback whales trying to attract mates. They spent the morning and early afternoon feeding and now start to warm up their vocal chords for a night of singing.

Tube sponges filter water for food.

Opening up

The sand anemone has been buried in sand for most of the day, keeping its tender tentacles hidden from nipping fish. As the light decreases, the anemone stretches out its stinging arms ready to catch food during the night.

Seeking shelter

Algae-eating fish, like the yellow tang, hide in crevices in the reef at night to avoid predators. Hawaii's Humuhumunukunukuapua'a have a special spine that springs up to wedge them tightly into their hiding place, making it difficult for predators to pull them out.

08:00 09:00 10:00 11:00 12:00 13:00 14:00 15:00 16:00 17:00 18:00

161

Coral collection

Australia's Great Barrier Reef is the world's most extensive coral reef system and the largest living structure on Earth. It can be seen from space, yet it is made up of billions of tiny animals, called polyps. Each coral is a colony of polyps, and each polyp has microscopic plantlike algae that live inside its body. These produce food for the polyp, while the polyp provides a safe home for the algae.

Underwater world

Reefs are complex, rainbow-colored habitats, with nooks and crannies that teem with many thousands of creatures. About one-quarter of the world's fish species rely on coral reefs for their survival. The Great Barrier Reef is made up of nearly 3,000 reefs and 900 islands.

Corals settle

Tiny coral larvae, carried on ocean currents, settle on a rocky surface and change into polyps. Each polyp produces a small amount of calcium carbonate (limestone), which forms a hard protective skeleton around its soft body. The polyps start to divide to form a colony of identical polyps.

The tentacles sting prey and sweep it into the polyp's mouth.

The hard skeleton protects the soft body inside .

Food travels down into the stomach where it is digested.

Building a reef

Many species of coral have settled and are becoming enormous colonies. They grow into different shapes—some are large, treelike branches, while others form flat shelves or big, brainlike balls. The hard coral skeletons build up over time to form limestone reefs, with new colonies growing on top of those that have died.

Competing for space

Space on the reef is limited. Coral colonies compete for positions with the best light and water conditions. They can even stretch out stringlike tentacles to digest their neighbors.

These two coral colonies, one brown, one green, are fighting for space.

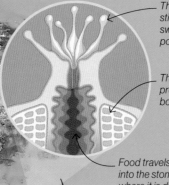

6,000 YA

6,000–5,000 YA

3,000 YA

Protecting the reef

The Australian Government announces a conservation plan to protect the reef that includes "seeding" it with corals that have been grown to cope with higher water temperatures and spraying tiny droplets of salt water into the air to attract moisture and create low-lying clouds to shade and cool the reef. The plan also includes funding to change farming practices that pollute the reef.

2020

A devastating storm

A cyclone passes near the reef. The storm's high winds produce powerful waves that smash into large areas of coral in their path, reducing them to rubble.

Recovery of the reef

Scientists diving on the reef discover that its corals have visibly started to recover eight years after the cyclone. The number of hard limestone skeletons created by the reef's coral polyps has increased by 400 percent since 2014.

2018

Coral bleaching

As sea temperatures rise due to global warming, corals become stressed and expel the algae that live inside them. Without algae, corals turn white and become damaged. This is called coral bleaching.

Algae

Healthy coral
Tiny algae living inside the polyps convert sunlight into food for the coral. Algae give corals their color.

Algae leaving the coral

Stressed coral
The polyps expel most of their algae, starving the coral of food. The coral can survive like this for a couple of months.

2009   **2014**   **2017**

The reef forms a natural barrier between the Australian coastline and the open ocean.

Bleached coral
If water conditions remain poor, the coral will expel any remaining algae. In this bleached state, corals are likely to become diseased or die.

Reef growth grinds to a halt

Scientists measure the growth of the reef and find that it is only growing at a quarter of the rate it was before the cyclone struck five years previously.

Bleaching across the reef

Higher sea temperatures cause bleaching across the reef. Up to 90 percent of corals in the north of the Great Barrier Reef are bleached, while those in the south have not been as badly affected because of slightly lower ocean temperatures.

Four days after it is fertilized, a tiny embryo is developing inside a transparent egg.

Each fertilized egg is just a few millimeters across.

All ribbon eels are born male. About seven days after hatching, a young eel is silvery and almost transparent.

Young males develop a stripe that changes from black to bright blue as they mature.

The female's larger body allows her to use energy to produce eggs.

Changing color

It might look as if these four images are of different creatures, but they are actually all stages in the life of a ribbon eel. Found in parts of the Indian and Pacific Oceans, ribbon eel eggs and larvae are tiny and almost transparent, but when they become adults, they transform into something much more colorful. Males turn an eye-catching blue and yellow, then when they reach a body length of 4.5 ft (1.3 m), they turn completely yellow and transform into females, capable of laying their own eggs.

Egg spawning

Around the time of a full moon, a dominant male clownfish prepares a nesting site by clearing a spot on a rock near an anemone. The female inspects it and then lays up to 1000 eggs there.

The eggs are only around 0.1 in (3 mm) long and change their color as they develop.

Keeping anemones close

Clownfish have a close relationship—called mutualism—with anemones, which are relatives of jellyfish and live their lives fixed to rocks. The anemones' stings provide protection from predators, while the clownfish in turn protect the anemones from parasites, keep them clean, and never try to eat them. Clownfish are also covered in a special thick mucus layer to protect them from the anemones' stings.

Shortly afterward

Caring for the eggs

The male clownfish passes over the eggs and fertilizes them. He then looks after the eggs, protecting them from parasites and keeping them clean.

The father cares for the young and will usually eat any eggs that are damaged or infected.

Clowning around

Recognizable for their distinctive stripes, clownfish reside in the coral reef. They live inside sea anemones—animals with stinging tentacles that look a bit like plants. Unlike most animals, all clownfish start their lives as males, and they have the ability to change their sex. They live in groups headed by a dominant female—if she dies, the largest male will then transform into a female and take charge.

Clownfish eyes become visible a couple of days before they hatch..

Days 6–10

Larvae hatch

The eggs hatch after 6–10 days. They hatch into tiny, translucent larvae, which are all male. They float off into the open ocean for the next couple of weeks, growing as they feed on microscopic plants and animals. Many are eaten by larger fish.

Clownfish communicate through popping and clicking noises, which they make by smacking their teeth together.

There are 29 species of clownfish, each with different coloring, but almost all of them have vertical stripes.

Years 5–10

Becoming female
When the female of the group dies, the dominant male will change its sex and turn into the new dominant female. Then, the next biggest male will grow and become its new partner. .

Days 24–31

Juveniles
The little clownfish start to look like small versions of their parents, beginning to display their distinctive stripes. These juveniles find a reef and start to look for a social group to join.

First few years

Maturity
As males grow bigger, they gain more status in the social hierarchy on the anemone. The largest male is dominant, and the only one allowed to mate with the female.

Hatching

Tiny salmon, called alevins, hatch from eggs. To avoid predators, they hide in the gravel on the bottom of a lake or river. For six weeks or more, they gain all their nutrition from yolk sacs attached to their bellies.

Yolk sac

Egg

Winter

Late winter–Early spring

Small fry

When the yolk sac is used up, the little salmon—now called fry_ emerge from the gravel, swim to the surface, and begin feeding on tiny floating animals called zooplankton.

Death

After spawning, the male will look for other females to mate with. For about a week, the female remains close to her redd, defending it. Eventually, she dies, and the male dies soon after. Nutrients from their decaying bodies return to the ecosystem.

After spawning

Fertilization

As the female lays her eggs, a male swims alongside, fertilizing them with his sperm. This process of releasing and fertilizing eggs is called spawning. The female then fans the gravel with her tail, to bury the eggs.

Fall

Hazardous journey

Returning salmon face many dangers, especially bears that wait for them to pass upstream. But there are simply too many salmon on the move for the bears to catch all of them. "Salmon ladders," like steps or passways, are often added when dams are built, to help the fish "climb" the structures that would otherwise block their way.

Choosing a nest site

A female salmon carefully chooses a spot in the riverbed gravel to lay her eggs. She shakes her tail from side to side to create a hollow, or redd, and lays 500–1,000 eggs in it. She repeats this process four or five times.

Late summer

Early summer

Fry grow

Salmon fry are in danger of being eaten by larger fish, but dark vertical markings on their skin help provide camouflage. As they grow, the fry eat a greater variety of food, including aquatic insects and shrimplike animals called amphipods.

Early spring

Hunted by predators

The fry grow into smolt in the freshwater lake. As they grow bigger, they become targets for larger predators, including hungry fish, otters, and birds of prey such as ospreys and bald eagles.

1–2 years

Bald eagles swoop down to grab salmon with their talons.

Swimming salmon

Young sockeye salmon live in freshwater lakes and rivers in North America. When they are older, they swim several hundred kilometers to the Pacific Ocean. Fish that move between fresh water and salt water at different stages of their life are called anadromous. After several years growing at sea, sockeyes' bodies become red and their heads turn green. Incredibly, they find their way back to where they started life. There they breed—and die soon afterward.

Smolt migrate

From about a year old, the salmon start to migrate downriver to the Pacific Ocean, where there is more food. They taste chemical changes in the water to find their way and seem to remember this information for their return journey.

Spring of year 2

Life at sea

Once in the ocean, the salmon feed on zooplankton (tiny animals that swim near the surface), other fish, and even small squid. After a year, some males—called jacks—return to the river where they hatched. However, most sockeyes stay at sea for longer.

Spring

Return migration

After two or three years, most adult salmon begin to return to their birthplace, guided partly by interpreting Earth's magnetic field and the position of the sun. They turn brilliant red with green heads, a sign that they are ready to mate.

1–3 years later

Grizzly fishing

A grizzly bear eagerly waits for a catch as sockeye salmon try to jump over Brook Falls in the Katmai National Park and Preserve, Alaska. Grizzlies compete with each other for the best fishing spots in June and July as the salmon migrate back to their spawning sites. The most successful bears can catch more than 30 salmon in a day.

Bitter winter

It is -60°F (-51°C) and ice 5 ft (1.5 m) thick has formed on the mighty Yukon River. A snowshoe hare, with its white winter coat, sits motionless as wolves walk nearby on a path carved through the snow.

Life under the ice

Beneath the winter ice, among the pebbles on the riverbed, salmon eggs hatch as alevins. They are tiny and each alevin has a yolk sac attached to it, which will be its only source of food for weeks.

January

February

Year on the Yukon River

The Yukon River is 1,979 miles (3,185 km) long. It is a shallow and slow-moving river that runs through Canada and Alaska. There are extreme seasons this far north, with cold winters that last for six months every year, and short, intense summers. Animals that live here year-round have adapted to the conditions—some hibernate throughout the winter months, while others breed in the spring to give their young a better chance at surviving the winter.

Summer play

A family of river otters comes out to play and enjoy the sunshine—they are more active in the summer when the water is not iced over. The mother floats and tumbles with her pups—all good practice for learning to hunt frogs and fish.

July

Winding river

The Yukon River starts in the hills of the Canadian Yukon Territory. It winds around wooded islands and through mountains. As it enters Alaska, it widens into a vast wetland area before weaving its way to the Bering Sea.

Fireweed in bloom

Blooming pink fireweed flowers cover the banks of the river in August. Butterflies, bees, flies, and beetles rely on these flowers for their food, drinking the sweet nectar and pollinating each plant as they travel between them. The insects in turn are eaten by amphibians, such as frogs.

August

Birds prepare their nest

High up in an old conifer tree, two ospreys return in late March to the same nest they have used for many years. The nest is nearly 5 ft (1.5 m) wide. They work together to get it ready for their eggs, which will be laid in April, by making repairs and lining it with moss, bark, and grass.

Spring melt

The days are quickly getting longer and warmer. Snow melts, and the thick ice on the river breaks into chunks the size of bulldozers. As these are swept downriver by other ice sheets, some get pushed on to the shore, destroying anything in their path.

March

April

Start of summer

Summer begins and the days are long, with only a few hours of darkness. Conditions in the river are ideal—the water is warm but not too hot—and the adult salmon start their long migration upriver to spawn, leaping up waterfalls.

Calving season

Female moose give birth to their calves in May to give them time to feed up their young before the harsh winter. The young are left in a safe place for short periods while the mothers go off to feed and rest. However, there are threats nearby—grizzly bears are on the hunt, hungry after their long hibernation.

Mats of green algae float freely, providing food for small fish.

June

May

Spawning ends

A female salmon laid her eggs weeks ago and has been defending her nest ever since. She has not eaten in months and is weak. A grizzly bear plunges into the river, seizes her, and carries her ashore to eat.

Feeding the next generation

The smell of salmon carcasses fills the fall air. Bears and wolves pull the salmon to the riverbanks, eat their favorite parts, and leave the rest for scavengers. Insect maggots feed on the remains. These insects will go on to feed the next generation of salmon.

Freeze up

By mid-November, a thin layer of ice has formed on the river. Snowshoe hares and ptarmigans turn white in winter so they are better camouflaged against the snow and ice.

The dead of winter

Night is dark and long in the northern reaches of the river in December. A natural light show known as the aurora borealis (northern lights) takes place in the sky above, while below grizzly bears hibernate and otters swim under the ice to search for food.

September

October

November

December

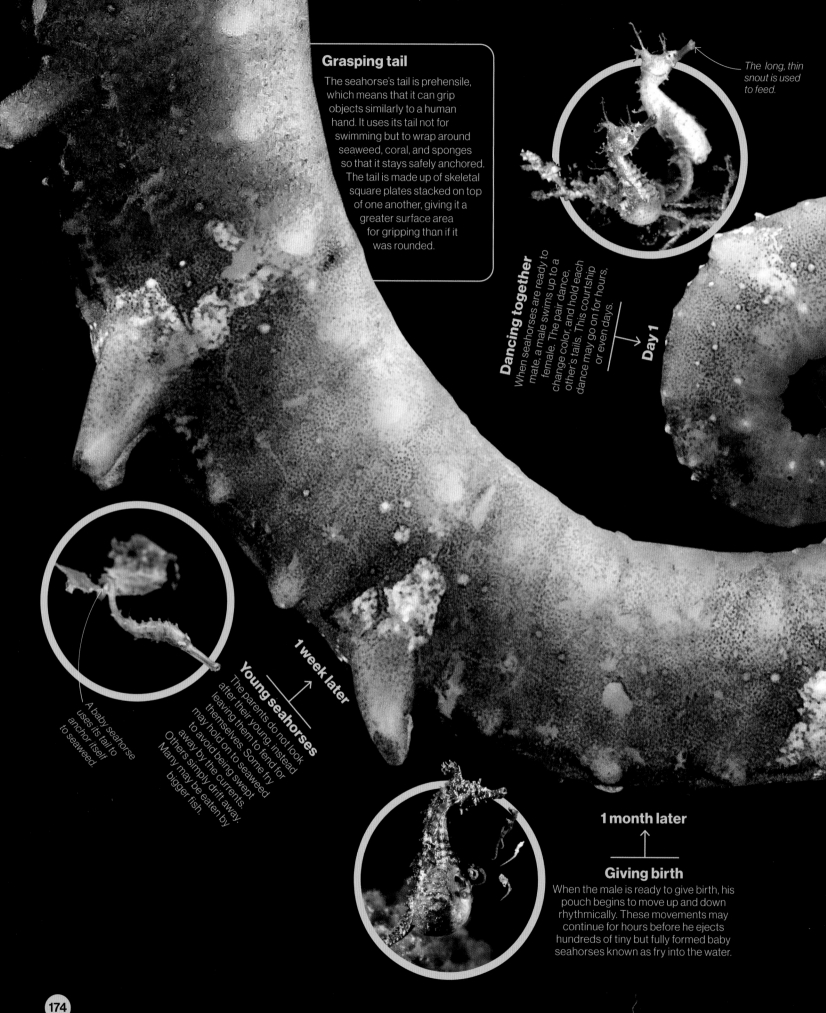

Grasping tail

The seahorse's tail is prehensile, which means that it can grip objects similarly to a human hand. It uses its tail not for swimming but to wrap around seaweed, coral, and sponges so that it stays safely anchored. The tail is made up of skeletal square plates stacked on top of one another, giving it a greater surface area for gripping than if it was rounded.

The long, thin snout is used to feed.

Dancing together

When seahorses are ready to mate, a male swims up to a female. The pair dance, change color, and hold each other's tails. This courtship dance may go on for hours, or even days.

Day 1

Young seahorses

The parents do not look after their young, instead leaving them to fend for themselves. Some fry may hold on to seaweed to avoid being swept away by the currents. Others simply drift away. Many may be eaten by bigger fish.

1 week later

A baby seahorse uses its tail to anchor itself to seaweed.

Giving birth

When the male is ready to give birth, his pouch begins to move up and down rhythmically. These movements may continue for hours before he ejects hundreds of tiny but fully formed baby seahorses known as fry into the water.

1 month later

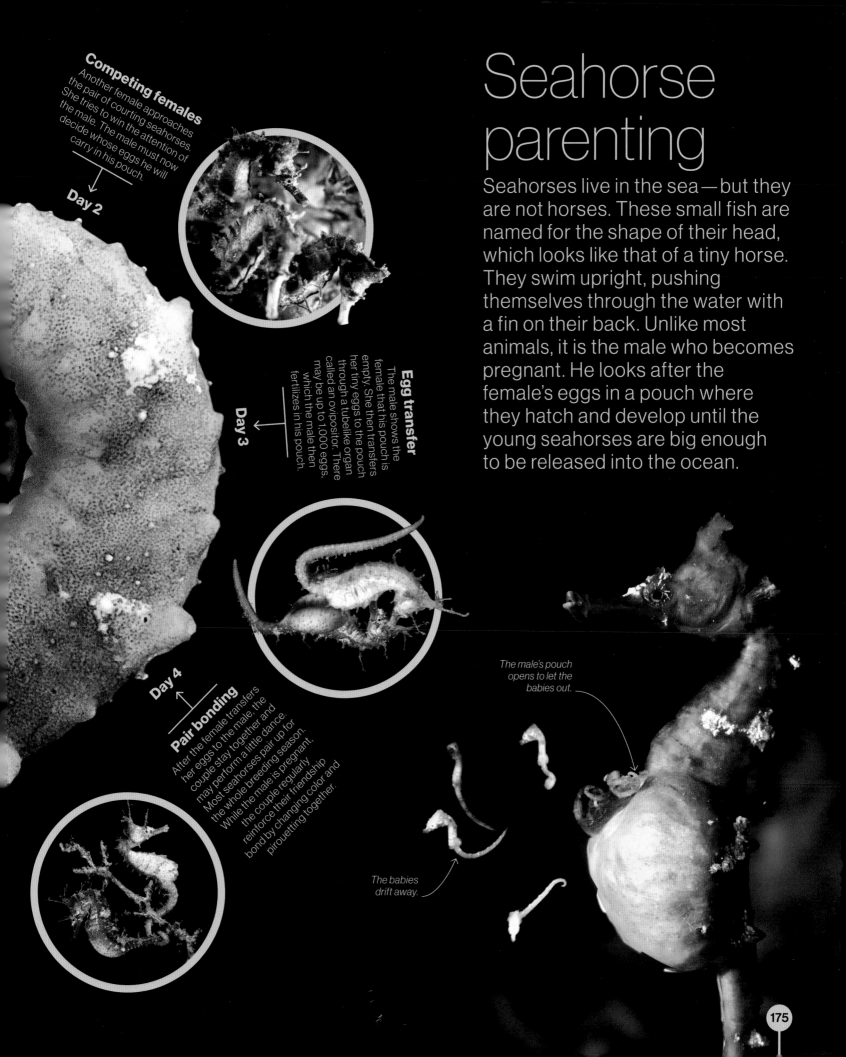

Seahorse parenting

Seahorses live in the sea—but they are not horses. These small fish are named for the shape of their head, which looks like that of a tiny horse. They swim upright, pushing themselves through the water with a fin on their back. Unlike most animals, it is the male who becomes pregnant. He looks after the female's eggs in a pouch where they hatch and develop until the young seahorses are big enough to be released into the ocean.

Competing females

Another female approaches the pair of courting seahorses. She tries to win the attention of the male. The male must now decide whose eggs he will carry in his pouch.

Day 2

Egg transfer

The male shows the female that his pouch is empty. She then transfers her tiny eggs to the pouch through a tubelike organ called an ovipositor. There may be up to 1,000 eggs, which the male then fertilizes in his pouch.

Day 3

Pair bonding

After the female transfers her eggs to the male, the couple stay together and may perform a little dance. Most seahorses pair up for the whole breeding season. While the male is pregnant, the couple regularly reinforce their friendship bond by changing color and pirouetting together.

Day 4

The male's pouch opens to let the babies out.

The babies drift away.

Day 1

Birth

A pregnant female waits for high tide before she swims into shallow nursery waters in a tropical estuary called a mangrove swamp. There, she gives birth to up to 18 shark pups, which are 20–30 in (50–76 cm) long.

Day 2

Pups

After birth, the mother swims back out to sea and the young shark pups must fend for themselves. They stay in the shallow waters and hide from predators, including adult lemon sharks, in the roots of the mangrove swamp.

From pup to predator

Lemon sharks are named for their slightly yellow color, which helps them blend into sandy habitats. Some species of sharks are solitary, but lemon sharks can be highly social, gathering in groups with other lemon sharks their own size. Like most other sharks, lemon sharks give birth to live young. To do so, they return to their birthing grounds in shallow mangrove waters around the coasts of the Americas and West Africa.

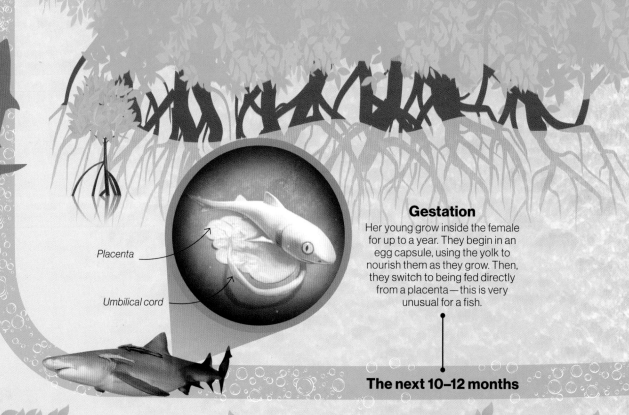

Placenta

Umbilical cord

Gestation

Her young grow inside the female for up to a year. They begin in an egg capsule, using the yolk to nourish them as they grow. Then, they switch to being fed directly from a placenta—this is very unusual for a fish.

The next 10–12 months

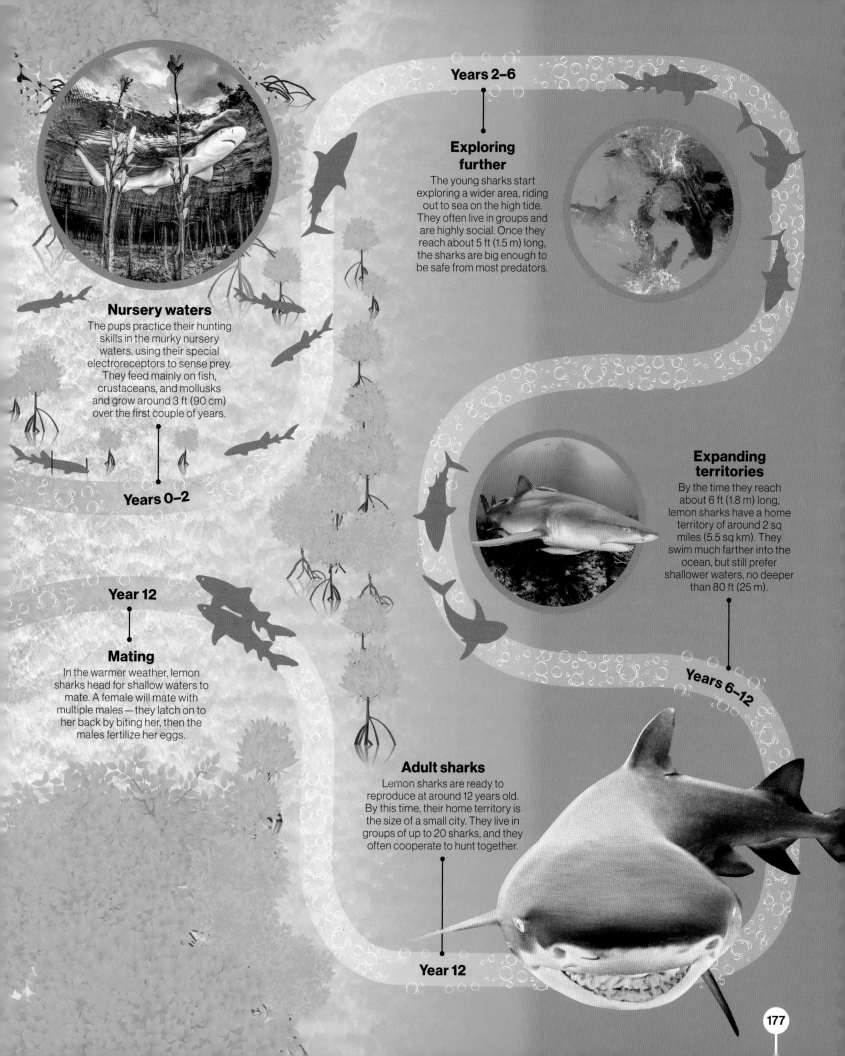

Nursery waters

The pups practice their hunting skills in the murky nursery waters, using their special electroreceptors to sense prey. They feed mainly on fish, crustaceans, and mollusks and grow around 3 ft (90 cm) over the first couple of years.

Years 0–2

Exploring further

Years 2–6

The young sharks start exploring a wider area, riding out to sea on the high tide. They often live in groups and are highly social. Once they reach about 5 ft (1.5 m) long, the sharks are big enough to be safe from most predators.

Expanding territories

By the time they reach about 6 ft (1.8 m) long, lemon sharks have a home territory of around 2 sq miles (5.5 sq km). They swim much farther into the ocean, but still prefer shallower waters, no deeper than 80 ft (25 m).

Years 6–12

Year 12

Mating

In the warmer weather, lemon sharks head for shallow waters to mate. A female will mate with multiple males—they latch on to her back by biting her, then the males fertilize her eggs.

Adult sharks

Lemon sharks are ready to reproduce at around 12 years old. By this time, their home territory is the size of a small city. They live in groups of up to 20 sharks, and they often cooperate to hunt together.

Year 12

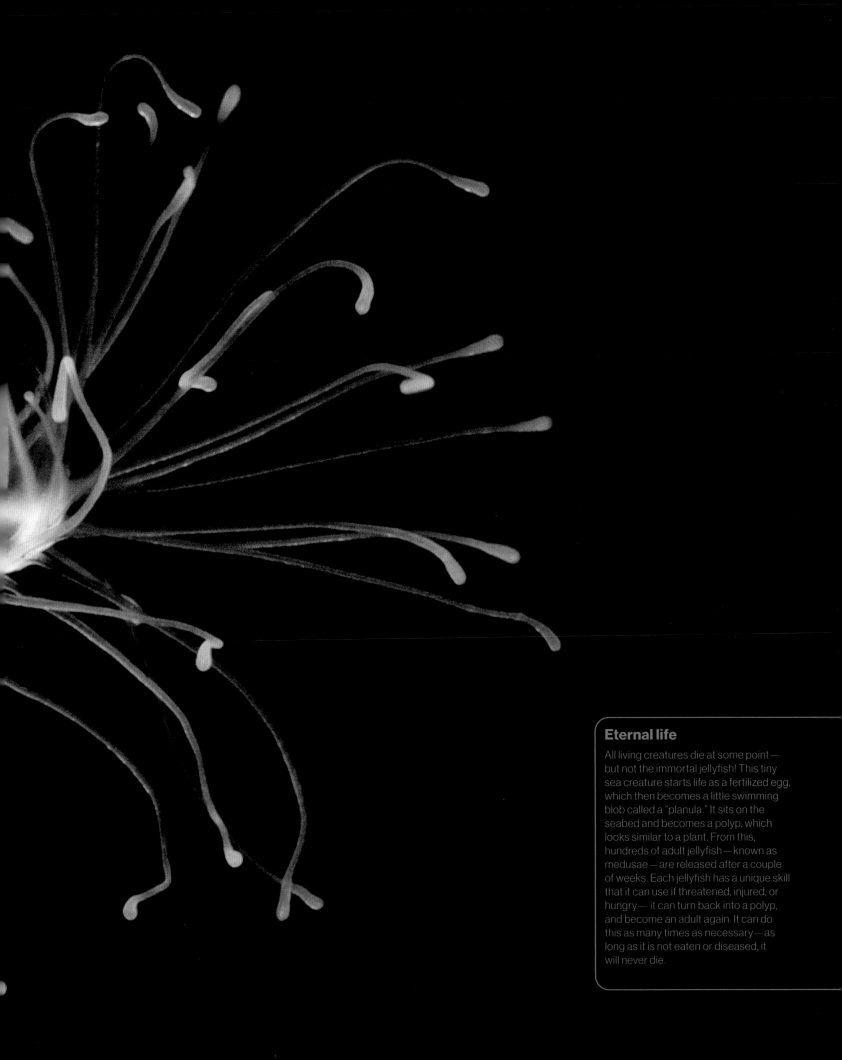

Eternal life

All living creatures die at some point—
but not the immortal jellyfish! This tiny
sea creature starts life as a fertilized egg,
which then becomes a little swimming
blob called a "planula." It sits on the
seabed and becomes a polyp, which
looks similar to a plant. From this,
hundreds of adult jellyfish—known as
medusae—are released after a couple
of weeks. Each jellyfish has a unique skill
that it can use if threatened, injured, or
hungry— it can turn back into a polyp,
and become an adult again. It can do
this as many times as necessary—as
long as it is not eaten or diseased, it
will never die.

A female emerges from her den inside a rock crevice.

The male may use sensitive chemical sensors on his suckers to detect the female's chemicals.

The female stores the male's sperm in her mantle—a cavity behind her head where all her vital organs are.

Each egg is about the size of a grain of rice.

Finding a home

A female giant Pacific octopus becomes ready to mate when she is between three and five years old. She selects a suitable ocean den, a spot that must be hard for predators to reach.

Day 1

Attracting a male

With her home ready, the female looks to attract a male. Nobody knows for certain how she does this, but most probably she releases a chemical into the water to indicate that she is ready to mate. Sometimes, more than one male may be attracted, and she must then choose one.

About day 2–5

Male transfers sperm

Once the male has been chosen, he uses his mating arm, called a hectocotylus, to transfer two packets of spermatophores (sperm) to the female. She stores these until she is ready to fertilize her eggs.

About day 6

Laying eggs

The female chooses when to fertilize her eggs—it may be right away or up to seven months later. She lays the fertilized eggs one by one and attaches them to the roof of her den in strings. She may lay more than 50,000 eggs.

Day 7

Eight-leg life

Though it starts life the size of a grain of rice, a giant Pacific octopus can grow larger than any other octopus species. Each limb is able to grow almost 16 ft (5 m) long, and the heaviest giant Pacific octopus on record is a whopping 600 lbs (272 kg)—almost as heavy as two panda bears. Giant Pacific octopuses have the most complex brains of any invertebrate and can change color and even texture to blend in with their surroundings.

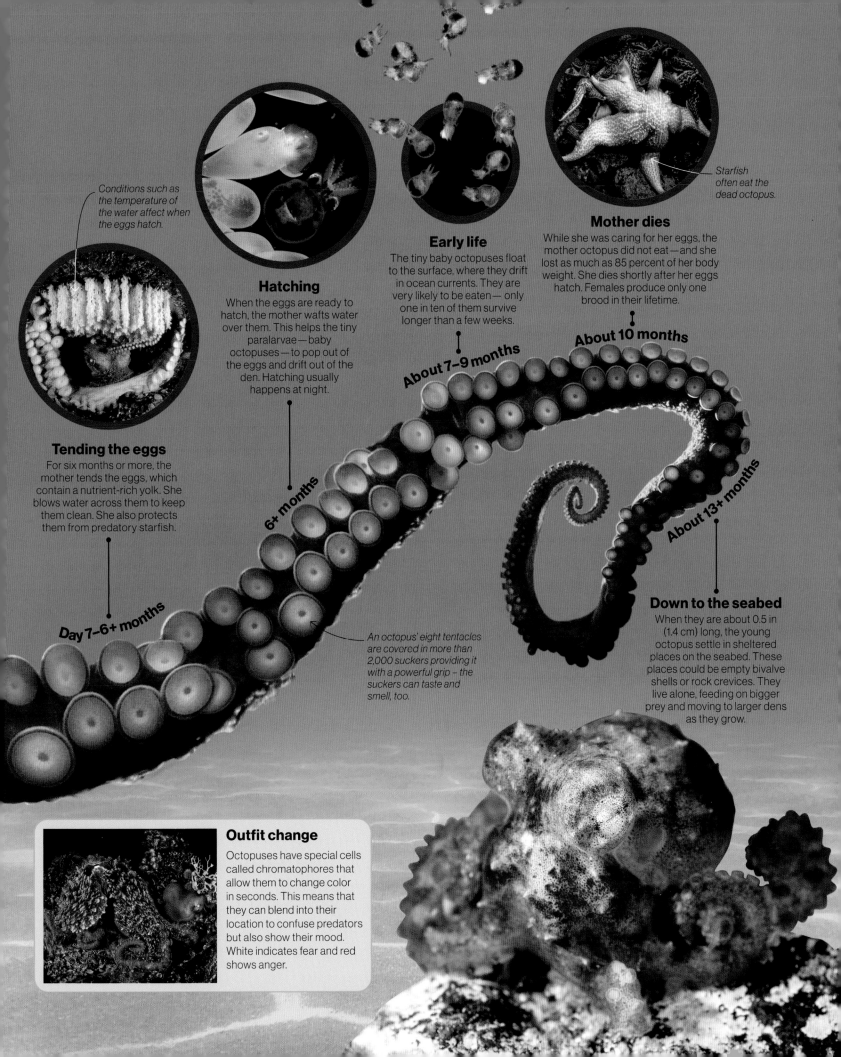

Conditions such as the temperature of the water affect when the eggs hatch.

Starfish often eat the dead octopus.

Hatching

When the eggs are ready to hatch, the mother wafts water over them. This helps the tiny paralarvae—baby octopuses—to pop out of the eggs and drift out of the den. Hatching usually happens at night.

Early life

The tiny baby octopuses float to the surface, where they drift in ocean currents. They are very likely to be eaten— only one in ten of them survive longer than a few weeks.

Mother dies

While she was caring for her eggs, the mother octopus did not eat—and she lost as much as 85 percent of her body weight. She dies shortly after her eggs hatch. Females produce only one brood in their lifetime.

About 10 months

About 7–9 months

Tending the eggs

For six months or more, the mother tends the eggs, which contain a nutrient-rich yolk. She blows water across them to keep them clean. She also protects them from predatory starfish.

6+ months

About 13+ months

Day 7–6+ months

An octopus' eight tentacles are covered in more than 2,000 suckers providing it with a powerful grip – the suckers can taste and smell, too.

Down to the seabed

When they are about 0.5 in (1.4 cm) long, the young octopus settle in sheltered places on the seabed. These places could be empty bivalve shells or rock crevices. They live alone, feeding on bigger prey and moving to larger dens as they grow.

Outfit change

Octopuses have special cells called chromatophores that allow them to change color in seconds. This means that they can blend into their location to confuse predators but also show their mood. White indicates fear and red shows anger.

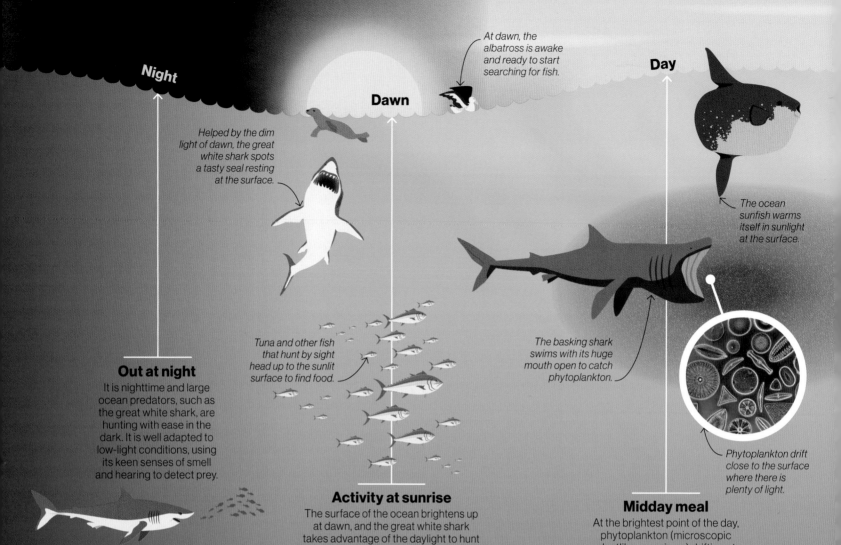

Night

Dawn

Day

At dawn, the albatross is awake and ready to start searching for fish.

Helped by the dim light of dawn, the great white shark spots a tasty seal resting at the surface.

The ocean sunfish warms itself in sunlight at the surface.

Tuna and other fish that hunt by sight head up to the sunlit surface to find food.

The basking shark swims with its huge mouth open to catch phytoplankton.

Phytoplankton drift close to the surface where there is plenty of light.

Out at night

It is nighttime and large ocean predators, such as the great white shark, are hunting with ease in the dark. It is well adapted to low-light conditions, using its keen senses of smell and hearing to detect prey.

Activity at sunrise

The surface of the ocean brightens up at dawn, and the great white shark takes advantage of the daylight to hunt a while longer. Marine animals such as tuna, which use their sense of sight to find food, swim up from deeper waters toward the surface to hunt. Above the water, seabirds such as the albatross begin hunting for fish.

Midday meal

At the brightest point of the day, phytoplankton (microscopic plantlike organisms) drifting at the surface create food using the sun's energy in a process called photosynthesis. The world's heaviest bony fish, the ocean sunfish, sunbathes in the daylight.

24 hours in the ocean

The largest migration in nature takes place in Earth's oceans. Each night, billions of fish and microscopic marine animals called zooplankton swim up from the dark depths to lighter, shallower waters, balancing the need to find food with the importance of staying hidden from predators.

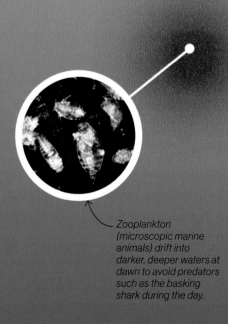

Zooplankton (microscopic marine animals) drift into darker, deeper waters at dawn to avoid predators such as the basking shark during the day.

The albatross glides on its enormous wings all day, landing on the water only to feed.

The albatross sleeps on the water's surface.

Night

Dolphins sleep floating on the water's surface, a behavior known as logging.

Day

Dusk

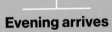

A group of dolphins, known as a pod, hunts fish near the surface during the day.

Evening arrives
At dusk, birds rest on the water's surface. Underwater, the great ocean migration begins, with many species including salps and lanternfish swimming up to the water's surface to feed throughout the night.

Zooplankton migrate upward to feed at night, safe from predators that rely on sunlight to hunt.

Sperm whales sleep vertically— they pop up for air about once every 15 minutes.

Changing tides
The tide is falling. The oceans rise (high tide) and fall (low tide) about once every 12 hours, depending on the location. The changing tides influence the daily feeding habits and movement of fish, and this in turn influences dolphins and seabirds who follow the tides to catch fish.

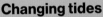

Night falls
The tide has risen, and with no sunlight the surface of the water is in darkness again. Larger zooplankton also drift upward, from the depths of the sea, to feed on phytoplankton. Dolphins and sperm whales rest at the surface.

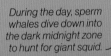

During the day, sperm whales dive down into the dark midnight zone to hunt for giant squid.

Little is known about giant squids, as they spend most of their time in the deep, dark waters of the midnight zone.

Ocean zones
Earth's oceans are divided into zones according to the level of sunlight they receive. Ninety percent of all marine life lives in the sunlight zone, the area closest to the surface where there is lots of light and plenty of plankton to eat. The twilight zone gets less sunlight—many species hide from predators here during the day before swimming up to the surface to feed at night. The midnight zone and the abyss are in total darkness, too deep for light to reach. Only the toughest of sea creatures are found at these chilly depths.

Sunlight zone 0–650 ft

Twilight zone 650–3,300 ft

Midnight zone 3,300–13,100 ft

Abyss 13,100–21,300 ft

Death

↑

Whale dies

A whale is an air-breathing mammal and must always return to the surface to breathe. When a whale dies of old age, it is usually near the surface.

A few days after death

↑

Floating on the surface

Soon after death, the whale's huge body starts to decompose. This releases gases that blow the carcass up like a balloon. The inflated body floats on the surface, and seabirds and sharks come to scavenge.

A buildup of gases in the body may make the whale explode.

A few hours later

↑

Whale sinks

Eventually the whale's body breaks open, and the gases inside leak out. The whale now starts to sink slowly to the bottom of the sea. It can take many hours for the carcass to reach the ocean floor.

ON/AROUND CARCASS

Hagfish

Octopus

Six-gill shark

Rattail fish

Scavengers

The first animals to reach the whale fall are scavengers, which come to eat the blubber, organs, and muscle. This deep in the ocean, there is no light from above, so the scavengers find the whale fall in the dark water from its smell.

Whale fall

When a whale dies, its giant body eventually sinks all the way to the bottom of the sea, creating a "whale fall." Deep down in the cold and dark ocean, the whale's carcass provides a feast for hundreds of animals on the empty seabed. This sudden and huge food supply can last decades. Every part of the whale is eaten—from the blubber (fat) to the bones.

Five years after death

Marine snow

Most food arrives on the sea floor as "marine snow." Creatures in deeper waters rely on this shower of flakes made from dead material from the plants and animals that live up near the surface. One whale fall contains the same amount of food as about 2,000 years of marine snow.

ON/AROUND CARCASS

Grooved tanner crab

Hesiod worm

Amphipod

Giant isopod

Eelpout

ON/IN SURROUNDING SEDIMENT

Sea pig

Brittle star

Ampharetid worm

Stripped skeleton

The whale fall is now a skeleton, and worms and shellfish scrape the last scraps of flesh from the remains. Meanwhile, small creatures such as sea pigs and brittle stars move in to live around the whale fall, surviving on nutrients from the carcass.

ON/AROUND CARCASS

Rubyspira snail

Adipicola mussel

Bone-eaters

Only the hard parts of the whale's bones remain. These are eaten by shellfish and zombie worms that bore inside to reach the nutrients in the bones.

ON/AROUND CARCASS

Pom pom anemone

A new home

Most of the whale's bones have crumbled to dust, but a few chunks of hard material are left. These hard surfaces create a platform for sea creatures, such as anemones, sponges, and corals, to set up home.

Seven years after death

50 years after death

50 years and beyond

Deep-sea octopuses are attracted to the food available at the whale fall.

Zombie worms boring into the bone give the carcass a hairy appearance.

The bone-eaters release sulfur chemicals into the water, which are consumed by yellow-colored bacteria.

Splish splash!

A mobula ray splashes back to the water after making a spectacular leap out of the Sea of Cortez, off the coast of Mexico. Mobula rays beat their wide, flat fins together to swim—a method that looks more like a bird flying. Every year, tens of thousands of them gather in huge shoals. When in these big groups, the rays often breach the surface and jump up to 6.5 ft (2 m) in the air. Scientists do not know for sure why they do this, but it might be to attract a mate.

MOBULA RAYS JUMPING

Monumental migration

The Christmas Island red crab—found only on Christmas Island and the Cocos (Keeling) Islands in the Indian Ocean—makes one of the most remarkable mass migrations. Every year, millions of crabs leave their homes in the middle of their islands to mate and lay eggs in the ocean. So many crabs make the migration that they bring road traffic to a standstill.

LARVAE

For two weeks after laying eggs, the female incubates the eggs in a special brood pouch on her abdomen.

Hatching
Guided by the moon and the high tide, the female heads into the ocean and releases her eggs at the same time as all the other females. The eggs hatch immediately, and the swirling clouds of larvae are swept out to sea by the currents. Hatching all at once gives the greatest number the best chance of survival.

Day 28

Egg laying
After mating, the male has a swim, before starting the long journey home again. The female remains in the burrow. After three days, she will lay up to 100,000 eggs. Egg-laden females then leave their burrows when the moon reaches its last quarter.

Day 17

Picking a mate
The larger male crabs are first to arrive at the beach. They begin digging and defending burrows. When the females arrive, they have a quick dip in the ocean and then choose a male with a burrow that appeals to them.

Days 8–16

Mating season begins
As soon as the first monsoon rains arrive at the beginning of the wet season, the forest-dwelling crabs begin their march to the sea. Millions of crabs scuttle distances that are vast for them, with road traffic often having to stop.

Day 1

Larval stage
The larvae spend around 3–4 weeks at sea, growing and changing. At this stage they are most at risk from predators, like rays and whale sharks. Eventually they change from larvae into shrimplike creatures, called megalopae.

Days 28–56

Megalopae
The megalopae drift back into the shallow waters close to the beach, where they spend a few days bobbing around. Then they metamorphose once again, changing into young crabs the size of apple pips. At this point, they are ready to return to land.

Day 60

First journey
Thousands of young crabs begin their own long march from the sea to the forest in the center of the island. This journey can take them nine days. Once they arrive, they spend most of their time hiding in burrows and molting as they continue to grow.

Day 63

Adults
After 4–5 years living in the forest, eating dried leaves, fruit, and seeds, the crabs are big enough to join the yearly mating migration themselves.

Years 4–5

Crabs are covered in a hard protective exoskeleton, also known as a carapace.

If a crab loses a limb, sometimes they can regrow a new one.

Frogspawn

Most female frogs lay their eggs, called "frogspawn," in water. All frog eggs are surrounded by a protective jelly, which clumps the eggs together. Glass frogs are a type of tree frog that instead lay their eggs on leaves overhanging streams.

Day 1

A clutch of eggs from a glass frog consists of around 28–30 eggs. Other species can lay up to 4,000 eggs.

Tiny tadpoles

Inside each egg, a tadpole grows quickly and soon has tiny eyes and a flat tail. Glass frog tadpoles grow especially long, muscular tails, which makes them strong swimmers—essential once they hatch and drop into the fast-flowing stream below.

Weeks 0–2

Tadpole to frog

Frogs are amphibians—a group of cold-blooded, vertebrate (backboned) animals that start life in water as larvae, and then go through a series of changes (called "metamorphosis") to become air-breathing adults. Frog larvae are called tadpoles and have a tail but no legs, and once they are adult frogs, they have four legs but no tail. Each frog species makes these changes at different times.

Two legs

Each tadpole looks and behaves like a tiny fish—it breathes through gills, and its long tail flicks sideways to propel it through the water. After a few weeks in the water, two small buds emerge from the bottom of the tadpole's body, which grow into its back legs.

Weeks 4–6

Four legs

The tadpole grows two front legs and now looks like a tiny frog with a tail. It feeds on plants and algae in the water, and its gills are absorbed into its skin as its lungs begin to develop.

Weeks 8–10

Translucent skin on the underside of glass frogs is a form of camouflage.

Froglet

Once the tail shrivels away and the lungs are fully developed, the tadpole is called a froglet. It leaves the water, although its skin must remain moist as its lungs receive oxygen from water through the skin. The round toe pads of glass frogs enlarge to help them cling to branches, and emit a mucus that allows them to "stick" to leaves.

Week 16

Growing tadpoles

The nutrient-rich yolk inside each egg provides the tadpole with food until it is ready to hatch. The tadpoles continue to grow and have now developed broad bodies as well as long tails.

Week 2

Frog breeding

With more than 4,000 frog species identified in the world, it is not surprising that different frogs reproduce in different ways.

Grey foam-nest tree frog

At mating time, the female grey tree frog lets out a fluid on a tree branch above water. She works the fluid into a foam and lays her eggs inside it. Males then secrete their sperm into the foam to fertilize the eggs.

Poison dart frog

Poison dart frog females lay their eggs in moist leaf litter and stay on guard beside them. When the tadpoles hatch, the adults then carry them to the nearest body of water.

Tadpoles emerge

Once the tadpoles have reached their optimum size— which is about 1.33 in (34 mm) long for glass frog tadpoles— they are ready to leave their eggs on the leaf. Each tadpole uses its head to push its way out of the egg and drops into the water below, where it will usually burrow beneath rocks on the riverbed to avoid being eaten by predators.

Weeks 2–3

Forward-facing eyes of glass frogs enable them to see prey directly in front of them.

Adult frog

A fully mature glass frog grows to just 1 in (30 mm) long but can jump an impressive 10 ft (3 m) and live for 14 years. It prefers to hunt at night and eats insects and spiders. All frogs return to the water's edge to mate and lay eggs.

Week 20+

Risking life and limb

Dropping tails and losing legs can help some animals escape from predators. Amphibians such as the Japanese fire-bellied newt have the amazing ability to grow back the lost parts of their body. They can recreate fully functioning legs, tails, and even eye lenses.

Loss of limb

Newts are hunted by fish and birds, which may swallow them whole or perhaps eat a leg. While the newt may escape with its life, the loss of a limb makes it harder to walk, swim, climb—and feed.

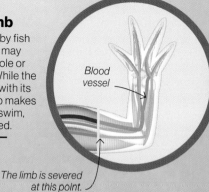

Blood vessel

The limb is severed at this point.

Start

Every limb can regenerate.

The fire-bellied newt can regrow new eye lenses.

40 days

Keeping a low profile

While a limb is regrowing, a newt will not be as active as usual because regeneration uses up a lot of energy. Until the process is complete, the newt will be more vulnerable to predators and so it may rest in a sheltered place to stay safe.

Nerves have regrown

New leg

The new leg looks like an exact copy of the original—and more importantly, it works just as well. The new muscles and bone allow the newt to move it; new nerves mean it is sensitive to touch; and new skin protects it from germs.

Blood clots

Red blood cells stick together and liquid blood turns into a solid clot in just a few minutes. A hard scab forms on top to stop blood from escaping from the newt's body. Without this, the animal will bleed to death.

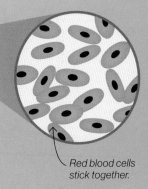

Red blood cells stick together.

Regeneration in other animals

Amphibians are not the only animals that can regrow parts of their body. Most species of lizards can grow a new tail if they lose theirs in an accident or a fight. Some species of starfish can even break themselves in half and regrow the limbs to create two new starfish.

This arm is starting to regrow.

Starfish are able to grow a new arm.

Flatworms can grow a new head.

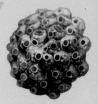

Sea squirts can grow a whole new body.

10 minutes later

Skin grows over

A new layer of skin forms over the wound, protecting the damaged tissue. At the same time, stem cells — cells with the potential to form any kind of tissue — begin to multiply.

Stem cells

1–2 days

3–12 days

The tail regrows if a predator bites it off.

Mound of stem cells

The multiplying stem cells form a mound called a blastema. The blastema will produce all the new tissues inside the regrowing limb.

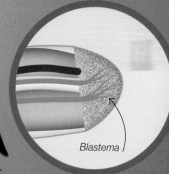
Blastema

20 days

30 days

Taking shape

The blastema produces different types of cells that will form bone, nerves, blood vessels, and muscles. These begin to arrange themselves, and after about 20 days, the shape of the regrowing limb is visible for the first time.

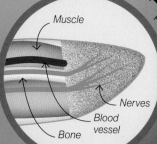
Muscle
Nerves
Blood vessel
Bone

Mini leg

A new limb has grown from the wound. Although it is tiny, it is shaped like a normal leg, and the knee and toes are clearly visible. It has working nerves and muscles, and the newt is able to move it.

Sand and surf

Leatherbacks are the world's largest turtles, growing up to 8.5 ft (2.6 m) long. These remarkable reptiles swim thousands of miles every year, between warm nesting sites and cooler waters in search of food. They mainly eat jellyfish and dive to depths of 3,280 ft (1,000 m) in search of them. Females come ashore only to lay their eggs in the warm sand of tropical beaches, and males never leave the ocean.

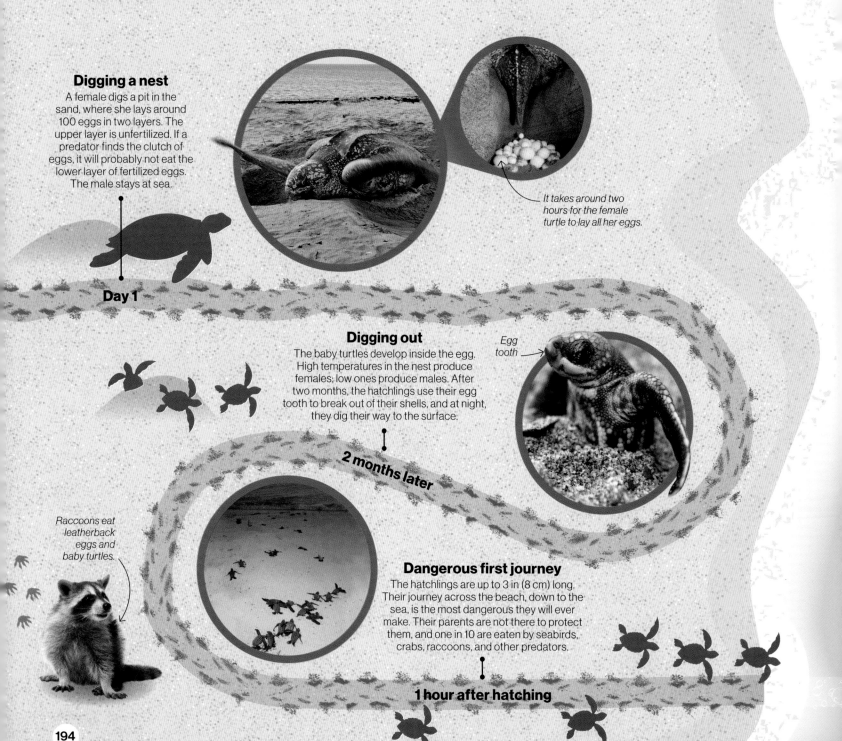

Digging a nest

A female digs a pit in the sand, where she lays around 100 eggs in two layers. The upper layer is unfertilized. If a predator finds the clutch of eggs, it will probably not eat the lower layer of fertilized eggs. The male stays at sea.

It takes around two hours for the female turtle to lay all her eggs.

Day 1

Digging out

The baby turtles develop inside the egg. High temperatures in the nest produce females; low ones produce males. After two months, the hatchlings use their egg tooth to break out of their shells, and at night, they dig their way to the surface.

Egg tooth

2 months later

Raccoons eat leatherback eggs and baby turtles.

Dangerous first journey

The hatchlings are up to 3 in (8 cm) long. Their journey across the beach, down to the sea, is the most dangerous they will ever make. Their parents are not there to protect them, and one in 10 are eaten by seabirds, crabs, raccoons, and other predators.

1 hour after hatching

Ready to mate

Leatherback turtles reach maturity between 5 and 15 years old. Once ready to mate, female leatherbacks return to shore. The males swim close to the beach and try to mate with as many females as possible. Leatherback turtles can live for up to 50 years.

Females come ashore every two or three years to lay their eggs.

Males never return to shore.

Years 5–15

Finding cool waters

When they are about 3 ft (1 m) long, the turtles migrate to cooler waters where there are more jellyfish. We know this because they are now big enough to be fitted with tracking devices.

Years 5–15

Strong swimmers

Leatherback turtles have tough, leathery skin on the surface of their shells. Seven ridges along the upper shell (carapace) provide stability in the water. Long front flippers make them powerful swimmers, and their paddle-shaped back flippers help them dive deep.

Ridged shell

Paddle-shaped back flipper

Very long front flippers

Adrift in the ocean

The young turtles' tiny flippers cannot carry them far, and they are swept along in ocean currents. They grow bigger over the next year, but many are eaten by fish. Fewer than one in 10 make it to the end of their first year.

The lost years

Scientists are still learning about what young leatherback turtles do in their first few years because they are too small to track. But we do know they face dangers: some are caught in fishing nets and others die after swallowing plastic bags.

Jellyfish are the favourite prey of leatherback turtles.

Year 1

First few years

Day in the life of a lizard

Chameleons are a type of lizard superbly adapted to life in the trees, where they spend most of their time. Their toes are fused together to form Y-shaped feet that function like gripping tongs. Their strong, curling tails act like a fifth limb, helping chameleons move and balance with ease on narrow tree branches. Chameleons are active during the day and sleep for up to 12 hours at night.

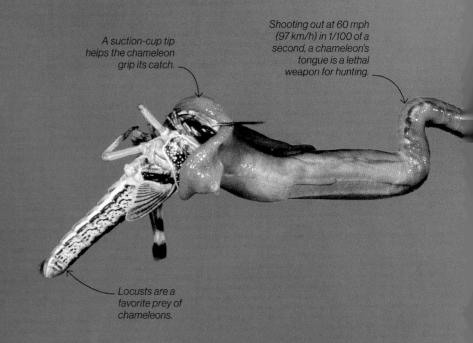

A suction-cup tip helps the chameleon grip its catch.

Shooting out at 60 mph (97 km/h) in 1/100 of a second, a chameleon's tongue is a lethal weapon for hunting.

Locusts are a favorite prey of chameleons.

Early morning

Slow to get going

A chameleon is always a slow-moving creature, but it is especially sluggish before it has a chance to warm up after the cool night. A cold-blooded animal, the chameleon starts the day by warming itself basking in the sun's rays. Luckily, the lizard is well camouflaged, helping it to avoid predators as it creeps slowly around in the treetops.

Late morning

First drink

High up in the trees, away from rivers or lakes, the chameleon finds fresh water wherever it can. It does most of its drinking in the morning, when dew has collected on the leaves overnight, or straight after a rainfall, when water droplets are still dripping from the branches above.

Midday

Looking for lunch

The chameleon's eyes can each move and focus independently of the other. This useful ability lets it use one eye to search for food and the other to keep an eye out for predators, such as birds of prey and snakes. The eyes protrude outward from the sides of the chameleon's head, giving it all-around vision. It can spot prey up to 30 ft (9 m) away.

The colorful panther chameleon from Madagascar is one of more than 200 species of chameleon.

Early afternoon

Shedding skin

An adult chameleon sheds its layer of old, dead skin about once every eight weeks. It takes about an hour to shed the skin, and the chameleon may use branches or its feet to scratch off the dead layer. This process allows the lizard's body to grow bigger.

Late afternoon

Time to fight

Males are protective of their territory. When a male wanders into another male's area, it can often lead to conflict. The two males may face each other and change into vibrant colors as a warning. If neither backs away, they might fight, and the lizard that loses will retreat to live several branches lower down in the trees.

Evening

Ready for bed

The chameleon finds a comfortable branch for the night and settles down. It generally sleeps for about 12 hours per night from sunset to sunrise. As the chameleon drifts off to sleep, its bright colors fade to avoid the attention of predators and its body temperature drops in the cool night air.

Year in the life of a grass snake

The grass snake is a reptile that lives in woodlands, wetlands, and grasslands across Europe and parts of Asia. It is rather timid and will slip away if disturbed by humans. Grass snakes are not venomous but use sneak attacks and their ability to hunt in water and on land to capture their prey. Like many reptiles, they hibernate over the cold winter months, often in warm spots that are hard to find.

Finding a mate
Spring is the time when grass snakes seek mating partners. Males go in search of females and form writhing "balls" of up to eight males and one or two females. These mating clusters sometimes continue for two hours before the snakes go their separate ways.

April–May

Grass snakes eat their prey, such as this frog, whole.

First meal
Grass snakes are strong swimmers. They can hunt a wide variety of prey, in fresh water as well as on land, including frogs, toads, and newts. In early spring, they also take advantage of small fish that are spawning and easier to catch. Some grass snakes are able to catch ducklings and even small mammals.

March–April

Shedding skin
Grass snakes continue to grow through their lives. They shed their skin when it does not fit any more. Males shed their skin twice a year, but females shed their skins only once, just before they lay their eggs.

Adults emerge
At the end of the long winter, a grass snake wakes up from its hibernation after the first few warm days of spring. It basks in the sunshine to get warm, then goes looking for its first meal of the year.

March–April

Newt

A grass snake hides until it is the right time to strike.

Hunting

Starting in late spring, newts move to ponds to mate, which makes it easier for grass snakes to hunt them. Though they do not have any venom, grass snakes use surprise and their ability to hunt on land and also in water to their advantage. They swallow their prey whole, often while it is still alive!

May–June

Laying eggs

About two months after mating, pregnant females lay their eggs in piles of warm, rotting vegetation. Young females may lay between seven and 15 eggs, while some of the oldest— those at least 10 years old— can lay up to 40.

After hatching, a young grass snake can immediately look after itself.

June–July

Hatching eggs

The eggs hatch about 10 days after they are laid. The little snakes that emerge are about 5.9 in (15 cm) long. They are miniature versions of their parents, even down to their coloring.

June–July

Preparing for winter

Fall is a good time for grass snakes to hunt as there are many young animals who are not wise to their predators' tactics. But juvenile snakes may themselves fall victim to larger predators, including domestic cats, herons, and badgers. If threatened, a grass snake may trick a predator by curling up and playing dead.

The snake pretends to be dead by lying motionless with its mouth open.

September–October

Hibernation

As winter approaches each grass snake must find a good spot to hibernate in over the winter. It must find a relatively warm, moist and frost-free spot to burrow into, such as an old rabbit's compost heap or root system. Most young snakes die in their first winter because they are not warm enough.

October–March

Egg-eating snake

Snakes do not have arms and cannot chew, so when it comes to eating, they need to find ways to work around these limitations. Some species of snakes have developed ways to feed either mostly or only on eggs. These egg-eaters have jaws that can open and separate to allow them to surround their food, and their bodies are able to stretch to two and a half times their normal diameter to swallow it. Once fed, the snake may have to fast for a long period until the next bird nesting season.

Egg-eating snakes have no teeth, as teeth would get in the way of the egg.

These snakes can eat eggs as big as a chicken's egg.

2

Special bones in the lower jaw separate sideways to help the mouth open wider.

3

Flexible skin between the snake's scales stretches.

4

Once swallowed, powerful muscles push the egg down into the snake's throat.

5

Special downward-pointing spines in the snake's backbone crack the egg.

6

The egg's nourishing contents are squeezed down into the snake's stomach.

7

The snake cannot digest the egg shell, so it is regurgitated as a crushed pellet from its throat.

Full nest

A couple of months after mating, the female lays her eggs in the nest and covers them in sand. The female will lay between 25–80 hard-shelled white eggs, which will incubate for around 80–90 days. Several females will often nest close to each other to help protect the young.

Mating

Mating takes place during the dry season, when the risk of nest flooding is low. Males fight each other and try to attract a female with noisy displays to show their size and strength—bellowing, blowing water out of their noses, and slapping their snouts on the water. Once they have mated, the female digs a nest on the riverbank. Males mate with several different females.

Protective watch

After laying her eggs, the female enters a trancelike state and watches over her nest. She eats rarely, or not at all, during this time. A male will often be nearby, keeping an eye out for hungry monitor lizards and other predators eager to feed on the eggs.

Crocodile eggs are only slightly bigger than a chicken's egg.

Day 1

2 months after mating

2–5 months after mating

Life on the river

Nile crocodiles live in freshwater habitats in Africa, and they may live for as long as 100 years. They feast mainly on fish, occasionally snapping up any larger animals that come their way, including zebra, baby hippos, and even porcupines. Despite their fearsome reputation, female crocodiles are attentive parents—they fiercely guard their eggs and protect their hatchlings from predators.

Early years
The mother leads the hatchlings to the river, sometimes carrying them gently in her powerful jaws. She will keep her young close for two years, protecting them from predators and carrying them on her back.

Growing up
After two years, the young crocodiles leave their mother's protection. Some form hunting groups with other juveniles of a similar size. They eat insects and small fish and grow about 12 in (30 cm) a year.

Adulthood
Crocodiles are fully grown once they have reached around 8.2 ft (2.5 m). This usually takes 10–15 years. They spend most of their time resting, only hunting when hungry. Females will breed every 2–3 years. Crocodiles can live for up to 70 years.

Time to hatch
When they are ready to hatch, the tiny crocodiles start squeaking from inside the eggs. The mother responds by digging away the sand, and each hatchling uses its egg tooth to break out of its egg. The new crocodiles are 12 in (30 cm) long.

5 months after mating

Years 0–2

Years 2–10

Years 10–15

Hunting strategy
Crocodiles are ambush predators. They wait patiently, hidden in the water, and if a wildebeest or zebra comes close enough, the crocodile launches out of the water and drags it under to drown it. Saltwater crocodiles, found in Australia and Southeast Asia, have the strongest bite in the animal kingdom.

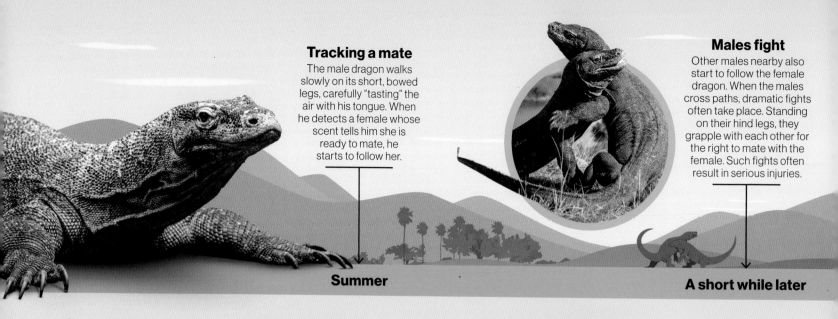

Tracking a mate

The male dragon walks slowly on its short, bowed legs, carefully "tasting" the air with his tongue. When he detects a female whose scent tells him she is ready to mate, he starts to follow her.

Summer

Males fight

Other males nearby also start to follow the female dragon. When the males cross paths, dramatic fights often take place. Standing on their hind legs, they grapple with each other for the right to mate with the female. Such fights often result in serious injuries.

A short while later

A dragon's life

With its long forked tongue, sawlike teeth, muscular tail, and razor-sharp claws, the Komodo dragon is a fearsome-looking reptile. At nearly 10 ft (3 m) long and weighing as much as 330 lb (150 kg), it is the world's largest living lizard. It feeds on both the rotting flesh of dead animals and live prey and will attack animals as large as buffalo.

Leaving the burrow

The baby dragon digs its way to the surface. There, it has to fend for itself because the mother provides no more parental care after hatching. Many young dragons die in their first few weeks in the outside world.

A few hours after hatching

Year 1

Dangerous time

Young Komodo dragons are small enough to be eaten by other predators—including larger Komodo dragons, civet cats, snakes, and wild boar. For safety, they live in trees, and siblings may stick together in small groups.

Young dragons hide up in tree branches for the first months of their lives.

Sneaky dining

By their second year, dragons are big enough to move down from the trees and live on the ground. They hunt and eat small lizards, snakes, birds, and insects, and sometimes even creep up to snatch bites of the kills made by adult dragons.

Year 2

Mating time

After fighting off any competition, the male shows the female he wants to mate by rubbing his chin on her, scratching her back, and licking her. If he is too rough, she bites and slaps him with her tail.

August

New-laid eggs

The female lays up to 30 eggs and buries them in either the abandoned burrow of another animal or a burrow the dragon has dug herself. She is protective of her eggs, guarding the burrow from thieves such as wild dogs or other Komodo dragons.

September

Female Komodo dragons may create decoy burrows to confuse egg thieves.

Fearsome hunters

Komodo dragons sniff out prey by flicking out their tongues, which can smell as well as taste. They grab their victims with their powerful jaws, thrashing them about. Komodo dragons have venom in their saliva, which weakens and ultimately kills larger prey once bitten. Small victims are swallowed whole, usually headfirst.

Breaking free

When it is time to hatch, a young dragon uses its egg tooth to break out of the egg. This is hard work for the tiny animal—now just 2 in (5 cm) long—and it rests in its eggshell before finding its way out of the burrow.

April

Komodo dragons have fairly poor vision and hearing but a powerful sense of smell.

Reaching maturity

By the time they reach eight years old, Komodo dragons can be 10 ft (3 m) long—big enough not to have to worry about predators any more. They are now able to mate and may go on to live up to 30 years old.

Year 8+

Building a bower

The male flame bowerbird found in the rainforests of New Guinea has vibrant feathers to attract a female, but that is not his only distinctive feature. He builds an elaborate arena, known as a bower, out of twigs and leaves, and dances for a potential mate. If the female bowerbird is unimpressed, she will look for another mate, so the male must work hard to meet her standards.

Plastic pollution

Satin bowerbirds are found in Eastern Australia. Males used to decorate their bowers with blue flowers, berries, feathers, and snail shells. However, with so much plastic litter discarded in their habitat, they now choose bright blue plastic bottle tops, spoons, and drinking straws, which litter the ground around their bowers for years.

First twigs

The male bowerbird begins construction on the forest floor. He pokes long twigs into the ground firmly to create the structure for the curved walls of the bower.

Day 1

Building the structure

He reinforces the walls by filling the gaps with short twigs. The walls are far enough apart for the female to peer through. He then builds a platform for her to stand on when he performs.

Day 3

Finishing touches

To decorate his bower, the male collects colorful objects from the forest, such as empty snail shells, seeds, and berries. He places them carefully around the bower.

Day 4

The female flame bowerbird has olive-green and pale yellow feathers.

Purple petals add a burst of color to the bower.

Day 7

Nesting

The female builds a nest without the male's help. She lays just one egg, which hatches after 19–24 days. Once the chick has hatched, the female cares for it by herself. The male goes back to attracting potential mates at his bower.

Day 6

Show time!

The female has chosen the bower and takes her place on the platform and waits. The male performs. He sings and dances, wiggling his bright yellow wings to impress her. If she likes his performance, she will mate with him. If she is not attracted to him, she will fly away.

Day 5

Female inspection

Now that the bower is ready, the female bowerbird visits the bower while the male is away. She walks in from the back and inspects the male's side of the platform. She will also visit the bowers of other birds to see how they compare.

Empty snail shells are often used for decorating a bower.

A female cuckoo resembles a sparrowhawk, a bird of prey, so she frightens reed warblers away from their nests.

A few weeks before

Nest search

After mating in spring, the female cuckoo searches for a host nest in which to lay her egg. She visits several nests before picking her favorite. The chosen nest belongs to a reed warbler, a common victim of the cuckoo's sneaky parenting strategy.

Sneaky egg switch

In a fleeting visit, the female cuckoo pushes out one of the eggs from the reed warbler's nest, replacing it with her own. Some birds do notice the cuckoo's unusual egg and abandon their nest, but in most cases, they begin to care for it.

Killer instinct

The cuckoo egg is more developed than the reed warbler's eggs, so it hatches first. The naked and blind cuckoo chick instinctively wriggles its body underneath each of the other eggs and, using its back, pushes them out of the nest one by one.

Around 12 days before hatching

A cuckoo's egg is larger than the host's eggs but is a similar color.

Day 1

The chick removes the other eggs; as a result, it now has no competition for food.

The male has gray feathers, while the female can have gray or brown feathers.

The males uses his two-note cuckoo call to attract a female.

Nest intruder

The common cuckoo is a brood parasite, a type of animal that depends on other animals to raise its offspring. Rather than building its own nest, the cuckoo hunts for one belonging to an unsuspecting host bird and deposits its own egg. During the summer, the female can lay up to 25 eggs, each in different bird nests!

The reed warbler brings back food for the cuckoo chick.

Independence

In fall, the fully grown cuckoo heads south to spend the winter in Africa. When fully mature in two years' time, it will return to where it hatched to breed and another reed warbler will be tricked into raising the next cuckoo chick.

Time to fledge

Three weeks after hatching, the cuckoo chick fledges (leaves the nest) for the first time. The reed warbler still provides it with food, at the nest, for the next two weeks. Once the young cuckoo learns to fly, it leaves the nest permanently and hunts by itself for a few months.

A big chick

The cuckoo is now the only chick in the nest and grows fast. It begs for food, making a noise that sounds like a nest full of chicks. The reed warbler brings the cuckoo chick food as if it were its own.

The cuckoo is so large that it struggles to fit in the nest.

Day 14

Day 21

A few months later

Sneaky stick insects

Cuckoos are not the only animals to trick other species into raising their young. Australian walking stick insects lay eggs that look like seeds with tasty tips. Ants take the eggs to their nest and eat the tips but leave the rest. When the walking stick insect hatches, it resembles an ant. It exits the nest, leaving the ants unaware that there was an intruder in their midst.

Day in the life of a spoonbill

Covered in pink and white feathers, the roseate spoonbill is one of the most striking birds found along the coast of Texas and Florida and in wetlands throughout Central and South America. Its flat, spoon-shaped bill (beak) allows it to find food in the murky water without needing to see, so it can feed during daylight and in darkness too.

Early morning

Late morning

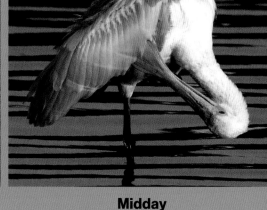

Midday

Early start
At first light, groups of spoonbills wade slowly, swinging their bills from side to side under the water's surface to feel for crustaceans, aquatic insects, and small fish. Spoonbills share their habitat with other birds, such as egrets.

Leisurely breakfast
Spoonbills spend most of the day eating in coastal areas, mangroves, lagoons, or mudflats. As they feed, they keep in touch with each other by uttering quiet grunts. If one bird notices a predator, it raises the alarm to warn the others.

Freshening up
Taking a break from feeding, spoonbills preen (tidy) their feathers to keep them in good condition. They use their bill to remove parasites, clean their feathers, and arrange stray ones back into the right place.

The pink color of the roseate spoonbill's feathers comes from the pink pigments found in crustaceans, their main source of food.

Early afternoon

Pairing up

In the breeding season, spoonbills pair up. The male collects twigs, and the female uses them to build a nest in a tree overhanging the water. In the nest, the female will lay up to five eggs. After about 24 days, the eggs will hatch.

Late afternoon

Day sleeper

Spoonbills usually sleep standing in water or sometimes in a tree. By standing on one leg with their bill tucked under the feathers on their back, they reduce heat loss through unfeathered body parts, such as the head.

Evening

Late meal

Spoonbills do not need to feed in daylight because they find their food by touch rather than sight. So in the fading light of the evening—when fewer predators are hunting—they go out looking for food again.

Cold and quiet

There is a hush on the grassland and all is still. A thick blanket of snow covers the ground. Temperatures regularly drop to −40°F (−40°C). Huge bison, with thick woolly coats, push the snow with their massive heads to reach grasses below.

January

Finding a nest

With few trees on the prairies, burrowing owls instead search for dens abandoned by other animals, to nest in. They take full advantage of the open, treeless plains to hunt for mice, voles, lizards, and large insects.

February

Year on a prairie

The prairies are enormous areas of grassland found in the Americas. They are fairly flat, with few trees, and moderate rainfall. The prairies do, however, have distinct seasons. Snowy winters give way to carpets of spring flowers. Hot summers, alive with animals, turn to cool fall breezes.

Grasshopper attack!

The prairies are hot. The summer weather attracts thousands of grasshoppers to the prairies, where they munch through grasses and other plants. Birds such as Swainson's hawk take advantage and feast on the insects.

July

Flying seeds

The prairie plants have produced seeds. The fall breeze carries them across the vast open plains. Milkweed pods break open, releasing hundreds of seeds that are carried on the wind by their silky threads.

August–September

The rut

Shorter days and cooler temperatures mark the start of the breeding season, known as the rut, for tule elk. Males honk loudly to attract females and fight each other, by headbutting, to decide which stag is dominant.

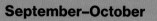

September–October

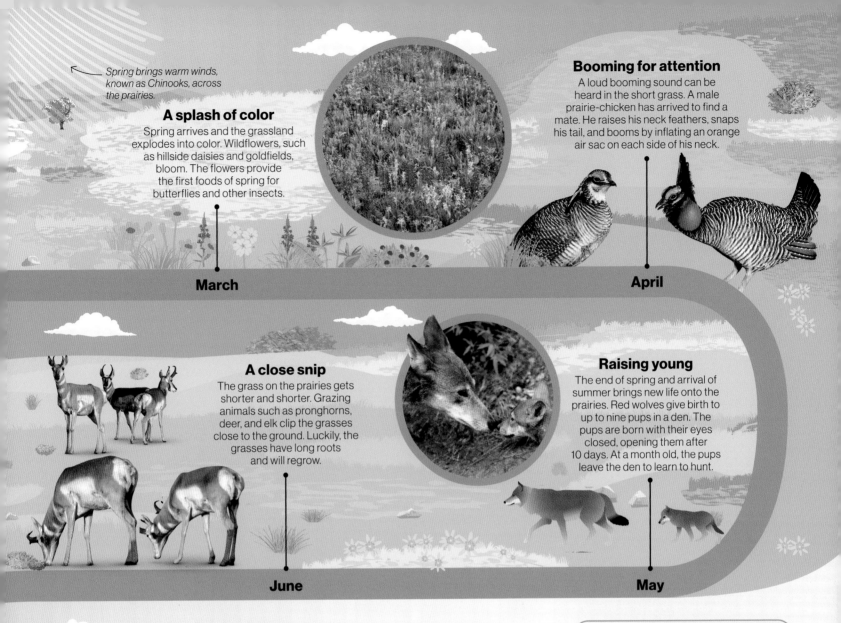

Spring brings warm winds, known as Chinooks, across the prairies.

A splash of color

Spring arrives and the grassland explodes into color. Wildflowers, such as hillside daisies and goldfields, bloom. The flowers provide the first foods of spring for butterflies and other insects.

Booming for attention

A loud booming sound can be heard in the short grass. A male prairie-chicken has arrived to find a mate. He raises his neck feathers, snaps his tail, and booms by inflating an orange air sac on each side of his neck.

March

April

A close snip

The grass on the prairies gets shorter and shorter. Grazing animals such as pronghorns, deer, and elk clip the grasses close to the ground. Luckily, the grasses have long roots and will regrow.

Raising young

The end of spring and arrival of summer brings new life onto the prairies. Red wolves give birth to up to nine pups in a den. The pups are born with their eyes closed, opening them after 10 days. At a month old, the pups leave the den to learn to hunt.

June

May

Turning brown

The days and nights are cool and many animals, such as Swainson's hawk, have migrated south to find warmer weather. The grasses have all dried up and the landscape is brown.

Snow tunnels

The snow arrives and the prairies are quiet once again. Some animals hibernate, but the prairie vole stays active throughout the winter. It burrows tunnels through the snow to move about and find food.

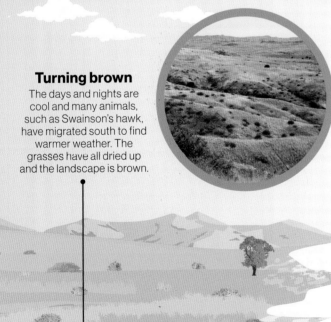

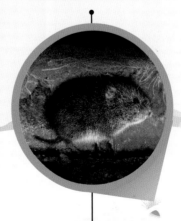

A carpet of color

The Carizzo Plain, which lies 100 miles (160 km) northwest of Los Angeles, is the largest native grassland in California. Each spring, this huge grassland becomes a patchwork of bright colors as the meadow flowers cover the rolling hills with oranges, yellows, greens, and purples.

November

December

Inside an egg

The nourishing yolk shrinks as the growing embryo feeds from it. The white helps to protect the embryo. The allantois allows the embryo to breathe and gets rid of its waste.

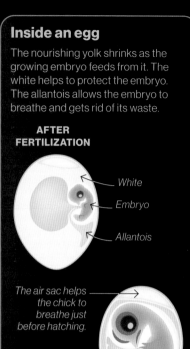

AFTER FERTILIZATION

White
Embryo
Allantois

The air sac helps the chick to breathe just before hatching.

JUST BEFORE HATCHING

From egg to adult

Unlike most mammals, which grow inside their mother's body, birds develop inside eggs. And, though an egg may seem small and fragile, it contains everything a baby bird needs for a healthy start to its life. Inside the egg, the embryo (unhatched bird) starts as a single cell that divides many times to form the different parts of the chick. After hatching, some birds—such as ducks and gulls—can leave the nest fairly soon. Others, such as the barn owl, need some extra time to develop.

Feeding

Barn owl chicks cannot hunt for their own food, so they must rely on their parents to bring them food. The male parent hunts small mammals, which are ripped apart by the female parent and fed to the chicks.

Barn owl eggs hatch after about 32 days of incubation.

Day 1

Day 1

Days 3–5

Day 7

Hatching

After fertilization, the egg is incubated (warmed) by a parent. When it is ready to hatch, the chick wriggles to weaken the eggshell and then strikes at it with its egg tooth—a sharp projection on its beak. It creates a hole and then widens it to get out.

Out of the egg

The tiny chick is helpless, hardly able to stand, and begs for food when it hears a parent close by. Barn owl eggs hatch several days apart, so the oldest chick in the nest can be four times heavier than the youngest.

Eyes closed

Barn owl chicks do not open their eyes for several days. They primarily use sound to communicate with each other and their parents. Each chick makes a soft chittering sound, especially when cold, or when they are seeking attention.

Soft down

After about a week, the chick opens its eyes. It now has a coat of soft feathers called down that protects the chick. Despite this, it is still unable to keep itself warm, so it relies on its mother to make sure it does not get cold.

Learning to fly

For young barn owls, as with many birds, the first flight may end in an uncomfortable heap. However, they are quick to learn basic flight control and can soon land without causing themselves injury.

A barn owl's eyesight is about twice as sharp as that of humans, and they are better able to see movement at night.

As the young owl tests its wings, it sends little bits of fluff and feathers in all directions.

The barn owl can twist and rotate its head more than 270° to focus on a sound.

Week 3

Week 8

Week 10

Week 12

On the move

By this time, the chick has developed a thicker covering of down, which enables it to keep itself warm. This frees the mother up to help with hunting. The chicks squabble over food and move around more than before.

Ready to fly

Before flying from the nest, the chick must have a full set of feathers. It becomes active and restless while it waits, exercising its wings and looking outside, absorbing what it can about the world outside before it starts learning to fly.

Sharp hearing

After much practice, the chick is now a steady flier. It focuses on learning to hunt, using its senses and its instinct to guide it. Its sense of hearing improves and will be crucial for when it must do all its hunting alone.

Hunting alone

By now, the chick is an expert hunter. Its parents gradually give it less food. After 12 weeks, the chick leaves its parents' nest to find its own area to nest and hunt on its own—it is now an adult owl. It can breed in its first year, and eggs are laid in the spring.

Wandering albatrosses fly vast distances without using much energy, by soaring on strong winds.

Egg laying

Once every two years—in December or January—the female lays a single egg, which is white with small dark spots. At least 4 in (10 cm) long, it is more than twice the size of a large chicken's egg.

Incubation

The egg must be kept warm, at 91°F (33°C), in cold and windy conditions. Both parents take turns to sit on the egg for 2–3 weeks each, while the other flies out to sea to feed. They incubate the egg for up to 83 days.

January

Courtship

The colony is busy with noisy calls, much energetic wing-stretching, and bill clattering. Young birds, eager to find themselves a suitable mate, compete against other birds for female attention, space, and materials to build their nests.

February

Joining the colony

With their long wings and short legs, wandering albatrosses are heavy and clumsy and find it difficult to move about on the ground. They have to nest on land but need a long open space where they can run into the wind to take off and fly again.

December

November

Both parents have a patch of hot, bare skin they uncover to keep the egg warm.

An albatross snatches fish with its hooked bill while swimming, or lunges 3–6.5 ft (1–2 m) into the water to grab them.

These huge birds are 43–53 in (110–135 cm) long with a whopping wingspan of 8–11.5 ft (2.5–3.5 m).

Hatching

The chick may take four days to break free of its shell. Covered in thick, white down, it looks like a little woolly penguin with beady eyes and a small beak. The chick depends on its parents for warmth, protection, and food.

March–April

Feeding the chick

For the first 30 days, parents feed their chick every 2–4 days. Later, each parent takes turns flying farther out to sea, traveling vast distances before returning with a massive meal for the chick.

April–October

Flying at last

After growing for about 10 months, the young albatross can fly. It learns from older birds where to look for food and how to catch it. After leaving the nest, it may not touch land for years, but will sometimes float on the ocean if the wind is weak. It becomes an adult at around 11 years old.

10 months later

Freedom at sea

The wandering albatross has the widest wingspan of any bird. These wings allow them to spend long periods at sea, where they can spend up to 20 days at a time covering up to 9,300 miles (15,000 km), looking for fish, squid, and crustaceans to eat. They are not always on their own, though—in the breeding season, they live in colonies near the Antarctic Circle.

Partners for life

Once in a pair, wandering albatrosses stay together for life. They return every year to the same spot to nest. Climate change has meant stronger winds around the Antarctic Circle, so the smaller females now fly faster, but for shorter distances. As a result, they stay closer to the nest for longer when incubating, so the survival rate of chicks may improve.

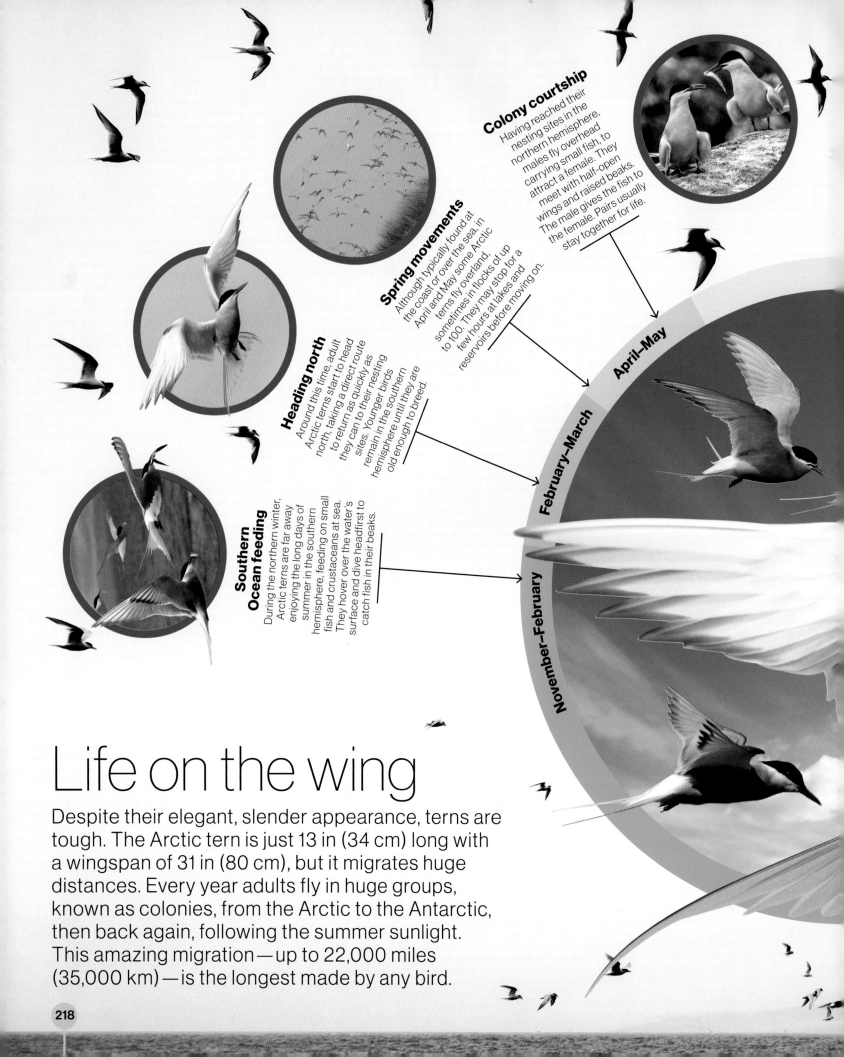

Colony courtship
Having reached their nesting sites in the northern hemisphere, males fly overhead carrying small fish, to attract a female. They meet with half-open wings and raised beaks. The male gives the fish to the female. Pairs usually stay together for life.

Spring movements
Although typically found at the coast or over the sea, in April and May some Arctic terns fly overland, sometimes in flocks of up to 100. They may stop for a few hours at lakes and reservoirs before moving on.

Heading north
Around this time, adult Arctic terns start to head north, taking a direct route to return as quickly as they can to their nesting sites. Younger birds remain in the southern hemisphere until they are old enough to breed.

Southern Ocean feeding
During the northern winter, Arctic terns are far away enjoying the long days of summer in the southern hemisphere, feeding on small fish and crustaceans at sea. They hover over the water's surface and dive headfirst to catch fish in their beaks.

April–May

February–March

November–February

Life on the wing

Despite their elegant, slender appearance, terns are tough. The Arctic tern is just 13 in (34 cm) long with a wingspan of 31 in (80 cm), but it migrates huge distances. Every year adults fly in huge groups, known as colonies, from the Arctic to the Antarctic, then back again, following the summer sunlight. This amazing migration—up to 22,000 miles (35,000 km)—is the longest made by any bird.

Warming the eggs
Arctic terns lay between one and three eggs. The parents warm them by sitting on them before they hatch. The nests are simple hollows in sand or rocks. The eggs hatch about 21–23 days after they are laid.

May–June

Tiny chicks
Each chick breaks free from its egg using an egg tooth—a sharp protrusion on its bill that falls off soon after the chick hatches. The tiny terns stay close to the nest for four weeks, eating fish brought by their parents. They can fly from 25 days old.

June–July

Returning south
Flocks drift slowly from north to south in autumn, without the urgency to breed that hurries them on in spring. Birds flying from North America may reach South Africa in about four months.

August–October

Arctic terns glide for much of their time during migration.

The ideal nesting site
The nesting sites of Arctic terns can be found on bare, open coasts all around the northern hemisphere, as far south as Britain and Nova Scotia, Canada. Colonies vary in size: some may consist of just a few pairs, while others might have more than 1,000. Colonies are normally very noisy, but just before leaving to migrate north or south, the birds fall silent for a short period—this behavior is known as the "dread."

March–April

Long journey

Adult emperor penguins return to their breeding ground, after having swum hundreds of miles out to sea. It is a long trek—up to 125 miles (200 km) over ice and snow to get there. They walk very slowly at less than 1 mph (1.6 km/h), sometimes speeding up by "tobogganing" downhill on their flat bellies.

March–June

Arrival

The male emperor penguins reach the breeding ground first, as the long winter begins. They make no nests but return to the same place each year. When their female mates arrive, the pairs greet each other by bowing, raising their bills, and waving their wings.

May–June

Egg laying

Each female emperor penguin lays one egg, which is quickly passed to the male. He keeps it safe and warm on his feet, tucked under a roll of fat, known as a brood pouch.

Emperor penguin eggs are about 4.7 in (12 cm) long and 3 in (8 cm) wide.

Penguin sizes

There are about 20 living species of penguins. The largest is the emperor and the smallest is the little penguin. Large species tend to live in very cold regions, especially Antarctica, while smaller species make their homes in warmer regions.

Emperor penguin	Macaroni penguin	Little penguin
44 in (112 cm)	28 in (71 cm)	12 in (30 cm)

May–June

Female leaves

After laying the egg, the female returns to the sea. She needs to feed on krill (shrimps) and fish, often diving down to 165 ft (50 m) or more below the surface to find them.

May–August

Warming the egg

The males shuffle about with the egg on their feet and squeeze together for warmth in the severe winter conditions. Temperatures can plummet to as low as −76°F (−60°C), but each male incubates the egg (keeps it warm) at a steady 100°F (38°C).

July–August

Hatching

About 62 to 66 days after laying, the chick inside the egg hatches. Almost naked, it soon grows a thick layer of down (fluffy feathers). The male feeds the chick with a kind of cheesy "milk" from his throat, but the baby emperor will get its first decent meal only when its mother returns.

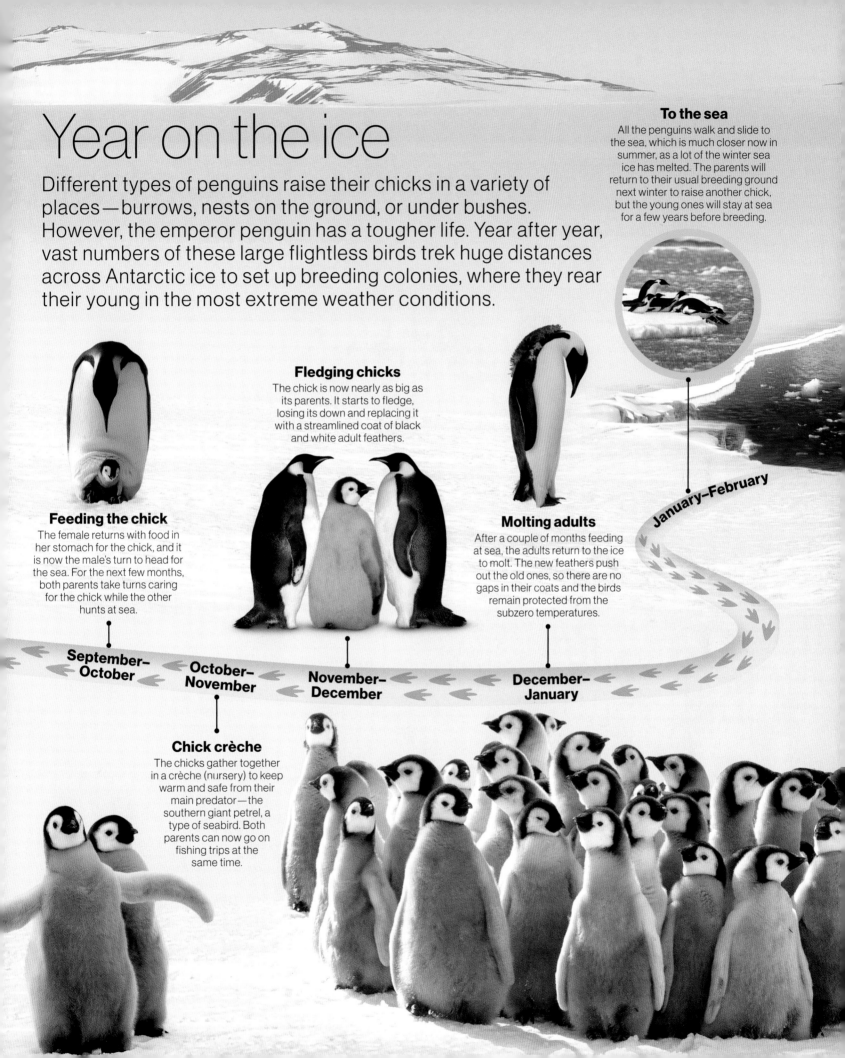

Year on the ice

Different types of penguins raise their chicks in a variety of places—burrows, nests on the ground, or under bushes. However, the emperor penguin has a tougher life. Year after year, vast numbers of these large flightless birds trek huge distances across Antarctic ice to set up breeding colonies, where they rear their young in the most extreme weather conditions.

To the sea

All the penguins walk and slide to the sea, which is much closer now in summer, as a lot of the winter sea ice has melted. The parents will return to their usual breeding ground next winter to raise another chick, but the young ones will stay at sea for a few years before breeding.

Fledging chicks

The chick is now nearly as big as its parents. It starts to fledge, losing its down and replacing it with a streamlined coat of black and white adult feathers.

Feeding the chick

The female returns with food in her stomach for the chick, and it is now the male's turn to head for the sea. For the next few months, both parents take turns caring for the chick while the other hunts at sea.

Molting adults

After a couple of months feeding at sea, the adults return to the ice to molt. The new feathers push out the old ones, so there are no gaps in their coats and the birds remain protected from the subzero temperatures.

January–February

September–October

October–November

November–December

December–January

Chick crèche

The chicks gather together in a crèche (nursery) to keep warm and safe from their main predator—the southern giant petrel, a type of seabird. Both parents can now go on fishing trips at the same time.

Hardworking wings

Hummingbirds' wings can beat up to 200 times every second, so fast that they produce the humming sound that gives the bird its name. Ball-and-socket shoulder joints allow them to swing their wings in ways other birds cannot, even allowing them to fly backward. They take up to 250 breaths a minute and drink energy-rich nectar from up to 2,000 flowers a day to power their superfast wings.

To fly slowly, the wings beat at a medium pace.

The bird straightens its wings and beats harder to fly faster.

The wings beat around the head to fly backwards.

The wings point downward and whip into a figure 8 shape.

FORWARD SLOW   **FORWARD FAST**   **HOVERING**   **BACKWARD**

Dry season

The Pantanal, during the short dry season, is an expanse of grassland spotted with small trees and bushes. Pink blossoms of the trumpet tree give flashes of color. Little rain falls, and the days are warm. Nights are cooler, which often brings fog. The ground is mostly dry.

Time to nest

A pair of bright blue hyacinth macaws have found a tree with an ideal hole to nest in. At 3.3 ft (1 m) long from tail tip to head, the hyacinth macaw is the world's largest flying parrot.

▶ Dry season (Mid-May–Mid-August)

Year in the wetlands

Wetlands are water-soaked areas where the land is flooded a lot of the time. The world's largest tropical wetland, known as the Pantanal, is in South America. It covers a huge area of flat grassland spanning parts of Brazil, Paraguay, and Bolivia. The Pantanal is home to many extraordinary plants and animals, including the world's largest rodent and more than 600 species of birds.

Wet season

It is hot and humid on the Pantanal, and huge thunderstorms cause sudden intense downpours of rain. Rivers burst their banks and flood the land, creating shallow lakes and swamps. The wet season has arrived.

Wet season (Mid-November–Late March) ◀

Time of plenty

Standing as tall as a 12-year-old child, the jabiru stork uses its long legs to wade through the waters of the wetlands. It uses its long beak to catch fish, frogs, snakes, and insects.

Time to move

Although a superb swimmer, the capybara (a giant rodent the size of a pig) moves to higher ground when the water levels rise. This animal spends its days grazing on aquatic plants.

Searching for food

The giant anteater roams the grassland in search of ants and termites. Sharp front claws can rip through a termite mound. Its giant tongue, as long as your arm, reaches inside to lap up the insects.

Reliant on the river

The stealthy jaguar stays close to a river during the dry season. It is usually searching for one of its favorite prey, the caiman. With the river's water levels low, a caiman has fewer places to hide from the jaguar's jaws.

A stealthy giant

The massive green anaconda (which is three times the length of an adult human) is more at home in the river than on land. It glides silently through newly formed pools of water, searching for prey, which it squeezes to death before swallowing whole.

Wetland fires

It's hard to imagine the rainy wetlands being affected by fire, yet small fires happen regularly. In recent years, however, fires in the Pantanal have been bigger than ever before. An area the size of 2.3 million football fields was scorched in 2020. Cutting down trees for farmland and climate change are the reasons for the giant fires.

Rainy season

Temperatures are rising, sometimes reaching a sweltering 104°F (40°C), and the rains pour throughout the season. The rivers fill and lakes appear across the grassland.

Rainy season (Mid-August–Mid-November)

Hunting for dry food

After leaving to escape the swampy waters of the wet season, a herd of white-lipped peccaries have now returned to the dry lowlands. These piglike animals snuffle around the fresh grass searching for fruit, nuts, fungi, and insects.

Wading through water

The marsh deer wades through shallow water, grazing on plants. Its widely splayed hooves are also partially webbed, which help this large deer to walk and swim through water.

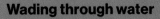

Intermediate season

The temperature drops and the rains start to ease off. The water on the land slowly flows back to the rivers and the land once again becomes grassland scattered with ponds. Mammals that had traveled to higher ground return to the lowlands.

Intermediate season (April–Mid-May)

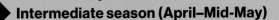

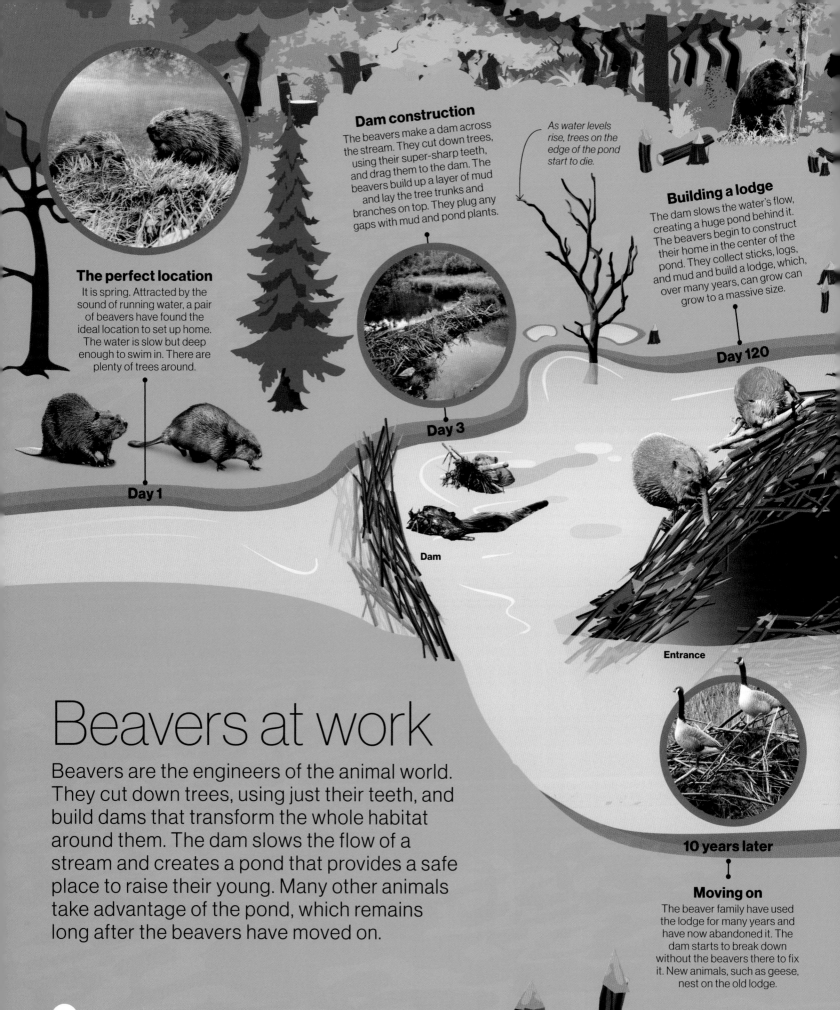

Dam construction
The beavers make a dam across the stream. They cut down trees, using their super-sharp teeth, and drag them to the dam. The beavers build up a layer of mud and lay the tree trunks and branches on top. They plug any gaps with mud and pond plants.

As water levels rise, trees on the edge of the pond start to die.

Building a lodge
The dam slows the water's flow, creating a huge pond behind it. The beavers begin to construct their home in the center of the pond. They collect sticks, logs, and mud and build a lodge, which, over many years, can grow can grow to a massive size.

Day 120

The perfect location
It is spring. Attracted by the sound of running water, a pair of beavers have found the ideal location to set up home. The water is slow but deep enough to swim in. There are plenty of trees around.

Day 1

Day 3

Dam

Entrance

Beavers at work

Beavers are the engineers of the animal world. They cut down trees, using just their teeth, and build dams that transform the whole habitat around them. The dam slows the flow of a stream and creates a pond that provides a safe place to raise their young. Many other animals take advantage of the pond, which remains long after the beavers have moved on.

10 years later

Moving on
The beaver family have used the lodge for many years and have now abandoned it. The dam starts to break down without the beavers there to fix it. New animals, such as geese, nest on the old lodge.

A finished home

The lodge is ready. Inside is a cozy chamber, which the beavers line with dry leaves. The chamber is built above water level so it never floods. The only entrance is underwater, making it extremely hard for predators to enter.

Day 140

Storing food

As the days get shorter and the cool weather sets in, the beavers start to collect their favorite plant food. They store it in an area of the pond not far from the lodge. This will be their winter food store.

Day 150

A long, cold winter

The beavers are ready for winter. They do not hibernate, but they do cuddle up inside their cozy, warm lodge during the cold months. Their thick fur keeps them warm, and they eat the food in their food store, which now lies beneath the ice.

Day 240

What is a keystone species?

A keystone species is a type of animal that makes a big impact on their habitat and environment. Beavers are a keystone species. With their dams and lodges, they create wetland habitats that would not otherwise exist. New plants grow and other animals make beaver ponds their homes as well.

Plants such as cattails grow at the edge of the pond.

Food store

The lodge contains three distinct chambers — a nursery for the young, sleeping quarters, and a feeding chamber.

Kingfisher

Day 365

Beaver babies

Spring has arrived and the weather is warm. The female beavers give birth to three or four babies, known as kits. After just three days, they start to sharpen their teeth on sticks their parents bring to them. They are getting ready to gnaw trees. The kits can swim within days of being born.

7 years later

Northwestern salamander

New habitat

The beaver pond and its side channels have attracted many new animals. Fish, frogs, and salamanders have set up home. New plants growing around the pond bring in more visitors, including songbirds, ducks, kingfishers, moose, and deer.

Electroreception

The platypus's extra-sensitive, velvety bill helps it find food in muddy water. The bill is able to sense the movement of other animals by picking up tiny pulses of electricity coming from their bodies. As the platypus sweeps its head from side to side on the dark riverbed, it detects these electrical signals and uses them to figure out the direction and distance of small prey, such as crayfish, worms, and insects.

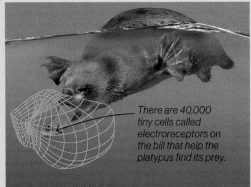

There are 40,000 tiny cells called electroreceptors on the bill that help the platypus find its prey.

Paddling platypus

The platypus looks like it is made from parts of different animals—when 18th-century British scientists first saw a specimen sent from Australia, they thought it was a hoax. They could not believe that a furry animal could have a ducklike bill, webbed feet, and a paddle-shaped tail. Unlike most mammals, platypuses lay eggs instead of giving birth to live young.

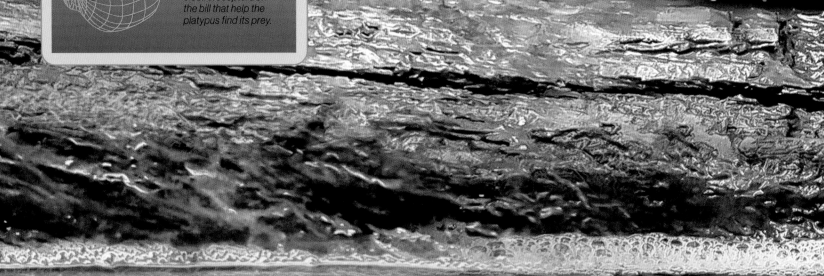

Late winter

Mating

Although platypuses live alone, the males search for females to mate with at this time. Unusually for mammals, they have a poisonous spike on their heels, which they may use to jab competing males.

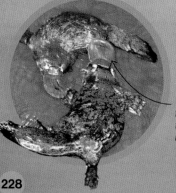

Before mating, the male holds the female's tail in its bill.

Early spring

Making a nursery

After mating, the female digs a large nursery burrow using the long claws on her front paws. She then carries in bedding of twigs and leaves using her tail and back legs.

Platypuses build deep burrows in muddy riverbanks.

2–4 weeks later

Laying eggs

The mother lays two or three small grape-size eggs, each coated in a leathery shell. She keeps the eggs warm by pressing them to her belly with her tail until they hatch, after around 10 days.

The platypus has hard pads in its bill instead of teeth to help grind and crush food.

Its thick, waterproof fur traps air, keeping the platypus warm and helping it to stay afloat.

10 days later

↑

Eggs hatch
Upon hatching, the blind, hairless newborns, known as puggles, will still need a lot of care from their mother. She spends most of her time with them in the burrow and will leave them to forage more regularly as they grow.

After hatching

↑

Providing milk
The mother feeds her puggles milk in the early stage of their lives by releasing milk directly through her skin and the puggles lick it off her fur. They are not ready to swim on their own yet.

4 months later

↑

Time to leave
The puggles feed on their mother's milk for around four months. By then, they are around 20 times the weight they were when they hatched. It is now time for them to leave the burrow and start finding their own food.

3 years later

↑

Reaching maturity
A young platypus continues to grow after leaving the burrow. It becomes a fully grown adult around the age of three, when it is ready to mate. A platypus can live for 12 years in the wild.

The baby platypus (puggle) uses a sharp protrusion called an egg tooth on its bill to cut through the shell.

By 14 weeks, a young platypus is covered in fur and can swim around 3 ft (1 m) per second through fast waters.

Long, webbed toes help the platypus paddle through water.

The waterproof tail is used for steering when swimming.

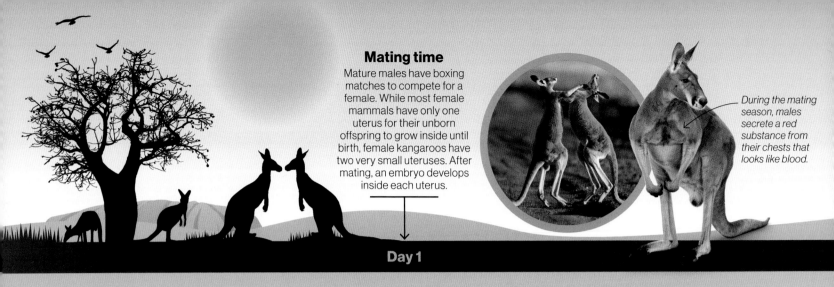

Mating time

Mature males have boxing matches to compete for a female. While most female mammals have only one uterus for their unborn offspring to grow inside until birth, female kangaroos have two very small uteruses. After mating, an embryo develops inside each uterus.

During the mating season, males secrete a red substance from their chests that looks like blood.

Day 1

Life on the hop

Famous for their hopping, kangaroos are a type of mammal called a marsupial. Marsupials are different from most mammals because they give birth to tiny, partially formed offspring (joeys). The joeys must then clamber up into a pouch on the mother's front, where they continue to grow until they are strong enough to survive. Red kangaroos, the largest marsupial, take almost two years to raise their young.

Short trips

The joey weighs about 4 lbs (2 kg), about as much as two bags of sugar, but it is still too small to keep up with the rest of the kangaroo herd (known as a mob). It climbs back into the pouch and is carried by its mother when it is time to move.

Month 6

Month 9

Out of the pouch

The joey is too big and heavy for the mother to carry. She stops the joey from climbing back into the pouch, but it still pokes its head inside to suckle her milk.

Next joey is born

After the older joey has left the pouch, the paused embryo restarts its development. Once born, it makes its way up to the mother's empty pouch, just like its sibling did several months earlier.

Different milks

The mother now has two developing offspring to feed. The mother provides different milks tailored for each joey's nutritional needs. The older joey is fed a thick, fatty milk, while the younger one receives a protein-rich substance.

The mother keeps watch. Kangaroos have only a few predators, including humans and wild dogs.

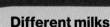

Month 10

Month 11

Pausing development

After growing for a week, one of the embryos stops developing. Kangaroos can pause a pregnancy to make sure that only one joey is born and enters the pouch at a time. The second embryo keeps growing.

Birth

The embryo that continued to grow is born after a short pregnancy—just roughly a month in the uterus. It is still very undeveloped, helpless, and hairless. It is the size of a jelly bean and weighs 0.04 oz (1 g)—about as much as a paper clip.

Week 1

Around month 1

First steps

Bigger and stronger, the joey is now much more active. It is strong enough to climb outside the pouch for short periods to explore, but it rarely travels far from its mother.

Joey suckles

Safely inside the pouch, the joey finds one of its mother's four teats. The teat swells up inside the mouth, so the joey cannot let go. It drinks constantly for two months, swallowing milk and breathing air at the same time.

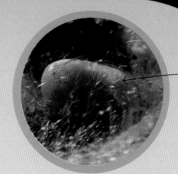

The joey is tiny and only partially formed.

Journey to the pouch

The joey needs to find its mother's pouch. Its back legs are only stumps, but its forelegs have two long claws, which it uses to haul itself from the birth canal to the mother's pouch. The mother licks a path through the fur to help the joey find its way.

Month 5

Month 3

A few minutes later

The next joey travels to its mother's pouch

New diet

The older joey weighs around 22 lb (10 kg). It is too large to just be fed milk and so it now starts to eat a more nutritious diet of solid food. Kangaroos are herbivores, meaning they eat only plants.

Red kangaroos can bound along twice as fast as a top human sprinter.

They hop on two enormous back feet.

Maturity

The older joey weighs 77–187 lb (35–85 kg). It is now fully independent.

Month 12

Months 18–24

Life in the slow lane

This brown-throated three-toed sloth is making its way back up its tree in Costa Rica, but it will take a while to get there. Sloths move incredibly slowly—an effect of their leafy, low-calorie diet and slow digestive systems. They simply do not have the energy to move faster so, to avoid predators, they sleep high up in the trees for about 15 hours a day, then wake up at night to eat..Their long, curved claws allow them to cling on to branches, but they can also be used to defend themselves if threatened.

Day in the life of a chimpanzee

Chimpanzees live in communities in tropical forests, woodlands, and grasslands in Africa. Each member of a chimp community has a different rank in the social hierarchy, with an alpha male at the top. Members of the group build close relationships with each other by working together to hunt, sharing food, playing, and grooming. They are active and busy during the day and spend the nighttime hours sleeping high up in the treetops.

Early morning

Breakfast

Chimps are busy eating from first thing in the morning. In fact, they spend much of their day, up to eight hours, searching for food. As omnivores, they eat both plants and animals. Their diet includes a mixture of fruits, nuts, flowers, and honey, as well as prey such as insects, frogs, and even monkeys and antelope.

Late morning

Brunch

Still hungry after breakfast, the chimps search for a small animal to eat. They find a young antelope. Working as a team, the chimps play different roles—chasers pursue the prey, blockers prevent it from escaping, and ambushers grab it. Once the antelope has been caught and killed, the chimps share the meal between them.

Midday

Snack time

Chimps snack throughout the day, and a sharp stick comes in useful for easily digging out tasty termite treats from a nest. Chimps use more tools than any other creature, except humans. Like humans, they have opposable thumbs, which means they can use their hands to grip and move objects with precision.

Early afternoon

Late afternoon

Evening

Play time

Chimps spend hours of each day playfully tickling, wrestling, chasing, kicking, and biting each other. They pull facial expressions to communicate and laugh when they find something funny. Baby chimps play solely with their mothers at first, but, as they get older, they play more often with other young chimps or alone.

Time to relax

Chimps regularly groom each other throughout the day to remove parasites and dirt. This behavior helps them to relax and strengthens the friendship bonds between them as well. Lower-ranked chimps often groom higher-ranking members of the group to win approval.

Ready for bed

As the day comes to a close, chimps climb high up in the trees where predators such as leopards cannot find them. In the treetops, they build comfortable nests by weaving together branches and leaves. They sleep through the night, getting about eight or nine hours of rest.

The making of a macaque

Also known as snow monkeys, Japanese macaques are found on three of the four Japanese islands—Honshu, Shikoku, and Kyushu. Because of the chilly temperatures in winter, they have learned to bathe in hot pools to keep warm. Macaques are very sociable animals, staying together in all-female and all-male groups known as troops. Infants stay with their mothers for a few years before settling into their new troops.

A young macaque will often copy its mother's behavior.

Day 1

Mating season

Mating season is typically from March to September. Adult macaques spend around two weeks away from their troops. Males and females feed, sleep, and mate together. They usually have several partners during this time.

5.5 months later

Birth

When the time comes to have her infant, a pregnant macaque usually goes to a quiet, secluded spot and gives birth on the ground. Her infant weighs about 1.2 lb (550 g)—the same as a loaf of bread—but it will grow quickly.

Weeks 0–3

Caring mother

The new mother carries her infant on her belly for the first few weeks of its life. She protects and grooms her baby, picking bugs from its fur, as well as suckling it with her milk.

Week 4

Hitching a ride

The infant stays attached to the mother and starts to ride on her back, grasping her fur with its fingers and toes. In some macaque troops, the father also helps with taking care of the offspring, but this behavior is rare among males.

This adult female is pregnant.

A heavy insulating coat keeps the macaques warm in winter.

Learning by copying

If one macaque discovers a behavior from humans that looks useful—for example, washing sweet potatoes before eating them, or fishing—other members of the troop will start doing it as well. And if the behavior is taken up by the majority of the troop, the adults will show it to the next generation of macaques.

Weeks 5–6

Solid food

The infant is suckling on its mother's milk but has also started eating solid food, such as leaves and fruit. For now, the mother forages (finds food) for her infant, but in a week or so, it will start to look for food by itself.

Months 3–4

Fast learners

Although still by its mother's side, the young macaque watches the older members of its troop to learn from them. At this stage, it is a speedy runner and climbs trees to find its own fruit, leaves, seeds, and insects to eat.

Month 7

Growing up

The young macaque is playful and rolls snowballs to throw at the members of the troop. Like the adults, it is very noisy. The young macaque suckles on its mother's milk until it is about two years old.

Years 4–5

Leaving the troop

Young females remain in their mother's troop, and males leave when they are four to five years old. They sometimes team up with a group of other adolescent males. They will be ready to mate when they are five years old.

Year in the life of an Alpine ibex

Herds of Alpine ibex live on the slopes of the European Alps, at heights of up to 10,800 ft (3,300 m). In winter, these wild mountain goats endure extremely harsh conditions, with freezing temperatures and snow covering the ground. They clamber up and down steep, rocky cliffs to find plants to eat. When the snow melts in spring, they migrate to lush green meadows to feed, and in summer the females give birth to their young.

The male's thick, curved horns can grow up to 3.3 ft (1 m) long.

Hooves that grip

Alpine ibex are so good at climbing near-vertical mountainsides because of their hooves, which are cloven (meaning divided in two) with two toes. Under each toe, a soft inner pad with a rubbery, nonslip surface is pressed against and grips on to the bump of a rock. As the animal presses its weight down, the soft inner pad and the hard outer wall of the hoof cup the bump of the rock, locking it in position.

Side view of hoof

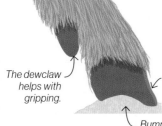

The dewclaw helps with gripping.

The hard outer wall acts like a cup over the bump of rock underneath.

Bump of rock

Hoof from below

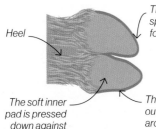

Heel

The two toes spread out for extra grip.

The soft inner pad is pressed down against the uneven rock surface.

The hard outer wall around each toe cups the rock beneath.

Rutting

The mating season begins and lasts about six weeks. Male ibex that want to mate strut around with their short tails sticking up, showing the white fur beneath. They fight, clashing horns to decide which ones are dominant and have the right to mate with a female.

December

Herd separates

Although winter is not yet over and snow blizzards may still sweep in, spring is not far away. The ibex divide into male and female herds again.

December–January

February–April

Pregnant female ibex

Mating

If a female ibex allows a male to mate with her and she becomes pregnant, she gives birth to a kid (baby ibex) five months later. The kid will be born in the middle of summer when there is plenty of food for the mother to eat.

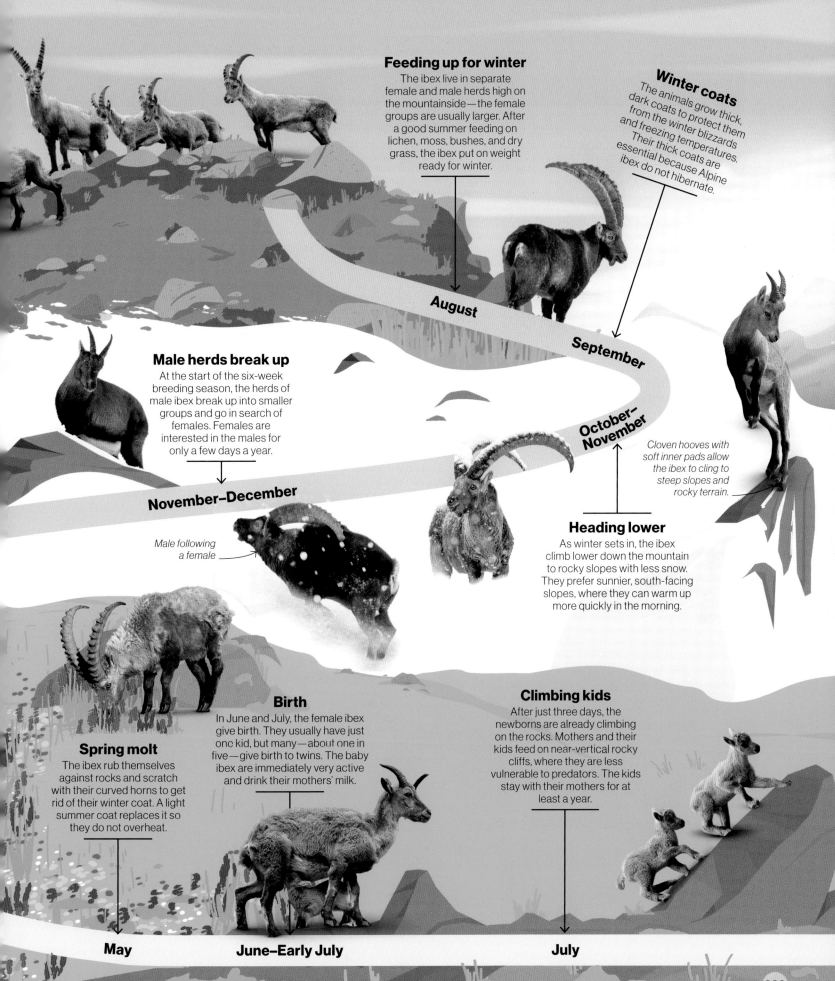

Feeding up for winter

The ibex live in separate female and male herds high on the mountainside—the female groups are usually larger. After a good summer feeding on lichen, moss, bushes, and dry grass, the ibex put on weight ready for winter.

Winter coats

The animals grow thick, dark coats to protect them from the winter blizzards and freezing temperatures. Their thick coats are essential because Alpine ibex do not hibernate.

August

September

Male herds break up

At the start of the six-week breeding season, the herds of male ibex break up into smaller groups and go in search of females. Females are interested in the males for only a few days a year.

October–November

Cloven hooves with soft inner pads allow the ibex to cling to steep slopes and rocky terrain.

November–December

Male following a female

Heading lower

As winter sets in, the ibex climb lower down the mountain to rocky slopes with less snow. They prefer sunnier, south-facing slopes, where they can warm up more quickly in the morning.

Spring molt

The ibex rub themselves against rocks and scratch with their curved horns to get rid of their winter coat. A light summer coat replaces it so they do not overheat.

Birth

In June and July, the female ibex give birth. They usually have just one kid, but many—about one in five—give birth to twins. The baby ibex are immediately very active and drink their mothers' milk.

Climbing kids

After just three days, the newborns are already climbing on the rocks. Mothers and their kids feed on near-vertical rocky cliffs, where they are less vulnerable to predators. The kids stay with their mothers for at least a year.

May

June–Early July

July

Hunting in the snow

Snow leopards face harsh conditions searching for prey during the coldest month of the year. However, they have broad paws for walking easily on snow and thick fur to keep them extra warm.

January

Winter trek

Wild Mongolian asses (known as khulan) feed on shrubs and plant roots during the cold winter. They can travel thousands of miles in just a few weeks to find food, covering as much as 27,000 sq miles (70,000 sq km) in a year.

February

Year in the Gobi Desert

The Gobi Desert in East Asia is the fifth largest desert in the world. It is known as a cold desert with its long, bitter winters and relatively mild summertime temperatures. The Mongolian word *gobi* means "waterless place," yet despite these harsh conditions, it is home to a surprising number of animals. Many species stay active in the desert all year round, while some creatures migrate or hibernate for a part of the year.

September

Falcons migrate

With their young fledged (matured), saker falcons that have bred in the Gobi Desert in the spring migrate to less arid (dry) climates in the south. They do not form large groups when migrating, preferring to make the journey on their own.

Change of coat

The fur on Pallas's cats grows thicker and longer to keep them warm throughout the bitterly cold winter months as they hunt in the snow. The fur loses its orange-to-red hues and turns a frosted gray.

October

Breeding season

Breeding, also known as rutting, for Bactrian camels happens throughout the winter. It is a stinky affair as the males spread their urine, which contains female-attracting hormones, all over their bodies using their tails.

March

Ready for spring

Temperatures in the desert begin to rise above 32°F (0°C) and the Gobi bear, a relative of the brown bear, has woken from its five-month-long hibernation. It will feed on roots, berries, and even insects.

April

Time for food

Out of hibernation, the Central Asian pit viper hunts rodents. It has heat-sensing pits between its nostrils and eyes, which can detect temperature differences of a few hundredths of a degree, helping it to track down prey, even at night.

May

In need of water

This hardy tree produces bright yellow flowers. It has a root system that goes down 16.5 ft (5 m) and branches that expand far and wide in order to capture as much water as possible when it rains.

August

Light rains

A few light showers have left long-lasting pools in the desert, called watering holes. Animals visit the watering holes often in the warmth of summer to drink. The rains bring color to the desert as new plants start to grow.

July

Summer flowers

Wild onions bloom in a sea of pink flowers. These plants are an important food source for many animals, including camels, khulan, tolai hares, and Gobi bears. Every part of the plant can be eaten, right down to the bulb.

June

Ready for winter

Much like their rabbit relatives, pikas are active in their burrows throughout the winter. They live in family groups and depend on food reserves—piles of mosses, branches, and nuts—they have gathered over summer.

November

Business as usual

Gray wolf packs continue to hunt through the winter, feeding largely on small mammals, such as pikas. In a month or two, the alpha male and female will mate to add a new generation of pups to the pack.

December

Rocky desert

The Gobi Desert is not covered in dunes like a typical desert. In fact, only 5 percent of it consists of sand. Its diverse landscape ranges from flat plains (steppe), valleys, and mountain ranges to salt marshes, lakes, and rivers. However, most of the desert is mainly bare rock and gravel with limited plants.

Day in the life of a meerkat

Meerkats are sociable mammals that live in close-knit family groups, known as mobs, of up to 50 individuals in the deserts of southern Africa. One dominant female (the matriarch) leads the mob, which has a strict social hierarchy. Meerkats are early risers, foraging by day and sleeping together in their underground burrow at night.

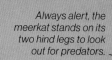

Always alert, the meerkat stands on its two hind legs to look out for predators.

Early morning

First hunt

Meerkats eat a variety of food, including insects, scorpions, small reptiles, and eggs. They dig in the sand to find their prey, spending at least five hours each day searching for food. Meerkats hunt in the early morning and late afternoon to avoid the hottest parts of the day.

Early morning

Keeping a lookout

While some meerkats leave the burrow in search of food, others take turns guarding the entrance. The lookout stands upright as it scans for predators, such as eagles. At the first sight of a threat, it barks a warning and the other meerkats run to safety in the burrow.

Late morning

Warming up

When meerkats emerge from their burrow for a day of digging, hunting, and playing, they often stretch out in the sunshine to warm themselves—all the time remaining alert for danger. When it gets too hot, they move to find shade.

Midday

Time for a nap

Meerkats sleep for 10–12 hours every day. They often huddle together for a nap during the hottest part of the day, either in a shady spot outside or inside their cool burrow. At night, they stay inside the burrow, which is a comfortable temperature and safe from predators.

Early afternoon

Cleaning and bonding

Meerkats of all ages and ranks spend time grooming each other to remove parasites and keep their fur in good condition. As well as helping them to stay clean, this behavior strengthens the bonds between meerkats and helps lower-ranking individuals win support from the higher-ranking mob members.

Late afternoon

Having fun

While the adults hunt and keep watch, pups spend most of the day play-fighting. Playmates leap on and pin each other to the ground. They run, chase, and sometimes nip one another. Pups do this to make friends and build trust, or just because it is fun!

The dry season

At the start of the year, the land is dry and grazers such as warthogs and zebras have to roam far and wide to find grass. The lions in turn travel long distances to follow their prey.

Prey is scarce at this time of year and lions must choose carefully when to attack.

January

Striking out alone

Juvenile male lions, about two to three years old, separate from the rest of the pride. They wander to another part of the plain and will attempt to take over another pride.

February

Living with lions

Living in groups called "prides," African lions roam the plains—huge areas of open grassland, such as the Masai Mara in Kenya. A pride may have up to 40 members—a dominant male, younger males, and females—living and working together to hunt. Life is tough in an environment where food is hard to find for many months of the year.

Babysitting

The cubs are growing fast. Adult females form a crèche (nursery), where cubs suckle milk from other females as well as their own mothers. This arrangement allows some mothers to hunt while their cubs are looked after.

Late August

Home alone

With hungry cubs now eating meat, the adult females spend more time hunting. They often leave the cubs hidden in the grass for long periods. This is a dangerous time for unaccompanied cubs, which may be spotted by hungry hyenas.

September

Learning to hunt

A few months old, the cubs travel with their mothers on hunting expeditions to watch and learn how prey are stalked and killed. Young lions do not actively take part in hunts until they are about a year old.

October–November

Time of plenty

The rainy season begins. The grass quickly grows and prey arrives to eat it. The lions have plenty to hunt, including buffalo. The females typically do most of the hunting for their pride, but an adult male might occasionally join in.

March–April

Heavy rains

The daily rains become heavier. If a pride's territory floods during the downpours, they may be forced to move away to find drier ground where it is easier to hunt.

April–May

Mating season

It is the end of the rainy season. At this time, females mate with the pride's dominant males, but this happens only every other year. In a pride, multiple females will become pregnant at the same time to ensure their cubs are born at similar times.

May–June

New pride members

Several females give birth around the same time after a pregnancy lasting about 3.5 months. At first, the tiny cubs cannot open their eyes and are completely dependent on their mother's milk to survive.

The Great Migration

Hundreds of thousands of grazing animals, such as wildebeest, start to migrate across the Serengeti in Tanzania and the Masai Mara in Kenya in search of lush vegetation to eat. Lions lurk behind trees and on riverbanks as they pass, waiting to pounce.

July

Early August

The mother stays with her cubs when the pride splits up.

The adult male lion leaves the pride alone to develop strength and become more mature.

The pride divides

The dry season begins and the wildebeest have moved on to find more food elsewhere. With less prey around to eat, the pride divides into smaller groups to give itself a greater chance of surviving through the tough dry season ahead.

December

Life at the water hole

Dramatic transformations happen every year at the Etosha National Park in Namibia. In the rainy season—between November and April—watering holes form that attract passing mammals and wading birds. The vegetation springs into life, making the landscape lush and green, with plenty to eat for everyone. During the drier months, these watering holes shrink or disappear completely, and the land turns brown and dusty. This leaves zebras, elephants, springbok, and many other creatures struggling to survive as food and water become harder to find.

Life on the hoof

The ground shakes with the thunder of hooves as more than a million wildebeest, joined by zebras and gazelles, make the Great Migration from the dry Serengeti Plains in Tanzania to greener pastures in Kenya. It is the largest overland migration in the world. By migrating each year, the wildebeest do not exhaust the food supply in any one area and avoid drought and starvation.

Predators and protection

Cheetahs, lions, hyenas, and wild dogs are all eager to make a meal of the new calves. Wildebeest mothers are alert to threats and put themselves between the predators and their young, shoving the predators away with their massive heads and horns. Herds bunch together, placing young calves in the center for protection.

A fresh start

About 80 percent of calves are born within a two- to three-week period, increasing their chance of survival as predators are overwhelmed by their numbers. The calves can stand and suckle minutes after being born and can run with the herd soon after that.

Grazing

Herds of wildebeest are spread out across the plains, feeding on grasses while keeping watch for predators as much as possible. The calves now depend less on their mother's milk as they eat more grass.

Massive migration

The Serengeti Plains are becoming dry and grass is scarce. Wildebeest gather to form a superherd—about 1.5 million animals altogether. Quite suddenly the annual migration begins, the ground shuddering with the impact of their hooves.

Joining others

The wildebeest move up into the central and western Serengeti. Zebras and gazelles join the herd as they travel. Approximately 3,000 lions live here, but for the herd, there is safety in numbers.

January

February

March

April

May

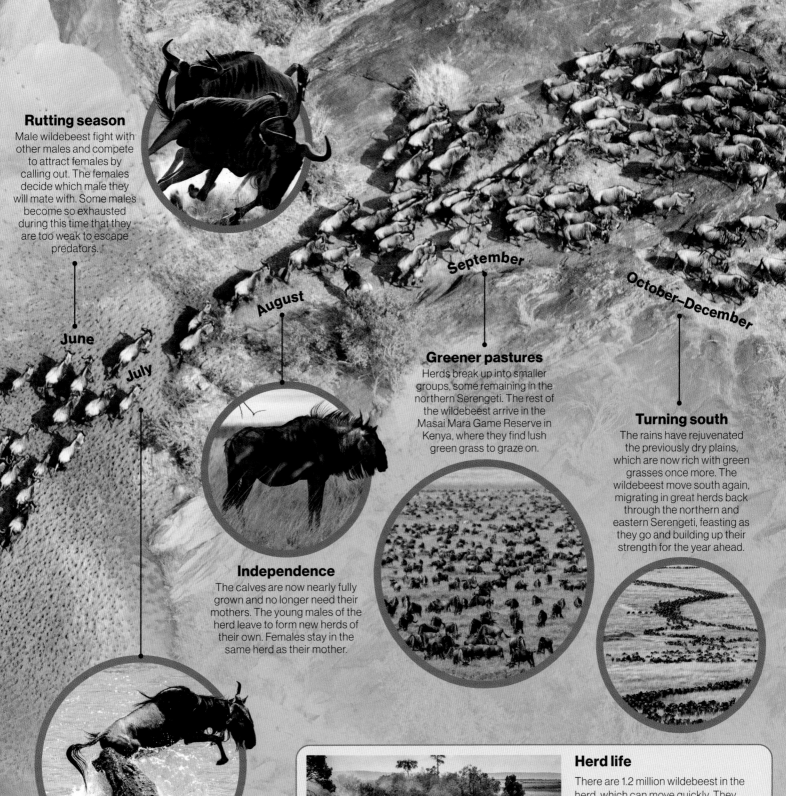

Rutting season

Male wildebeest fight with other males and compete to attract females by calling out. The females decide which male they will mate with. Some males become so exhausted during this time that they are too weak to escape predators.

June

July

August

September

October–December

Greener pastures

Herds break up into smaller groups, some remaining in the northern Serengeti. The rest of the wildebeest arrive in the Masai Mara Game Reserve in Kenya, where they find lush green grass to graze on.

Turning south

The rains have rejuvenated the previously dry plains, which are now rich with green grasses once more. The wildebeest move south again, migrating in great herds back through the northern and eastern Serengeti, feasting as they go and building up their strength for the year ahead.

Independence

The calves are now nearly fully grown and no longer need their mothers. The young males of the herd leave to form new herds of their own. Females stay in the same herd as their mother.

Crocodile crossing

The wildebeest at the front of the Great Migration stop as they reach the banks of the Mara River. It is a long drop into the river below, where Nile crocodiles lurk. Suddenly one wildebeest takes the leap and the rest follow behind. Most make it, but thousands do not.

Herd life

There are 1.2 million wildebeest in the herd, which can move quickly. They travel for up to 25 miles (40 km) a day, so up to 1,240 miles (2,000 km) a year. During the course of their migration, they cross two crocodile-infested rivers (the Mara and the Grumeti Rivers). They also need to eat a lot, since they require so much energy—the superherd consumes about 4,400 tons (4,000 metric tons; the weight of a blue whale) of grass every single day.

Living large

Hippopotamuses are social animals that live in Africa, south of the Sahara Desert. Apart from elephants, they are the heaviest land animals on Earth, weighing up to 5 tons. Hippos spend most of their time in herds of up to 30, with males and females, adults, and calves all together. They cool themselves in the water of lakes and rivers by day and graze at night, eating huge quantities of grass.

Grazing
By this time, the calf spends more time grazing out of water. It still gets additional nutrition from its mother's milk.

Months 5–6

Nursing
The hippo calf depends entirely on its mother's milk for the first few weeks of its life. It remains in the water while the mother goes to forage (find food). After a month, the baby will begin grazing with its mother.

Month 1

A hippo's jaws are 25 in (65 cm) wide. When it yawns, its mouth opens almost fully straight.

Weaning
Once it is about eight months old, the young hippo is eating more solid food than milk. Most calves are fully weaned (no longer drinking their mother's milk) by the time they are one year old.

Month 8

Oxpeckers eat ticks and other parasites that live on hippos' thick skin.

Teenage years
Young hippos grow to adult size quite quickly. Despite this, they will not be able to become parents themselves until they are at least five years old for females, or seven years old for males.

Years 5–7

Courtship

Usually during the dry season, the dominant male in a hippo herd searches for a receptive female to mate with. If he finds a partner, the couple mate in the water. The male may mate with several females.

Dry season

Quiet time

Once a female becomes pregnant, she stays with the herd until a week or two before giving birth. She then leaves the group and finds her own quiet space for a few weeks.

7.5 months after mating

Rejoining the herd

The mother and calf rejoin their herd after a week or two. The calf's father is very protective toward the females and young in his group. He will attack any animal he sees as a threat to them, including crocodiles, hyenas, lions, and leopards.

Weeks 1–2

Water birth

Female hippos usually give birth during the rainy season, and in the water. After giving birth, the mother nudges her newborn up to the surface to breathe—a calf can survive underwater for only 40 seconds, unlike adults, who can hold their breath for five minutes before needing to surface.

Day 1

Fully grown

Hippos may live for more than 40 years. Females of breeding age do not become pregnant each year—every second year is more usual. They often continue to give birth to calves well into their 30s.

Years 30–40+

Handling the heat

To keep cool under the scorching African sun, hippos spend most of their time wallowing in lakes and rivers, or lolling about in the mud. Their eyes, nostrils, and ears are on the top of their head so they can see, breathe, and hear while mostly submerged. Hippos even sweat an oily liquid that coats their skin and acts like sunblock; it also helps protect them from infections.

Some sandstorms can reach as high as 50 ft (15 m).

Weather drama

Strong winds suddenly come through, picking up the surface sand and carrying it in every direction. The sandstorm only about 10 ft (3 m) high forces animals to seek shelter but it passes quickly.

Early breakfast

A desert monitor lizard is looking for snakes, lizards, and rodents for its breakfast. It hunts for only a few hours in the early morning before spending the rest of the day hiding in its burrow to avoid the heat.

Morning dew

Addax antelopes rise early to take advantage of the cool morning and the dew that has collected on shrubs in the night. This is risky, though, as early morning hunters, such as African wild dogs, may be lurking.

03:00 **04:00** **05:00** **06:00**

02:00

Night hunter

4 deer's and 400 cm's prey, 84 deer's as deer's looking to its prey, 84 as cm's as deer's looking to its stinger to stun its prey. It lies in wait, emerging from its burrow at night and even senses a human.

01:00

00:00

24 hours in the desert

Across North Africa lies the Sahara, one of the harshest places on Earth. Yet this vast desert, which stretches over more than 3.5 million sq miles (9 million sq km), is home to many types of plants and animals. These tough species have adapted to the tiny amount of rain that falls each year; the scorching daytime heat; and the cool nights.

Cold deserts

The Sahara may be the world's most famous hot desert, but the planet's largest deserts are in Antarctica and the Arctic. These freezing cold, barren expanses are classified as deserts because of how little precipitation (rain or snow) they get each year and how inhospitable they are for plants.

23:00

22:00

21:00 **20:00** **19:00**

Unexpected danger

As the sun goes down, a horned viper lies half buried in the sand. The snake waits patiently for a small nocturnal rodent to come into striking distance.

Listening for prey

A fennec fox leaves its den to find food. Its big ears help to keep it cool during the day and its thick fur keeps it warm at night. The fox lowers its head from side to side, listening for prey crawling beneath the sand.

Darkness falls

Under cover of darkness, a jerboa leaves its burrow to find plants, soft seeds, and the occasional beetle to eat. It listens for danger with its big ears and can leap 17 times its body length to escape from nocturnal predators.

Shelter from the sun

A euphorbia plant provides some shelter for a fat sand rat as the temperature rises. The rodent would not dare nibble at its leaves and stem, however, as they are filled with a toxic sap to deter herbivores from grazing.

Basking time

A male common agama lizard warms itself in the sun to get the energy it needs to hunt insects. Its bright blue-and-red pattern attracts females and scares away male rivals.

Rising temperatures

The desert sand reaches a scorching 158°F (70°C), and Saharan silver ants come out to scavenge dead insects. The ants race across the hot surface at 2.8 ft (85 cm) per second—that's like you running at 400 mph (644 km/h)!

Being hairy is cool

Fast feet are not the only way Saharan silver ants stay cool in the searing heat of the desert. They are also covered in uniquely shaped hairs that allow body heat to escape while reflecting the warm rays of sunlight. The hairs reflect light like a mirror, and this effect gives the ants a silvery appearance.

The ant's head is covered in hair.

The hairs are hollow and triangular in cross section.

Bushy eyebrows and long eyelashes protect a dromedary's eyes from blowing sand.

07:00 08:00 09:00 10:00 11:00 12:00 00:00 13:00 14:00 15:00 16:00 17:00 18:00

This gazelle can run at 60 mph (96 km/h), but it cannot escape a cheetah.

Evening hunt

Out for its early evening hunt, a Saharan cheetah chases down a Dorcas gazelle. The big cat reaches a peak speed of 62 mph (100 km/h) during the hunt. It gets all the water it needs to survive from the gazelle's blood.

Hiding from the heat

As a small group of dromedaries (Arabian camels) shelter in the shade of a red acacia tree, another of its leaves drops to the ground. The tree is shedding its leaves after a long period of drought to conserve (keep) moisture until the rains come again.

Sound sleepers

A koala and her joey cling to a branch of a eucalyptus tree in the morning. Koalas can sleep for up to 22 hours a day and are usually most active at dusk, night, and dawn, but can move during the day if disturbed. They need so much sleep as they get very little energy from their diet of eucalyptus leaves. These leaves are also toxic, which means koalas' digestive systems require lots of energy, as they have to work extra hard to make the leaves safe to eat.

1.5–2 hours
Sperm whale

These whales spends only 7 percent of their time asleep. They take occasional "power naps" of about 15 minutes each, neither breathing nor moving. The whales sleep vertically with their tails down and heads just below the water's surface.

2 hours
Giraffe

On average, giraffes spend just 8 percent of their time asleep and even this is broken into five- or 10-minute naps throughout the day. They can sleep standing up—this means they are able to make a quick escape if a predator approaches.

2–3 hours
Elephant

African elephants sleep standing up or lying down. They usually snooze in groups, with some remaining awake to keep watch for predators while the others nap. They are able to remain awake for up to 46 hours.

10–12 hours
Owl

Most owls sleep during the day—at night they hunt mice and voles. They snooze perched upright on a branch or a rocky ledge. Their sleep is formed of a series of shorter naps rather than one long, unbroken sleep session.

9.5–11.5 hours
Chimpanzee

Like humans, chimps have one long period of sleep at night. When it is time for bed, most build tree nests from branches and leaves, although some prefer to snooze on the ground.

8–12 hours
Bearded dragon

These desert reptiles sleep when it is dark—they sleep more during the winter and less in summer. They may sleep on the ground, sometimes buried under a thin covering of sand, or even sleep vertically on a tree trunk.

16 hours
Tiger

Tigers sleep whenever they can—they never use any more energy than they absolutely have to. After making a large kill, a tiger will take a long sleep next to its prey, then resume its feast.

17 hours
Crocodile

Sleeping with one eye open is a behavior crocodiles share with many birds. It probably means that one hemisphere (half) of the brain is active and alert while the other dozes.

19 hours
Giant armadillo

Giant armadillos dig burrows to sleep in during the day. These mammals are mostly active at night, around dawn, and then again around dusk, when they hunt for termites, ants, and worms.

2.5–5 hours
Horse

By locking large joints in their limbs, horses can sleep standing up. For their first three months of life, foals spend about half the day napping, lying down. Once they are older, they sleep upright and for shorter periods.

4–5 hours
Ant

Although ants always seem to be active, they do sleep. A worker ant takes about 250 naps a day, each lasting just over a minute. This means that most ants in a colony are awake at any one time.

5–8 hours
Honeybee

Most honeybees sleep at night, when darkness makes it more difficult to forage for nectar and pollen. By day, they sometimes snooze inside flowers as well as in the hive.

8–12 hours
Giant panda

Pandas usually snooze for 2–4 hours at a time, although these rests may be longer in summer. They sleep on their side, back, or belly—and, unusually, they are able to poop while they sleep.

8–12 hours
Parrotfish

It is not always obvious when fish are napping, but parrotfish are an exception. They secrete mucus and use it to create a cocoon to sleep inside. This sac offers protection from predators.

8–10 hours
Sloth

Sloths move very slowly and rest often—their leafy diet does not give them much energy. They may sleep hanging from tree branches and often return to the same place to sleep.

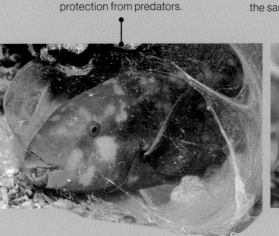

20 hours
Little brown bat

In summer, these flying mammals sleep all day and forage for insects for a few hours each night. They hibernate during the colder months of the year, with their heartbeats falling to just eight beats per minute.

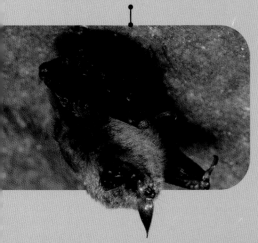

Sleep schedules

Sleep is vitally important for animals. If deprived of rest, they often become weak and lose the ability to control their temperature. How much of the day different animals spend asleep varies enormously. Some sleep in one solid block, while others sleep in short bursts, a few minutes at a time. Some animals even shut down one half of their brain while the other stays awake. It is tricky to research animal sleep in the wild, so there is still a lot that scientists do not yet know.

Night sight

There are fewer predators about at night, but with very little light, it is much harder to see. Tarsiers get around this problem by having huge eyeballs that gather as much light as possible. Each eye is as big as the tarsier's brain. The eyes are so large that they cannot move in their sockets, but tarsiers can swivel their heads in almost a full circle to see things around them. These adaptations make it easier for tarsiers to hunt at night and avoid bumping into predators.

Hunting in the dark

A nocturnal, tree-dwelling pink-toed tarantula hunts its prey, typically insects, frogs, and lizards. It strikes its victims from above with sharp fangs. If attacked by a predator itself, the tarantula flicks some of its hairs as a method of self-defense.

Last ones to bed

Before the sun rises, a family of pacas swim across a small stream to return to their burrow after a night spent searching for seeds and fruit on the forest floor. They are good swimmers but slow walkers. They will spend the day sleeping.

Early wake-up call

As daylight breaks, male howler monkeys begin to "howl." Their morning chorus grows louder and longer, drowning out any other sounds in the forest. They are letting others know where they are. Their calls can be heard 10 miles (16 km) away.

03:00   04:00   05:00   06:00

02:00

01:00

00:00

23:00

22:00

Midnight call

In the middle of the night, a male spectacled owl calls out to his mate. It sounds like a hammer hitting a tree, becoming quieter as the call goes on. She responds with a screech.

24 hours in the rainforest

Tropical rainforests are found in places near the equator. They are Earth's most varied habitats, a wet, warm home to millions of plant and animal species. Whether it is day or night, there are creatures awake and active—feeding, hunting, and finding shelter—while countless more hide and rest. The largest rainforest in the world is the Amazon in South America.

Layers of a rainforest

In the very highest branches of the tallest trees in a rainforest, the world is sunny and breezy. On the forest floor, it is dark, damp, and still. The closed canopy layer of thick, leafy trees prevents light from reaching the ground, transforming the world below into a very different place from the towering treetops.

Emergent layer
The leafy crowns of a few very tall trees soar above everything else.

Canopy layer
This is where most animals and plants in the rainforest live.

Understory layer
Only 5 percent of sunlight reaches the understory layer.

Forest floor
Only 2 percent of sunlight reaches the forest floor.

21:00   20:00   19:00

Night life begins

A kissing sound can be heard in the forest canopy. It is a furry kinkajou, making its "happy" call. This nocturnal mammal has a belly full of figs, which it will carry for up to 1 mile (1.6 km) before dispersing the fig seeds on the forest floor through its poop.

Darkness descends

With the rainforest now dark, pygmy round-eared bats awake and prepare to leave the shelter of their roost in an active termite nest high up in a tree. Their favorite food is insects, which they catch midflight using echolocation.

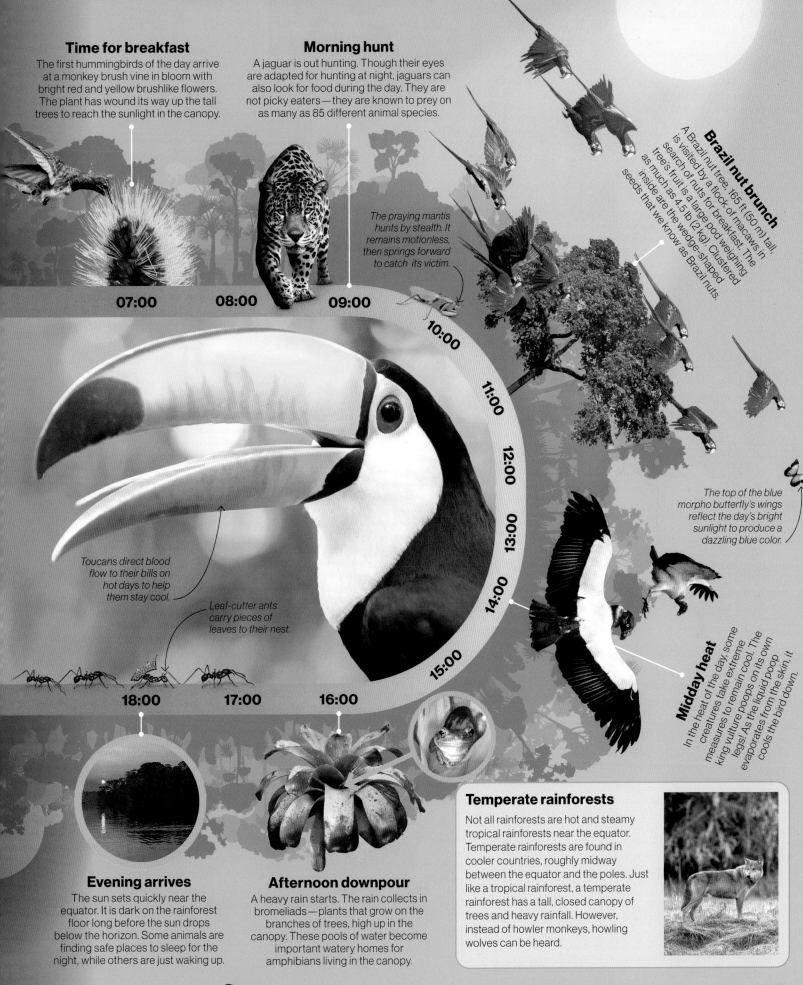

Time for breakfast

The first hummingbirds of the day arrive at a monkey brush vine in bloom with bright red and yellow brushlike flowers. The plant has wound its way up the tall trees to reach the sunlight in the canopy.

Morning hunt

A jaguar is out hunting. Though their eyes are adapted for hunting at night, jaguars can also look for food during the day. They are not picky eaters—they are known to prey on as many as 85 different animal species.

The praying mantis hunts by stealth. It remains motionless, then springs forward to catch its victim.

Brazil nut brunch

A Brazil nut tree, 165 ft (50 m) tall, is visited by a flock of macaws in search of nuts for breakfast. The tree's fruit is a large pod weighing as much as 4.5 lb (2 kg). Clustered inside are the wedge-shaped seeds that we know as Brazil nuts.

07:00 08:00 09:00

10:00

11:00

12:00

13:00

14:00

15:00

The top of the blue morpho butterfly's wings reflect the day's bright sunlight to produce a dazzling blue color.

Toucans direct blood flow to their bills on hot days to help them stay cool.

Leaf-cutter ants carry pieces of leaves to their nest.

Midday heat

In the heat of the day, some creatures take extreme measures to remain cool. The king vulture poops on its own legs! As the liquid poop evaporates from the skin, it cools the bird down.

18:00 17:00 16:00

Evening arrives

The sun sets quickly near the equator. It is dark on the rainforest floor long before the sun drops below the horizon. Some animals are finding safe places to sleep for the night, while others are just waking up.

Afternoon downpour

A heavy rain starts. The rain collects in bromeliads—plants that grow on the branches of trees, high up in the canopy. These pools of water become important watery homes for amphibians living in the canopy.

Temperate rainforests

Not all rainforests are hot and steamy tropical rainforests near the equator. Temperate rainforests are found in cooler countries, roughly midway between the equator and the poles. Just like a tropical rainforest, a temperate rainforest has a tall, closed canopy of trees and heavy rainfall. However, instead of howler monkeys, howling wolves can be heard.

Day in the life of a tiger

The Bengal tiger is the largest cat in the world. It roams around woodlands and the swamps of South Asia in search of prey, using its famous stripes to stay hidden among the dry grasses and bushes. Although it is active during the day, the Bengal tiger prefers to hunt at night when it can easily sneak up and attack its prey.

Early morning	**Late morning**	**Midday**	**Early afternoon**
Leaving marks	**Sending a message**	**Resting in the shade**	**Cooling down**
The tiger starts its day by patrolling its large territory, releasing a unique scent from its scent glands. By squirting urine, leaving poop, and scratching tree trunks, it warns other tigers not to approach its territory.	The tiger spends most of its time alone. While on its morning patrol, the tiger gives out a deep, powerful roar that can be heard far and wide in the forest, which tells other tigers to stay away.	The tiger uses the middle of the day to rest and digest its meal from the night before. It finds a shady place, perhaps in the low branches of a tree, to take a nap as the temperature heats up. To save energy, the tiger may spend up to 20 hours a day sleeping.	A quick dip helps the tiger cool down during the hottest part of the day. Unlike most other cats, the tiger is happy in the water, using its webbed paws and muscular body to swim. It will cross rivers and swamps to pursue prey.

The tiger's striped fur makes it hard for prey to spot it among tall grasses.

Late afternoon

Keeping clean

In the heat, the tiger lounges on the ground, cleaning its fur by licking it. Its tongue is covered in hard ridges that comb away dirt, ticks, and loose hairs. The saliva has antibacterial properties that prevent wounds from becoming infected.

Late afternoon

Ambush!

As it gets darker, the tiger goes in search of its next meal. Using its exceptional hearing and keen sense of smell, it tracks down a deer. The tiger creeps up on the deer, then attacks it side on, hoping to knock its prey over in one bound. Only about one in ten ambushes ends in a kill.

Evening

Dinner at sunset

The tiger hunts and kills its prey alone, with a single bite to the neck, which crushes the windpipe and snaps the spine. If the catch is a large animal, the tiger will not need to eat again for a while. In a single meal, a tiger can eat 88 lbs (40 kg) of meat.

Late night

In the shadows

Night falls but the tiger is still awake. Using its superb vision and hearing, and powerful sense of smell, it is back on the move to find more food in the dark. It growls quietly as it walks to warn other tigers to stay out of its way.

Mating time

Female pandas are fertile (able to become pregnant) for only a few days each year, so male pandas must find them during that time. Once they have found each other, the female will sit in a tree while the males fight each other on the ground for the chance to mate. Males and females do not remain together after mating.

New cub

Usually just one panda cub is born. At first, it looks more like a pink mouse than a panda. It is 900 times smaller than an adult and cannot see, hear, or crawl. The tiny, helpless cub gets all the energy it needs to grow from its mother's high-fat milk.

Safe space

A pregnant panda will search for a rock cave to build a cozy den inside. She spends her time making a nest out of bamboo, leaves, and bark, preparing a safe space to give birth and to nurture her new cub when it arrives.

Early stages

Over the first few weeks of its life, the cub grows fur, slowly opens its eyes, and can begin to hear. By about three weeks, the cub has its distinctive black and white markings.

First few weeks

3–5 months after mating

Just before birth

Day 1

Protecting the giant panda

Giant pandas have been considered an endangered species since the 1970s, when just 1,000 were thought to be left in the wild. In recent years, however, their numbers have been given a boost. Conservation projects, such as the Chengdu Panda Base in Sichuan province, have worked hard to protect the pandas' habitat and help them reproduce. This little cub, born at Chengdu, is just 10 days old.

Starting to move

After a few months of drinking its mother's milk, the young cub is strong enough to crawl. It soon becomes more active, starting to explore and play. The cub's eyesight and hearing improve, and tiny teeth begin to appear in preparation for eating solid food.

Independence

The panda becomes fully independent from its mother and sets out to find its own territory—usually an area around 3–7 sq miles (8–18 sq km). They still have some growing to do, so they spend around 10 to 16 hours a day eating. They need up to 88 lb (40 kg) of bamboo every day!

Months 2–5

Venturing out

The cub starts to eat bamboo like its mother, though it can take a while to get used to it. It learns to walk, run, swim, and climb. At this age, cubs are still vulnerable to predators such as wild dogs, snow leopards, and eagles, so the mother watches over it carefully.

Maturity

When they are fully grown (4 years for females, 6 years for males), giant pandas are ready to start reproducing. But as the bamboo forests where they live are often divided by roads and railroads, it can sometimes be difficult for adult pandas to find other pandas to mate with.

Months 6–18

Month 18

Years 4–6

Giant panda life

Pandas are large bears living in the remote, high bamboo forests of China, where their thick, waterproof black and white fur keeps them warm in the cool, misty mountains. They live slow, solitary lives, spending much of their day (up to 16 hours) eating bamboo—they must eat so much because this leafy plant contains very little nutrition for such large bears. Their big teeth and powerful jaw muscles help them grind up the tough plant stems.

Heavy sleeper

High in the mountains, a pregnant brown bear is hibernating in a warm den. There is deep snow outside, and the bear does not eat, drink, or go to the toilet for weeks at a time. Instead, she survives on her stored fat reserves.

Giving birth

In late January, the bear gives birth to two cubs, all while she stays fast asleep. The newborn cubs are tiny compared to their mother. They grow quickly thanks to their mother's fat-rich milk.

November

December

January

February

Year in the life of a brown bear

The brown bear is one of the world's largest land predators. It is found all over the northern hemisphere, wherever there are large areas of wild forest. Brown bears have no natural predators and spend a large part of each year fast asleep.

Fresh food

During the summer, a brown bear climbs to the highlands where there is plenty of food, including mushrooms and honey, and small animals it can hunt and kill to eat.

August

Putting on weight

As the highlands become cooler in fall, the bear returns to lower areas, especially river valleys. The bear needs to eat as much as possible—such as fish, nuts, and berries—to build up the thick layer of fat that it uses to survive the winter.

Building a den

Winter is not far away. The bear heads to high ground to dig a den among the roots of a large tree. The den is cozy, with a lining of dry leaves and soft moss.

September

October

Waking up

The mother bear wakes up in April as the snow outside begins to melt, and the days grow longer and warmer. The cubs stay close to the den, while their mother goes off to find food. Bears are omnivores, eating both plants and animals.

Looking for food

By late May, the bear cubs are strong enough to leave the den and live out in the open. The family heads to lower ground where the mother bear begins to teach her cubs how to look for their own food.

March

April

May

Fighting for mates

July sees the start of the mating season. Rival males may fight each other for mates during this period. The winner teams up with a nearby female, and they spend a few days together before going their separate ways.

Playing and learning

At this stage of their life, the cubs learn a lot by play-fighting. This helps them to develop hunting skills and teaches them how to treat other bears. The mother avoids other bears—she will not mate again until next year or the year after.

July

June

Hibernation time

As the first blizzards of winter arrive, the bear goes inside its den and falls into a deep sleep. It hibernates to avoid the freezing cold and because food is scarce. Pregnant females start hibernating earlier than males.

Thick fur keeps the brown bear warm all year round. It varies from blonde to black.

November

267

Seasons change

On the fringes of the bitterly cold polar regions of Earth is the tundra—where the ground below the surface is always frozen. Winters here are long, dark, and cold, but in the summer, the snow melts and the landscape is transformed into a riot of color and animal life. The Arctic fox is just one of many animals that must adapt to survive in this environment. In winter, its tawny brown coat changes to a thick, white fur coat that protects it from the cold and allows it to be camouflaged against the snow.

Arctic fox with winter coat

Arctic fox with summer coat

Spring melt

Spring has arrived in the forest. After a dark winter, the days start to get longer, and warmer temperatures melt the ice and snow. Conifer trees keep their leaves in winter, using the sun's energy to grow and to form seeds to reproduce.

Flooded forest

Much of the boreal forest is damp and swampy. The melted snow has nowhere to go. The soil is not deep, and in the far north, the deeper soil never thaws so meltwater floods the land.

▶ **Spring**

Year in a boreal forest

More than a quarter of all Earth's trees are found in the boreal forest—a band of cold, dark forest below the freezing Arctic, covering parts of North America, Scandinavia, and Russia. Here, summer is short and winter is tough. Both animals and trees must be hardy to survive the dramatic change of seasons.

Visitors arrive

The three-toed woodpecker pecks a hole in a tree to keep its young safe. It lives in the forest all year round, but in summer it is joined by overseas visitors. Over a billion birds of more than 300 species, including geese and sparrows, migrate here to breed.

Fall ◀

Fall color

As the cool weather arrives and the days shorten, brightly colored berries brighten up the landscape. Beneath the trees, shrubs burst with fruit, including lingonberries, crowberries, and cranberries.

Mushroom burst

Fungi beneath the soil are busy breaking down dead plant matter all year. But in the fall, the fungi burst out onto the surface as mushrooms. These are the fruits of the fungi that will spread seedlike spores to start new fungi networks elsewhere.

Return of the caribou

As winter approaches, tens of thousands of caribou trek 2,000 miles (3,200 km) to the boreal forest. They have spent the summer farther north in the treeless tundra, feeding and rearing their young away from the mating mosquitoes.

New life

After a two-month pregnancy, a female lynx finds a den beneath a bush or shrub. She gives birth to her kittens. They are blind at birth and depend on their mother completely until they are 12 weeks old.

Great fires

Every 50–150 years, a huge fire rages through the boreal forest. Often started by lightning strikes, these fires clear away the thick carpet of dead matter that has built up on the forest floor, making space for new growth. Some conifer species, such as the black spruce, need the heat of a fire to open their cones and release their seeds.

On the move

A buzzing sound is everywhere as millions of mosquitoes fill the air. The boggy, wet ground is the ideal spot for laying their eggs. Mosquitoes are an important food for many birds and fish.

Summer sun

Summer is warm but short in the boreal forest, with only 50–100 frost-free days. Plants and animals take advantage of the long daylight hours to find food and breed.

Summer

Winter freeze

The boreal forest is heading into winter. Days are short and temperatures may plummet to –76°F (–60°C). Snow once again covers the ground. In the northern part of the boreal forest, the sun sets in mid-November and is not seen again until spring.

Shedding snow

Many trees in the boreal forest are cone-shaped, which helps them to shake off fallen snow. Heavy snow can break branches and prevents the tree's needles from absorbing sunlight.

Finding warmth

Northern flying squirrels find old woodpecker holes or abandoned birds' nests and cuddle up in groups to keep warm. They venture out for only a few hours in the evening and early morning to find food.

Prepping for hibernation

The wood frog is getting ready for its hibernation. Its heart stops beating and it stops breathing. Although much of its body freezes, high levels of sugar in its cells stop it from dying, and it will thaw out again in spring.

Winter

Life as a young walrus

With its 3 ft (1 m) long tusks and a body that weighs more than most cars, there is no mistaking an adult walrus. The process of growing into a 1.5-ton mammal takes up to 15 years, and a lot of shellfish. When they are not diving in search of food, walruses haul their great weight out of the water to rest on sea ice.

January–March
Year 1

Males gather

Adult male walruses (known as bulls) form noisy groups close to herds of females. The bulls compete for the right to mate with the females (known as cows), bellowing, snorting, and jousting with their long, pointed tusks.

January–March
Year 1

Mating season

If they are ready to reproduce, female walruses join a displaying bull in the water and they mate. The most successful bulls may mate with more than 20 cows. A walrus pregnancy lasts for 15 or 16 months.

April–June
Year 2

Giving birth

In spring or early summer, females give birth—usually to a single pup each. A newborn pup weighs 99–165 lb (45–75 kg) and grows quickly, feeding on its mother's milk, which is rich in fat and protein.

2 months later

Growing pup

Nursing female walruses gather in herds of up to 50, staying apart from males and other females. Their pups grow by 4–6 inches 10–15 cm) every month. By the time they are two months old, the pups are strong swimmers.

A walrus's tusks keep growing throughout its life.

Walrus colonies

Global climate change means less of the Arctic Ocean is covered with sea ice in summer. As a result, walruses are hauling themselves out on to land more often. One of the largest colonies, of 40,000 walruses, can be found in summer on a beach near the village of Ryrkaypiy in Russia. The noise and smell of such huge colonies attracts their natural predators—polar bears.

Month 6

Protective parent

Pups eat their first solid food when they are about six months old, though they continue to drink their mothers' milk too. Their mothers are still very protective, sheltering the pups between strong fore flippers when on shore. In the water, a pup will often ride on its mother's back.

Years 0–2

Staying close

Pups accompany their mothers on hunting trips in search of shellfish, marine worms, and squid. As they get older, pups eat more solid food and rely less on their mothers' milk.

Year 2

Splitting up

Young walruses eat only solid food by about two years old. By this time, their mothers may be about to give birth again. Young female walruses leave their mothers' herd, but young males usually stick around for longer.

Years 6–7

Ready to mate

Female walruses are ready to have pups of their own by the time they are six or seven years old. In order to mate, males must compete with older, stronger bulls, so most are unlikely to reproduce successfully until they are fully grown, around 15 years of age.

Mating season

Summer has arrived, and the days are long. After searching for a mate for several weeks, a male polar bear picks up the scent of a female and he begins to follow her. If she is ready to breed, they will mate.

Early May

Male polar bears can reach up to 10 ft (3 m) long—at least twice the size of females.

Arctic survivor

Throughout the year, polar bears face freezing conditions in the Arctic. They are well equipped to survive the cold. Their large, webbed, flat paws act like nonslip snowshoes, allowing them to chase after seals on slippery ice and thick snow, and their long claws are handy for catching fish in a place where food is tricky to track down. Their thick coats keep them warm all year round.

Giving birth

Inside the den, the female gives birth to one or two cubs, or sometimes even three, but this is rare. They weigh about 1 lb (500g) and measure 12 in (30 cm) long. The cubs are hairless and they cannot see or hear.

December–January

The den stays warm because the bears' body heat is trapped inside.

Growing up

During their first couple of months, the cubs open their eyes. They grow fur and teeth, and begin to walk. Staying in the den, the mother is devoted to her cubs. They huddle close to her to stay warm.

Venturing out

The mother and cubs go on short trips from the den to get used to the cold outside. She often stops to rest and nurse her cubs, carrying them on her back to protect them from the deep snow and freezing water.

December–March

April

Sticking around

The pair stay close to each other for a few days after mating, then the male wanders off—he will not come back again. The female will spend the eight months of her pregnancy alone.

Late May

A polar bear's hair is hollow and clear, which allows it to absorb sunlight and retain heat.

Digging a den

To prepare for the arrival of her cubs, the female digs a den, where she will rest over the winter. She will not eat for several months, instead relying on fat reserves built up in the summer.

October–November

Hunt to survive

The female hunts throughout the summer, catching seals at breathing holes in the ice. It is crucial that she builds her strength for the winter ahead. She will need the nutrients to produce milk for her cubs once they are born.

May–October

Food for the family

It is time for the mother to go and hunt to feed herself. Her cubs go with her and they eat meat for the first time, but they will still be dependent on her milk for another two years and will not leave her until the age of three.

May

Going for a swim

Polar bears regularly swim between huge slabs of ice and have been known to cover 62 miles (100 km) of water. A thick layer of fat keeps them warm in the freezing water. They dive in pursuit of seals, using their front paws to paddle like a dog. They can stay underwater for up to three minutes.

Hunting on ice

A lone polar bear hunts on an ice floe in the Arctic Circle near Svalbard, Norway. Polar bears are the largest carnivores on land. They can sniff out their prey from miles away and are able to swim long distances in freezing water to reach it. Their habitats are coming under increasing pressure, however, due to climate change.

As the planet heats up, icy environments are melting, forcing the animals who depend on them into finding new ways to survive.

Glossary

Accretionary wedge In geology, sediments piled up during the process of subduction at the edge of a continental crust.

Adaptation A special feature of an animal or plant that helps it survive and reproduce in its environment.

Agriculture Growing crops and raising animals for food.

Algae Simple, plantlike organisms that live in water and make food by photosynthesis.

Alpha male/female The dominant member of a group of animals.

Ammonite A marine mollusk with a coiled shell and octopus-like tentacles that was common in the Mesozoic Era.

Ancestor Animal to which a more recent animal is related.

Angiosperm A flowering plant that bears ovules, later seeds, enclosed in ovaries.

Antennae Pairs of "feelers" attached to the head of an invertebrate animal, used for sensing its surroundings. The singular is antenna.

Anther The male part of the flower, found on the stamen, that contains the pollen.

Anthocyanin A pigment found in plants that may appear red, purple, blue, or black.

Antibacterial A term for a substance that kills bacteria or prevents their growth.

Aquatic Living or growing in or near water.

Asteroid A small, irregular solar system object, made of rock and/or metal, that orbits the sun.

Atmosphere The layer of gas that surrounds a planet. Also the outermost layer of gas around the sun or a star.

Aurora Patterns of light that appear near the poles of some planets. Solar wind particles are trapped by a planet's magnetic field and drawn into its atmosphere, where they collide with atoms and cause them to give off light.

Axis The imaginary line that passes through the center of a planet or star and around which the planet or star rotates.

Bacteria Microscopic single-celled organisms with no cell nuclei. Bacteria are the most abundant organisms on Earth.

Bark The protective outer layer or "skin" of the trunk, branches, and roots of a tree. This layer overlays the wood and protects the plant from water loss, cold, and other types of damage.

Biennial Plants that germinate and produce leaves in the first year, then flower and set seed in the second year.

Bill The hard part of a bird's mouth, used for feeding, preening, and sometimes as a weapon in self-defense. The bill is flat and rounded on the end. It differs to a beak, which is pointed on the end.

Bivalve A mollusk such as a clam, with two half shells joined by a hinge.

Blizzard A wind storm in which snow is blown into the air by very strong winds.

Blubber The thick layer of fat that protects some animals (such as whales and seals) from the cold.

Bract Small, leaflike structure typically found at the base of a flower. It can resemble normal foliage (leaves).

Breed To produce babies (young or offspring). A breed is also a distinct type of domesticated species, such as an Arabian horse.

Brood Group of young birds from the same nest.

Brood parasite A bird that tricks another bird into raising its young. Many cuckoos breed this way, laying their eggs in the nests of different species.

Burrow A hole in the ground that some animals (such as rabbits) live in.

Caldera A large crater at the top of a volcano. Volcanic calderas are produced by the collapse of a magma chamber or by an explosive eruption that removes the upper part of the volcano.

Camouflage Colors or patterns on an animal's skin or fur that allow it to blend with its surroundings.

Carnivore A meat-eating animal.

Carrion The flesh of dead animals.

Caterpillar The larva of a butterfly or moth.

Catkin An unbranched and often pendulous (hanging) flower cluster.

Cell The smallest existing unit of living matter.

Chemical Any element or compound. Water, iron, salt, and oxygen are examples of chemicals.

Chlorophyll A green substance in plant cells that absorbs light energy for making food in the process of photosynthesis.

Chloroplasts Tiny bodies in plant cells that contain chlorophyll.

Chrysalis The pupa of a butterfly; a hard casing inside which a caterpillar goes through metamorphosis.

Climate The pattern of weather and seasons a place experiences in a typical year.

Climate change Long-term changes in average temperatures and weather across Earth that can happen naturally or, more recently, as a result of human activity.

Clone An organism that is genetically identical to its parents and siblings.

Coast Thin strip of land where the land meets the sea or ocean.

Cocoon The soft casing in which a larva develops into the next stage of its life.

Colony A group of animals (such as penguins) that live together.

Comet An object made of dust and ice that travels around the sun in an elliptical orbit. As it gets near the sun, the ice starts to vaporize, creating a tail of dust and gas.

Contaminate To infect something by touching it or mixing with it.

Continent One of Earth's large landmasses. There are seven continents altogether: North America, South America, Europe, Asia, Africa, Oceania, and Antarctica.

Coral Small marine organisms that live in seabed colonies protected by hard skeletons. The skeletons of corals build up over time to form coral reefs.

Core The innermost and hottest part of Earth, made of iron and nickel.

Cotyledon The food-containing seed leaf situated within the embryo of a seed. Cotyledons supply nutrition to a plant embryo in order for the seed to germinate.

Crater A bowl-shaped depression (dent) on the surface of a planet, moon, asteroid, or other body.

Crèche A group of young animals about the same age, produced by different parents. One or more adults guard the crèche. This behavior is found in penguins and lions.

Crepuscular Active in twilight (when the sun is below the horizon).

Crevice A fracture or opening in a rock.

Crust The thin, solid outer layer of a planet or moon.

Crustacean An animal that has a hard shell, a pair of limbs on each body segment, and two pairs of antennae.

Cultivate To grow, breed, or improve a plant for its produce.

Cyanobacteria Single-celled organisms that can make sugars from carbon dioxide using energy from sunlight.

Dam A structure built across a river to restrict the flow of water.

Debris Bits of broken-up and loose material.

Decay The rotting of plant or animal matter by the action of bacteria or fungi.

Deciduous Referring to a tree that sheds its leaves in the fall and grows new ones in the spring.

Deforestation The cutting down of forests so that the land can be used either for crops, rearing animals, homes, or roads.

Descendant The offspring of a particular animal or family.

Desertification The transformation of a formerly more fertile region into desert.

Detritivore An animal or organism that feeds on dead or decomposing matter.

Digestive system The organs inside an animal's body that break down food and drink to release nutrients and energy for the body.

Dispersal The manner in which seeds are transported away (dispersed) from the parent plant that produces them. The main methods of dispersal are wind, water, animals, and mechanical (such as exploding seed capsules).

Diurnal Active during the day and sleeping at night.

DNA Deoxyribonucleic acid. The chemical that stores genetic information inside living cells.

Domesticate To train or breed animals or plants to be useful to humans.

Dominant A term for the most important or powerful animal in a group.

Dormant Not active for a period of time.

Drought A long period with little or no rain, often leading to water shortages.

Echolocation Locating objects by bouncing sound waves off them.

Ecosystem A community of animals and plants and the physical environment that they share.

Electron A negatively charged particle that occupies the outer part of an atom. Moving electrons carry electricity and generate magnetism.

Embryo A very early stage in the development of an animal or plant. Animal embryos are microscopic.

Environment The natural world all around us, including land, air, and living things.

Eon A large span of time in geological history. Earth's history is divided into four eons, which are subdivided in turn into eras and periods.

Epoch An interval of time in the geological timescale that is smaller than a period. An example is the Pliocene.

Equator The imaginary line around the center of a planet, halfway between its north and south poles.

Equinox The occasion when the sun is vertically overhead at a planet's equator and day and night have equal duration for the whole planet.

Erosion The process by which Earth's surface rock is worn down and carried away by wind, water, and/or glaciers.

Eruption The discharge of lava, gases, and other material from a volcano.

Eukaryote An organism made out of a complex cell or cells containing nuclei and other structures that are enclosed in membranes. All animals, plants, and fungi are eukaryotes.

Evaporation The change of a liquid into a gas by escape of molecules from its surface.

Evergreen Describes a tree that bears leaves all year round.

Evolution The gradual change of species over generations as they adapt to a changing environment. For example, humans evolved from apes.

Evolve Change, over many generations, to form new species. Humans evolved from apes.

Exoskeleton The tough, armorlike outer "skin" of some kinds of invertebrate. Insects, spiders, and crabs have an exoskeleton.

Extinct No longer existing on Earth.

Fault line A long crack in the ground, where Earth's plates have moved against each other.

Fertilize In a plant or female animal, cause an egg to join with a sperm (male) cell to create an embryo.

Flock A group of birds or mammals assembled together.

Forage To wander in search of food.

Fossil The remains or impression of a prehistoric plant or animal, usually preserved in rock.

Fruit The fertilized, ripe ovary of a plant containing one or more seeds—for example, berries, hips, capsules, and nuts. The term is also used for edible fruits.

Fungus A plantlike living thing, such as a toadstool or mold, that does not make its own food but lives on decaying plants and animals.

Gas giant A large planet composed of mainly of helium and/or hydrogen. Jupiter, Saturn, Uranus, and Neptune are gas giants.

Glacier A slow-moving mass of ice, formed from accumulated snow, on land.

Gene A length of code on a DNA molecule that performs a specific job. Genes are passed on from one generation to the next.

Generation Refers to all members of an animal or plant species born and living at around the same time.

Genetic Relating to genes.

Genetic code The arrangement of bases in a DNA molecule. The genetic code tells a cell how to convert the sequence of bases into a sequence of amino acids, from which proteins can be built.

Geology The scientific study of Earth's physical formation and structure. Geologists examine our planet's history, and the ongoing processes that are acting upon it.

Germination The growth of a small plant from a seed.

Geyser A jet of boiling water and steam that rises at intervals from the ground. It is powered by hot rocks heating groundwater.

Global warming A rise in the average temperature of Earth's atmosphere, caused largely by increasing levels of carbon dioxide from burning fossil fuels.

Glucose A compound made by plants during photosynthesis. Glucose is a sugar and is used for energy.

Gorge A deep valley, often with a river running through it.

Gravity The force that pulls all objects that have mass and energy toward one another. It is the force that keeps moons in orbit around planets, and planets in orbit around the sun.

Greenhouse gas A gas in Earth's atmosphere that traps heat, like a greenhouse, and warms the planet.

Grooming Brushing and cleaning fur.

Gymnosperm A plant with seeds that develop without an ovary to enclose and protect them while they mature. The majority of gymnosperms are conifers, whose seeds form and mature within cones.

Habitat The place, or type of place, where a plant or animal lives naturally.

Hemisphere One half of a sphere. Earth is divided into northern and southern hemispheres by the equator.

Herbivore An animal that eats plants.

Hibernate To go into a deep sleeplike state, usually during the winter.

Hierarchy A social grouping of animals, in which the members have different levels of importance. The most dominant animals are usually at the top of the hierarchy, and the most submissive ones at the bottom.

Hominin A scientific term for species very closely related to humans, including chimpanzees and our recent ancestors, but not gorillas or other apes.

Host An animal or plant that a parasite lives on.

Hyphae Long strandlike cells that collectively make up a mushroom and mycelium.

Ice age A period in which global temperatures were low and ice covered much of Earth's surface.

Ice floe A large lump of floating ice, usually drifting on the ocean.

Incubate To keep an egg warm so that it develops. Birds keep their eggs warm until their chicks are born.

Industrial Revolution A period in history, starting in the 18th century, when new machinery and power sources triggered a boom in manufacturing industries, causing US and European cities to expand rapidly.

Infection The term used when disease-causing organisms such as bacteria invade and multiply in a plant or animal.

Inflorescence A cluster of flowers arranged around a single axis (stem). There are many different types, based on the way the flowers are arranged.

Invertebrate An animal without a backbone.

Juvenile A young animal that is not yet able to reproduce.

Lagoon Area of shallow pondlike water.

Landmass A large body of land such as a continent.

Larva The immature wormlike form that hatches from the egg of many insects. The plural is larvae.

Lava Hot, melted rock that comes out of a volcano.

Lichen A plantlike organism, made from a fungus combined with algae, that grows mostly on rocks or tree trunks.

Life span The length of time an animal, plant, or organism lives.

Lithosphere The solid, hard outer layer of a planet or moon.

Magma Hot, molten rock deep underground. It turns into igneous rock when it cools and hardens.

Magnetic field A field of force created by a planet, star, or galaxy that surrounds it and extends into space.

Magnetism The invisible force of attraction or repulsion between some substances, especially iron.

Mammal A warm-blooded animal that feeds its young on milk produced by the female.

Mantle A thick layer of hot rock between the core and the crust of a planet or moon.

Mast year When some species of trees and shrubs produce more fruit or nuts than normal. This happens about every 5–10 years.

Mating The term used when animals pair up to breed.

Matriarch The female in charge of a group of animals.

Mature Old enough to breed or be fertilized.

Metabolism The term for all the processes within a cell that provide energy for life.

Metamorphosis Process by which some animals transform themselves into a different form from youth to adulthood. For example, a caterpillar to a butterfly.

Microorganism A living thing that can be seen only with a microscope. Bacteria are the most common type of microorganism. Also called a microbe.

Microscopic Very small and can be seen only under a microscope.

Migration Movement of animals from one place to another according to the seasons, usually to find food or to breed.

Mineral A naturally occurring solid chemical. Rocks are made of mineral grains locked together.

Molecule A particle of matter made of two or more atoms bonded together.

Mollusk An invertebrate (animal with no backbone) with a soft body, a specialized foot for moving around, and often a hard shell. Mollusks include slugs, snails, squid, and octopuses.

Monsoon A pattern of winds, especially in southern Asia, that blow from one direction for about half of the year, and from the other direction for the other half. The term is also used to refer to the heavy rains carried by these winds at certain times of the year.

Mold A type of fungus that grows best in moist, warm conditions, especially on food and decaying organic material.

Molt Shed feather, hair, or skin to make way for new growth.

Mudflat Muddy area of ground exposed at low tide, but under water at high tide.

Multicellular Comprised of more than one cell.

Mutualism When two different organisms are helpful to each other—for example, bees and plants.

Mycelium Main body of most fungi, formed from a branching network of fine, threadlike cells known as hyphae.

Natural selection The process by which animals and plants best adapted to their way of life survive and pass on their characteristics, leading to gradual change (evolution) of a species.

Natural variation Refers to the differences within a single plant species in the wild.

Neutron A subatomic particle that does not have an electrical charge. It is found in all atomic nuclei except those of hydrogen.

Nocturnal Active at night.

Nuclear fusion A process in which two atomic nuclei join to form a heavier nucleus and release large amounts of energy.

Nucleus The central part of an atom, or the part of a cell that stores genes.

Nutrients Chemical compounds that plants and animals need in order to survive and grow.

Offspring The young of a person, animal, or plant.

Omnivore An animal that eats both plants and other animals.

Orbit The path taken by an object in space around another when affected by its gravity. The orbits of planets are mostly elliptical in shape.

Organism An individual member of a biological species.

Ovary In plants, the lower, wide, vessel-like section of the female part of a flower that contains one or more ovules. After fertilization, the ovules become seeds and the ovary develops into a fruit.

Oxygen A gas contained in the atmosphere that is breathed in, or absorbed, by almost all living creatures to release energy from food.

Parasite An organism that lives on and feeds off another organism, called the host. A parasitoid is an insect that lives on or in another organism, such as an animal, and eventually kills it.

Particle An extremely small part of a solid, liquid, or gas.

Perennial A plant with a life cycle that spans several years.

Period A unit of time that is a division of an era—the Triassic Period is a part of the Mesozoic Era.

Photosynthesis The process by which plants use sunlight, water, and carbon dioxide from air to make food molecules.

Pigment A substance that colors other materials.

Planetesimal A small clump of rock and/or ice that came together when our solar system was forming. Planetesimals merged to form larger asteroids and planets.

Plankton Tiny, free-floating organisms that live in the surface of oceans and lakes.

Plateau A large area of relatively flat land that stands above its surroundings.

Pollen The small grains, formed in the anther of seed-bearing plants, which contain the male reproductive cell of a flower.

Pollinator An insect or other animal that carries pollen from the male part of a plant to the female part of the same or another plant.

Pollution Waste that has been dumped in water, in the air, or on land. Pollution can have a negative effect on the environment.

Population The number of a single species of animal in a particular place.

Predator An animal that hunts, kills, and eats other animals.

Preening When a bird cleans and smoothes its feathers with its beak.

Prey An animal that is hunted, killed, and eaten by a predator.

Pride A group of lions.

Primordia In biology, an organ or structure in its earliest stage of development.

Proboscis A mammal's nose that is extended and mobile, such as the trunk of an elephant. Also a tubelike mouthpart used by some insects to suck up liquid food.

Proton A particle in the nucleus of an atom that has a positive electric charge.

Protostar Star in its early stages of formation.

Pupa An insect at a transformation stage between the larva and the adult. The plural is pupae.

Pupate To become a pupa. At this stage, a chrysalis (hard case) or a cocoon (soft case) may be formed around a larva.

Quark A type of subatomic particle from which protons and neutrons are made.

Rainforest Dense, tropical woodland that gets very heavy rainfall.

Regurgitate Bring back food that is not completely digested from the stomach to the mouth.

Reptile A class of vertebrates that breathe air and are usually cold-blooded, such as snakes and lizards.

Rifting Two plates pulling apart to create a crack in the crust.

Sap Watery fluid found in plants. In trees, sap contains dissolved minerals that are carried from the roots to the leaves in tiny pipelines through the sapwood—an inner layer of soft wood.

Savanna A habitat of wide, open grasslands in a hot, tropical part of the world. It may have scattered trees. The largest savannas are in Africa and South America.

Scavenge To feed on animals that have been killed by others.

Seasons Yearly cycles of change that affect the weather, animals, and plants. The four seasons are spring, summer, fall, and winter.

Sediment Solid particles of rock or organic matter transported by water, wind, volcanic processes, or mass movement, and later deposited on the ground or on riverbeds or the seabed.

Seed The mature, fertilized ovule of a plant. Inside the seed case is the embryo and some stored food. Given the appropriate conditions for growth, a seed will grow and become a plant.

Shockwave A sharp movement of high pressure that may be caused by an explosion, earthquake, or something that moves faster than sound.

Siphon A tube used by aquatic mollusks to draw water into the body or pump it out.

Solstice When the sun is directly above either the farthest point north or the farthest point south of the equator that it ever reaches. At the Solstice, the hours of daylight are longest in one hemisphere while the hours of night are longest in the other.

Species A group of organisms with similar characteristics that can breed with each other to produce fertile offspring.

Spore A single reproductive cell that, unlike sex cells, is capable of developing without fusion with another reproductive cell. Therefore, spores do not require fertilization.

Stalactite A hanging, icicle-shaped structure formed in caves by dripping water with traces of rock in it.

Stalagmite A rising candle-shaped structure formed when stalactites drip on to the floor and leave traces of rock behind.

Stamen The male reproductive part of a flower. The stamen is a long, slender filament (stalk) with an anther at its tip.

Starch An odorless and tasteless white substance found in plants, especially grains and potatoes. It is used by plants as a source of energy.

Stigma The female part of the flower that receives the pollen.

Stromatolites These structures were created in shallow, warm water by sheets of blue-green algae and trapped sediments. Fossil stromatolites are evidence of early life.

Subatomic particle Any particle smaller than an atom.

Subduction The descent of an oceanic tectonic plate under another plate when two plates converge (meet).

Subgiant star A star that is significantly more luminous than a star of the same temperature and color.

Subtropical A term for a region with a slightly cooler climate than a tropical area.

Succulent A type of plant that has thick, fleshy leaves and/or stems adapted to store water.

Sunspot A cooler patch on the sun's surface that appears darker by contrast with its surroundings.

Supercontinent An ancient landmass, such as Pangaea, covering two or more continental plates.

Supereon Describes a time period that consists of more than one eon, such as the Precambrian.

Supergiant star The largest and most luminous type of star. Stars at least 10 times as massive as the sun swell into supergiants at the ends of their lives.

Supernova An exploding giant star.

Tectonic plate One of the large, slow-moving fragments into which Earth's crust is divided.

Temperate A term for a climate that is moderate, not extreme.

Terrain Area of land, usually with a particular feature, such as mountains, valleys, plateaus, or grassy plains.

Terrestrial Relating to land.

Territory An area occupied and defended by an animal or a group of animals.

Toxin A poisonous substance produced by bacteria, other microbes, and some plants and animals.

Tropical Relating to hot, humid regions.

Tsunami A fast-moving, often destructive sea wave generated most often by earthquake activity. It rises in height rapidly as it reaches shallow water.

Tundra A cold, treeless area near the North and South Poles, where soil remains frozen for most of the year.

Undergrowth Brambles, bushes, and short trees that grow beneath larger trees.

Upstream Movement in the opposite direction to which a river or stream is flowing.

Uterus The hollow, muscular organ in female mammals that houses a fertilized egg. Once implanted, the egg develops into an embryo and then a fetus.

Vegetation Types of plants found in an area of land.

Vein In plants, a vascular bundle (bundle of transport vessels) at or near the surface of a leaf and running through a leaf. Veins provide support for a leaf and are used to transport both water and food.

Venom Poisonous liquid produced by some animals such as snakes and scorpions.

Vertebrate An animal with a backbone.

Volcano An opening in Earth's crust where magma reaches the surface; also, a mountain that contains such an opening.

Wetland Tidal flat or swamp where the soil is permanently wet.

Wingspan Length between the tips of a pair of wings.

Wildfire Fire that starts naturally in a dry place or season. Climate change is making wildfires hotter and more frequent.

Index

Page numbers in **bold** indicate main entries.

Acknowledgments

Dorling Kindersley would like to thank the following people for their help with making this book:
Katie John for proofreading; Helen Peters for indexing; Edward Aves, Niki Dirnberger, Ben Morgan, and Carol Usher for editorial assistance; Joe Lawrence, Sammi Richiardi, and Jacqui Swan for design assistance; Sarosh Arif for reviewing the spread on human evolution; Isabel Thomas for additional writing; Steve Hoffman for fact-checking; Usman Toansari for supplying cutouts and shadows; Juhi Sheth and Vidushi Chaudhry for assisting with the jacket.

Smithsonian Enterprises:
Kealy Gordon, Product Development Manager
Jill Corcoran, Senior Director, Licensed Publishing
Brigid Ferraro, Vice President, Business Development and Licensing
Carol LeBlanc, President

National Museum of Natural History, Smithsonian:
Darrin Lunde, Collections Manager, Division of Mammals
Matthew Miller, Collections Volunteer Manager, Division of Paleobiology

Special thanks to Paige Towler

The publisher would like to thank the following for their kind permission to reproduce their photographs:

(Key: a-above; b-below/bottom; c-center; f-far; l-left; r-right; t-top)

2 Alamy Stock Photo: Jason Finn (clb). **Dorling Kindersley:** 123RF.com: Ana Vasileva/ABV (c); Twan Leenders (bc/frog). **Getty Images:** Peter Chadwick LRPS (cra). **Getty Images/iStock:** Derek Galon (cl). **naturepl.com:** Luiz Claudio Marigo (crb). **Shutterstock.com:** lewalp (bc/ladybird); Luca Nichetti (tr); Photoongraphy (br). **9 Getty Images/iStock:** nikonphotog (bc). **NASA:** Johns Hopkins University Applied Physics Laboratory/Southwest Research Institute (cl); JPL (tc). **Science Photo Library:** Ron Miller (cr). **10 NASA:** GSFC/CIL/Adriana Manrique Gutierrez (tr). **12-13 Science Photo Library:** Mark Garlick. **14 Science Photo Library:** Tim Brown (tr); Mark Garlick (c); Gregoire Cirade (bl). **14-15 Alamy Stock Photo:** Ryhor Bruyeu. **15 Science Photo Library:** Tim Brown (tr, cr); Mark Garlick (cl, clb, bl). **16 Alamy Stock Photo:** Matteo Omied (c); Science Photo Library (cra). **ESO:** ALMA (bl). **NASA:** JPL-Caltech (clb). **16-17 ESO:** L. Calçada. **17 Dorling Kindersley:** Dreamstime.com: Solarseven (br); Getty: Photodisc/StockTrek (crb). **NASA:** Johns Hopkins University Applied Physics Laboratory/Southwest Research Institute (bc); JPL-Caltech (tl); JPL (ca). **Science Photo Library:** GEMINI OBSERVATORY/LYNETTE COOK (cla). **Tim Wetherell – Australian National University**. **20-21 Dorling Kindersley:** Dreamstime.com: Doozydo. **20 Alamy Stock Photo:** Manuel Mata (br); Science History Images (cb). **Science Photo Library:** Mark Garlick (t); Ron Miller (bl). **21 Dorling Kindersley:** 123RF.com: Boris Stromar/astrobobo (br). **ESA:** (cb). **Science Photo Library:** Mark Garlick (tr, tl, c). **Shutterstock.com:** Michael Wyke/AP (bc). **22-3 NASA**. **24 Dreamstime.com:** Diego Barucco (crb). **Getty Images:** All About Space Magazine (cb). **25 Dorling Kindersley:** Satellite Imagemap/Planetary Visions (cra). **NASA:** GSFC (cb). **Science Photo Library:** Mikkel Juul Jensen (crb); Walter Myers (fcrb). **26 Getty Images/iStock:** marjorie anastacio (br). **Science Photo Library:** Ron Miller (bl). **27 Dreamstime.com:** Aleks49 (tl); Danicek (ca); Photographerlondon (cb); Alexander Marko (bl); Planetfelicity (br). **28-29 Shutterstock.com:** forestgraphic. **30-31 Shutterstock.com:** Artem Avetisyan. **32 Alamy Stock Photo:** Phil Degginger/Carnegie Museum (cr); Stocktrek Images, Inc. (bc). **Science Photo Library:** JAMES KUETHER (c). **33 Alamy Stock Photo:** Esteban De Armas (tr); Science Photo Library (cl). **Science Photo Library:** Richard Jones (cr); JAMES KUETHER (c). **Shutterstock.com:** vchal (br). **34-35 Dorling Kindersley:** Dreamstime.com:Evgeny Karandaev. **35 naturepl.com:** Alex Mustard (cra). **36 Getty Images/iStock:** nikonphotog (tl). **36-37 Getty Images:** hadynyah. **Getty Images/iStock:** mputsylo (b). **38-39 Science Photo Library:** TAKE 27 LTD. **38 Alamy Stock Photo:** World History Archive (cl). **Getty Images/iStock:** Elena Batkova (clb); Mimadeo (cb). **39 Dorling Kindersley:** Dreamstime.com: Adambowers (br). **Shutterstock.com:** Ian Dewar Photography (clb). **40-41 Dreamstime.com:** Amineah. **42-43 Dreamstime.com:** VanderWolfImages. **42 Alamy Stock Photo:** John Peter Photography (bl). **Getty Images/iStock:** Beboy_ltd (tr). **43 Dreamstime.com:** Albertoloyo (tr). **Getty Images/iStock:** alexey_ds (tl); farluk (tc). **44 Alamy Stock Photo:** World History Archive (tr). **Getty Images/iStock:** minoandriani (cr). **Forest Henderson. J. W. Valley, University of Wisconsin-Madison:** (ca). **44-45 Shutterstock.com:** Kues. **45 Alamy Stock Photo:** Keitma (tr); Alice Nerr (tl); Wirestock, Inc. (cla). **Dorling Kindersley:** Getty Images: Jim Sugar (br). **Dreamstime.com:** Photo263 (bl). **Science Photo Library:** Dirk Wiersma (cr). **Shutterstock.com:** ChWeiss (c). **46-47 Dorling Kindersley:** Dreamstime.com: Valentin Armianu/Asterixvs. **47 Alamy Stock Photo:** Sipa US (tr). **Getty Images/iStock:** PatrickPoendl (bl). **48-49 naturepl.com:** Luiz Claudio Marigo. **49 NASA:** (tr). **50-51 Getty Images/iStock:** trabantos. **52 Getty Images/iStock:** mputsylo (t). **Science Photo Library:** Dr Juerg Alean (bl). **52-53 Getty Images/iStock:** guenterguni. **53 Alamy Stock Photo:** Angus McComiskey (br); REUTERS (bc). **54 Nicholas J. Butterfield/University of Cambridge:** (bc). **NOAA:** P. Rona, OAR/National Undersea Research Program (NURP) (tl). **Shutterstock.com:** Tagliaferri Photography (cl). **54-55 Dorling Kindersley:** Dreamstime.com: Andreykuzmin. **55 Alamy Stock Photo:** Martin Hablutzel (clb). **Dorling Kindersley:** Dreamstime.com: Corey A Ford (tl). **Adrian Gonzalez/Eidorian Art** (crb). **Science Photo Library:** Sinclair Stammers (tr, c). **56-57 Dreamstime.com:** Domnitsky (c). **57 Alamy Stock Photo:** Zoonar GmbH (c). **Dorling Kindersley:** 123RF.com: madllen (fcrb); Dreamstime.com: Alexander Potapov (bc). **Getty Images/iStock:** Anagramm (crb). **Shutterstock.com:** Svetlana Zhukova (bl). **58 Dorling Kindersley:** Dreamstime.com: Callistemon3 (tr). **Dreamstime.com:** Delstudio (cra). **59 Prague National Museum:** (tl). **Professor Deming Wang:** (cr). **60 Alamy Stock Photo:** Nigel Cattlin (tc); Nature Photographers Ltd (tl); Lena Ivanova (cr). **Dreamstime.com:** Iva Vagnerova (ftl). **Shutterstock.com:** RachenArt (tr). **60-61 123RF.com:** meenna (cb). **Dorling Kindersley:** Dreamstime.com: Zoom-zoom (t). **Getty Images/iStock:** RamCreativ (b). **61 123RF.com:** nataliia2910 (ca). **Alamy Stock Photo:** Nature Picture Library (tl). **Getty Images/iStock:** blusezhou (tr); smirart (c). **Shutterstock.com:** Ethan Daniels (tc). **62-63 Alamy Stock Photo:** Susana Guzman. **64 Alamy Stock Photo:** Nigel Cattlin (bc); Zoonar GmbH (cr). **Science Photo Library:** Cordelia Molloy (cl). **Shutterstock.com:** Quang Ho (c); Juan M. Portillo (br); Tatiana Volgutova (c/leaves). **64-65 Shutterstock.com:** ElemenTxD (ca/hills); Roman Sigaev; Gizmort (b/soil); Kolonko (c/grass); SergW 72 10 (ca/trees); Kancerina (c/trees). **65 Alamy Stock Photo:** BigJoker (c); Hans Stuessi (cra); Washington Imaging (cra/seed pods); Deborah Vernon (fcr). **Dreamstime.com:** Kazakovmaksim (cra/seeds). **Garden World Images:** Trevor Sims (tc). **naturepl.com:** Mark Moffett/Minden (tr). **Shutterstock.com:** Tamara Kulikova (cl); I. Rottlaender (tl); Juan M. Portillo (clb/roots, cb/roots, crb/roots). **66-67 MerlinTuttle.org.** **66 MerlinTuttle.org:** (clb). **68-69 Shutterstock.com:** domnitsky (t/peel, c). **68 Alamy Stock Photo:** Carl Newman (cr). **Shutterstock.com:** domnitsky (c); GETSARA (tl); Ella Girsang (bc). **69 Alamy Stock Photo:** Tatiana Terekhina (clb). **Dreamstime.com:** Laupri (tr). **naturepl.com:** Nigel Cattlin (tl). **Shutterstock.com:** gresei (br/leaf); Svetlana Zhukova (c); Maria Kazakova1 (cb); V.S.Anandhakrishna (fbr); Photoongraphy (crb). **70 Alamy Stock Photo:** Vedat Kandemir (cla). **Tory Gordon-Harris:** (ca). **naturepl.com:** Phil Savoie (cra). **71 naturepl.com:** Holger Duty/BIA/Minden (cr). **72 Alamy Stock Photo:** Tomasz Klejdysz (cb); Tetiana Kolubai (c); Dario Sabljak (clb). **Getty Images:** Ed Reschke (cl). **72-73 Dreamstime.com:** Extezy. **73 Science Photo Library:** JACK K. CLARK/AGSTOCKUSA (cra). **74 Alamy Stock Photo:** Martin Shields (cra). **naturepl.com:** Mark Moffett/Minden (cr). **Shutterstock.com:** Joseph Jacobs (ca); Shulevskyy Volodymyr (br); papi8888 (fcla); Aedka Studio (cla); Narit13 (t/flowers). **74-75 Shutterstock.com:** Chatchai.J; Javier Volcan (leaves). **75 Shutterstock.com:** BBstockimage (tr); nnattalli (tc); Kaiskynet Studio (cla); ImagoPhoto (cl); NIKCOA (cb); LIKIT SUPASAI (b/leaf). **76-77 Dorling Kindersley:** Dreamstime.com: Zoom-zoom; Dreamstime.com: Mahira (c). **Shutterstock.com:** Ksena Shu (b). **76 Alamy Stock Photo:** Rick Lewis (ca). **Dreamstime.com:** Bimal Sarkar (tr). **Shutterstock.com:** PRASANNAPIX (clb). **77 Alamy Stock Photo:** Design Pics Inc (tc). **Dreamstime.com:** Vkarafill (br). **Shutterstock.com:** Thanakorn Hongphan (tl); wasanajai (tr); Natural_p (ca). **78 Dorling Kindersley:** 123RF.com: Karol Czinege/kayco (tr). **Getty Images/iStock:** Bobbushphoto (br); seven75 (tl); Mantonature (tc); evenfh (cr); Toshihiro Nakajima (c); mtcurado (cl); jeu (bl). **naturepl.com:** Jiri Lochman (bc). **79 Alamy Stock Photo:** FLPA (c). **Getty Images/iStock:** chuck (cr); JasonCordell (tl); KathrynWillmott (tc); JanJBrand (tr); RelaxFoto.de (cl); nplion (bl). **80-81 Alamy Stock Photo:** willy matheisl. **80 Alamy Stock Photo:** blickwinkel (cla); wonderful-Earth.net (tr); David Chapman (cl); Steve Bloom Images (cb); Gaertner (crb). **Getty Images/iStock:** artenex (cb/orchid); Piotr Krzeslak (tl). **81 Alamy Stock Photo:** blickwinkel (clb); Giedrius Stakauskas (crb). **Dorling Kindersley:** Dreamstime.com: Matthijs Kuijpers/Mgkuijpers (cb/dormouse). **Getty Images/iStock:** Andyworks; MichaelJay (tc). **82-83 Alamy Stock Photo:** Mint Images Limited. **84 Alamy Stock Photo:** Jenny Bailey (tr); mauritius images GmbH (crb); Zoonar GmbH (cr). **Dorling Kindersley:** 123RF.com: madllen (cl); iStock: Andyworks (fcl); 123RF.com: Oksana Tkachuk (c). **84-85 Getty Images:** ninochka. **85 Alamy Stock Photo:** FLPA (c); Photo Central (tc); imageBROKER (cr). **Getty Images:** Peter Chadwick LRPS (cl). **naturepl.com:** Ross Hoddinott (tl). **86 Alamy Stock Photo:** Nigel Cattlin (cra); C J Wheeler (fclb); Julian Eales (clb); Frank Teigler/Hippocampus Bildarchiv (crb, br); Richard Griffin (fcrb); Nature Photographers Ltd (bc). **Dreamstime.com:** Robert309 (bl/bud). **86-87 Shutterstock.com:** Faith Forrest (bark); Magenta10. **87 Dreamstime.com:** Domnitsky; Valery Prokhozhy (cla); Irina Kryvasheina (clb); Volodymyr Scherbak (bl). **Shutterstock.com:** Duncan Andison (tl); Madlen (tr, ca); Veniamin Kraskov (cr). **88 Alamy Stock Photo:** David Hosking (br); Natural History Archive (cr). **Getty Images:** Darrell Gulin (tc). **Courtesy of National Park Service, USA:** (bl); Jennifer Jerrett (bc). **naturepl.com:** Jeff Vanuga (tl). **89 123RF.com:** fishbgone (tc). **Dreamstime.com:** Harry Collins (c). **Getty Images/iStock:** Ericliu08 (br); Stuartb (cla). **naturepl.com:** Steven Fuller (cr); Jeff Vanuga (bl). **Jason Rothmeyer. 90 Alamy Stock Photo:** Linda Johnsonbaugh Arizona (cb); John Cancalosi (c); Jason Finn (clb). **Shutterstock.com:** Richard Trible (crb). **91 Alamy Stock Photo:** blickwinkel (ca); Jennifer Wright (clb); Martin Shields (cb). **Getty Images/iStock:** David Arment (cr); Foto4440 (tc); Matthew Jay Hartshorn (crb). **naturepl.com:** Tom Vezo (tr). **92-93 Getty Images/iStock:** abriendomundo. **93 Alamy Stock Photo:** Eleni Mavrandoni (br). **94 Dreamstime.com:** Lawrence Wee (tr). **95 Science Photo Library:** Pete Oxford/Nature Picture Library (tr). **96-97 Dreamstime.com:** Seadam. **98 Alamy Stock Photo:** Bob Gibbons (cb); Genevieve Vallee (crb). **99 Shutterstock.com:** Cre8 design (cb); Top Photo Corporation (crb). **100-101 naturepl.com:** Chris Mattison. **102-103 Getty Images/iStock:** Lemon_tm (cb). **Shutterstock.com:** Stephane Bidouze; stockvit (t). **102 Alamy Stock Photo:** Simon Burt (crb). **naturepl.com:** Michael Pitts (tr). **Royal Botanic Garden Edinburgh:** (fclb). **Shutterstock.com:** Wayne Lunn (clb). **103 Alamy Stock Photo:** Kevin Britland (cb); REUTERS (clb); Florapix (crb); Les Gibbon (fcrb). **Shutterstock.com:** Jamil Bin Mat Isa (cr); Samsujosssss (tr); suriya9999 (ca). **104-105 Dreamstime.com:** Vvoevale (c/leaves). **Getty Images/iStock:** Chet_W (c). **104 Dorling Kindersley:** Dreamstime.com: Alexander Potapov (c); iStockphoto.com: TomekD76 (tr). **Dreamstime.com:** Edmongin (cb); Valery Kraynov (br). **Getty Images/iStock:** Anagramm (ca). **105 Alamy Stock Photo:** IMAGES@ARTIST-AT-LARGE (ca). **Dreamstime.com:** Christian Weinkötz (tr); Wirestock (cra). **Getty Images/iStock:** Uum Nursihanto (cr). **Shutterstock.com:** Protasov AN (c). **106 Alamy Stock Photo**: Laura Romin & Larry Dalton (clb). **Dreamstime.com:** Gerald Deboer (c, cb). **Getty Images/iStock:** Gucio_55 (cr, crb). **naturepl.com:** Mark Moffett/Minden (bl); George Sanker (br). **107 Alamy Stock Photo:** All Canada Photos (c, ca); Henri Koskinen (tl); Christine Whitehead (clb); Naturepix (bl); Nature Picture Library (cb); Michelle Gilders (bc, cb/worm); Ernest Cooper (crb). **Dorling Kindersley:** Dreamstime.com: Steve Byland (tr). **108-109 Roman Uchytel. 109 Alamy Stock Photo:** Nature Picture Library (br); robertharding (c). **Dorling Kindersley:** (tc, cr); Dreamstime.com: Jean-edouard Rozey/Jeanro (cl). **Getty Images/iStock:** CathyKeifer (ca). **Shutterstock.com:** Patrick K. Campbell (bl); Jan Martin Will (cb). **110 Alamy Stock Photo:** Mohamad Haghani (bl). **Science Photo Library:** ANIMATE4.COM (bc); Friedrich Saurer (tc). **111 Alamy Stock Photo:** Panther Media GmbH (bl); Science Photo Library (tl). **Dorling Kindersley:** Dreamstime.com: Corey A Ford (tc). **Science Photo Library:** Roger Harris (br); Sebastian Kaulitzki (cr). **112-113 Shutterstock.com:** 7ynp100. **112 Dreamstime.com:** Mr1805 (tc). **113 Alamy Stock Photo:** Universal Images Group North America LLC (cr). **Dorling Kindersley:** 123RF.com: Mark Turner (cla). **Shutterstock.com:** Don Madden (fcr). **114 Alamy Stock Photo:** devi (br); Science Photo Library (bl). **115 Alamy Stock Photo:** MasPix (bl). **Science Photo Library:** Jaime Chirinos (br); Mark Garlick (ca). **Roman Uchytel:** (cr). **116 Dorling Kindersley:** Dreamstime.com: Corey A Ford (tc); Jon Hughes (tl). **Shutterstock.com:** Martial Red (c, cra). **116-117 Shutterstock.com:** vectortatu (t). **117 Shutterstock.com:** Alex Coan (tc); Martial Red (cla, crb). **118-119 Alamy Stock Photo:** Björn Wylezich. **119 Alamy Stock Photo:** Björn Wylezich (cra). **120 Alamy Stock Photo:** Corey Ford (crb); Friedrich Saurer (cr). **Dorling Kindersley:** James Kuether (tr); Harry Taylor/Royal Museum of Scotland, Edinburgh/Harry Taylor/Trustees of the National Museums Of Scotland (cla/Ichthyostega). **Getty Images:** Schafer & Hill (cla). **Science Photo Library:** Richard Jones (ftl, tl, tc); John Sibbick (ca). **121 Alamy Stock Photo:** FLPA (bc); Paralaxis (tr); IanDagnall Computing (c); FORGET Patrick/SAGAPHOTO.COM (cr); Panther Media GmbH (crb). **Science Photo Library:** Mark Garlick (ftl); Roger Harris (tree). **Roman Uchytel:** (cra). **122 Roman Uchytel:** (tl, tr, c, crb). **123 Roman Uchytel:** (tc, tr, cl, cr, bl, br). **124 Dorling Kindersley:** Dreamstime.com: Giovanni Gagliardi (t). **Getty Images/iStock:** Craig Lambert (bl). **Roman Uchytel:** (cla, ca, c, cr). **124-125 Dorling Kindersley:** 123RF.com: Jakub Gojda (b). **125 Getty Images/iStock:** evenfh (bc). **Roman Uchytel:** (cl). **126 Dorling Kindersley:** Dreamstime.com: Yobro10 (bl). **Roman Uchytel:** (fcl, cl, c/Phiomia, c, cr, fcr). **126-127 Dreamstime.com:** Alexei Averianov (t). **Roman Uchytel:** (c). **127 Alamy Stock Photo:** BIOSPHOTO (cra, fcrb/Asian). **Getty Images/iStock:** abadonian (fbr). **Shutterstock.com:** Dotted Yeti (ca, crb/mammoth). **Roman Uchytel:** (clb, cl, bl/Phosphatherium, bl/Barytherium, bc/Phiomia, bc/Palaeomastodon, bc/Mammut, bc/Gomphoterium, bc/Anancus, bc/Primelephas). **128 Getty Images/iStock:** SashaFoxWalters (bl). **129 Getty Images/iStock:** chubbyspud (bl). **130-1 John Gurche**. **132 Alamy Stock Photo:** BIOSPHOTO (tc); blickwinkel (tl); Image Professionals GmbH (c). **BluePlanetArchive.com:** Saul Gonor (bl); David Wrobel (cr); Masa Ushioda (br). **Getty Images:** Sandra Standbridge (tr). **Minden Pictures:** Steve Trewhella (bc). **naturepl.com:** Tony Wu (cl). **133 Dorling Kindersley:** Dreamstime.com: Sam D'cruz/Imagex (cr). **Getty Images:** Ignatius Tan (cl). **naturepl.com:** Brandon Cole (bl); Pete Oxford/Minden (tc); Michael & Patricia Fogden/Minden (tr); Hans Christoph Kappel (c). **Shutterstock.com:** GUDKOV ANDREY (tl). **134-135 Getty Images/iStock:** AsherDB. **134-135 Alamy Stock Photo:** Prisma by Dukes Presseagentur GmbH. **134 Alamy Stock Photo:** Chronicle (cb); Nature Photographers Ltd (tl). **naturepl.com:** Alex Hyde (bl, br). **135 Alamy Stock Photo:** Allan Cash Picture Library (bl); Chronicle (tc). **naturepl.com:** Kim Taylor (br). **136 Alamy Stock Photo:** blickwinkel (bc); mauritius images GmbH (bl); Nature Picture Library (br). **Dwight Kuhn:** (fbl). **136-137 Alamy Stock Photo:** Richard Becker (c). **Getty Images:** Sandra Standbridge (background). **naturepl.com:** Kim Taylor (tc). **Shutterstock.com:** Allexxandar (b); H.Elvin (cb). **137 naturepl.com:** Wild Wonders of Europe/Radisics (tc, tr); Solvin Zankl (br). **138 Alamy Stock Photo:** John Cancalosi (ca); B. Mete Uz (clb). **138-139 Getty Images/iStock:** Dimitris66 (t); mashuk (c); RamCreativ (b). **139 Alamy Stock Photo:** Tony Campbell (crb); Grant Heilman Photography (cra, cl). **Getty Images/iStock:** Kare (cb). **Getty Images:** Chip Somodevilla (tl). **140-140 Alamy Stock Photo:** Kim Karpeles. **140 Alamy Stock Photo:** All Canada Photos (cl, cb). **142-143 Getty Images:** Sylvain Cordier. **144-145 Alamy Stock Photo:** imageBROKER (c). **Getty Images/iStock:** Chainarong Prasertthai. **144 Dreamstime.com:** Tomatito26. **Getty Images/iStock:** Henrik_L (clb). **naturepl.com:** Premaphotos (br); Christian Ziegler/Minden (bc). **145 Alamy Stock Photo:** Imagebroker (c). **naturepl.com:** Nigel Cattlin (bc); Barry Mansell (tl); Mark Moffett/Minden (tc, clb); Piotr Naskrecki/Minden (tr); Martin Dohrn (ftr); Kim Taylor (crb). **147 Alamy Stock Photo:** Arterra Picture Library (tr). **148 Alamy Stock Photo:** Agencja Fotograficzna Caro (ca); unpick (tl, tr); Konstantin Nechaev (clb). **Dreamstime.com:** Verastuchelova (tc). **naturepl.com:** Ingo Arndt (cb); Stephen Dalton (bc); MD Kern/Palo Alto JR Museum (bl). **148-149 Getty Images:** Ed Peeters/EyeEm (c). **149 Alamy Stock Photo:** dpa picture alliance (ca, bc); Papilio (tc). **Getty Images/iStock:** Henrik_L (cra). **Getty Images:** Paul Starosta (bl). **naturepl.com:** Heidi & Hans-Juergen Koch/Minden (cb); Solvin Zankl (tl). **150 Alamy Stock Photo:** Nick Greaves (cb); Christopher Scott (tr); Nadine Klose (c); Travel South Africa - Chris Ridley (br). **naturepl.com:** Tony Heald (clb). **Shutterstock.com:** MR.PRAWET THADTHIAM (bl). **151 Alamy Stock Photo:** Roger Eritja (crb). **naturepl.com:** Nick Garbutt (cb); Linda Pitkin (tr); Nature Production (cla, ca). **Shutterstock.com:** AlexussK (bc); gaga.vastard (bl). **152 Alamy Stock Photo:** Andia (cra); Bob Gibbons (tc). **Dreamstime.com:** Palex66 (bl). **Science Photo Library:** CLAUDE NURIDSANY & MARIE PERENNOU (bc). **Shutterstock.com:** Martin Fowler (cb); lewalp (ftl, br); Keith Hider (cl); guy42 (cr); Yellowj (bl/leaf). **153 Alamy Stock Photo:** Dorling Kindersley ltd (cla); Derek Mitchell (tl); F1online digitale Bildagentur GmbH (bl). **Dreamstime.com:** Palex66 (cb). **Dean Heinze:** (br). **Science Photo Library:** CLAUDE NURIDSANY & MARIE PERENNOU (tr, c). **Shutterstock.com:** guy42 (cra); lewalp (ca, cr); Macronatura.es (fcr). **154-155 Shutterstock.com:** Yellowj. **154 Alamy Stock Photo:** Dirk Rueter (tl). **Dorling Kindersley:** original image (C) Tor Andreas Bakke (bc). **Studio Lindalu e.K.: Linda Lubbersen** (c). **155 Alamy Stock Photo:** Frank Blackburn (tr); blickwinkel (bc). **Alex Two Khek Teck:** (tl). **156-156 Alamy Stock Photo:** FLPA. **156 Alamy Stock Photo:** FLPA (tr). **naturepl.com:** Ripan Biswas (ca); James Dunbar (cl). **157 Alamy Stock Photo:** FLPA (tc). **naturepl.com:** Emanuele Biggi (tl). **158 naturepl.com:** Solvin Zankl (cla). **158-159 Dreamstime.com:** Tomatito26. **160 Alamy Stock Photo:** cbimages (tl); Stocktrek Images, Inc. (ca/fish eggs); Dominic Romer (clb); Tom Stack (cra). **Getty Images/iStock:** Divepic (bc); f9photos (tc). **naturepl.com:** Nature Production (br). **Shutterstock.com:** BlueRingMedia (crb); RLS Photo (cl); Rich Carey (ca). **160-161 Getty Images/iStock:** NatuskaDPI. **161 123RF.com:** grafner (cl). **Alamy Stock Photo:** BIOSPHOTO (ca). **Dorling Kindersley:** Linda Pitkin (tl); Jerry Young (bl). **Dreamstime.com:** Fredweiss (cr). **Getty Images/iStock:** Lingbeek (fcr); RibeirodosSantos (tc); slavadubrovin (crb). **naturepl.com:** David Fleetham (cb). **Shutterstock.com:** Porco_Rosso (tr). **162-163 Alamy Stock Photo:** Peter Adams Photography. **162 Alamy Stock Photo:** Erik Schlogl (clb). **Dorling Kindersley:** iStock: vlad61 (tr); iStock: strmko (cb). **naturepl.com:** Georgette Douwma (crb). **163 Alamy Stock Photo:** Juergen Freund (cl); Nature Picture Library (cb). **164-165 Dorling Kindersley:** Getty Images: Hal Beral. **164 BluePlanetArchive.com:** Tobias Friedrich (bl). **Daniel Zupanc:** (tl, cl). **166 Alamy Stock Photo:** Marli Wakeling. **naturepl.com:** Alex Mustard (c, cb). **Natacha Roux:** (br). **166-167 Shutterstock.com:** Adrien Ledeul (background). **167 Alamy Stock Photo:** blickwinkel (br); Underwater (tl). **naturepl.com:** Georgette Douwma (crb). **Natacha Roux:** (bl, bc). **168-169 123RF.com:** rhgdesign. **Getty Images/iStock:** sergio34 (sand); Dmitry Volkov (stones). **168 Alamy Stock Photo:** Design Pics Inc (cl); F1online digitale Bildagentur GmbH (br). **Getty Images/iStock:** seamartini (cla). **naturepl.com:** Alex Mustard (ca). **169 Alamy Stock Photo:** Minden Pictures (tc). **Dorling Kindersley:** Dreamstime.com: Moose Henderson (cra). **Dreamstime.com:** Lisaalisaill (b/sand). **naturepl.com:** Sergey Gorshkov/Minden (tl, tr). **Shutterstock.com:** CharacterFamily70 (br); topseller (bl). **170-171 Getty Images:** Rebecca Harding. **172 Alamy Stock Photo:** FLPA (crb); Minden Pictures (bl); imageBROKER (bc). **Getty Images/iStock:** John Adinolfi (tl). **Getty Images:** Jeff Foott (tr). **172-173 123RF.com:** nubephoto (t); rhgdesign (trees). **Getty Images/iStock:** Dmitry Volkov (stones). **173 Alamy Stock Photo:** mauritius images GmbH (crb); meanderingemu (tl). **Dorling Kindersley:** Dreamstime.com: Jean-edouard Rozey/Jeanro (bc); Chris Gomersall (t); Dreamstime.com: Ivan Kmit (br). **Dreamstime.com:** Miloslav Doubrava (bl). **Getty Images/iStock:** Derek Galon (c); seamartini (b). **Getty Images:** Mark Ralston/AFP (tc); Stefan Wackerhagen (cr). **174-175 Science Photo Library:** Dante Fenolio. **174 naturepl.com:** Magnus Lundgren (cl); Tony Wu (tr, bc). **175 Dorling Kindersley:** Dreamstime.com: Richard Carey/Richcareyzim (fbr). **naturepl.com:** Tony Wu (tc, c, bl, br). **176 123RF.com:** vadimmmus (tr). **BluePlanetArchive.com:** Jonathan Bird (bl). **naturepl.com:** Doug Perrine (ca). **Shutterstock.com:** allex wijaya (c). **176-177 Shutterstock.com:** Nong Amory (c); Tom Fricker Design (shark); kareemov (tree, leaves). **177 Alamy Stock Photo:** ArteSub (tr); WaterFrame (br). **Getty Images/iStock:** yfhishinuma (cr). **naturepl.com:** Shane Goss (tl). **Shutterstock.com:** tetiana_u (fcr). **178-178 BluePlanetArchive.com:** Alvaro E. Migotto. **180-181 Shutterstock.com:** Damsea; ND700 (c). **180 Alamy Stock Photo:** Andrey Nekrasov (tc). **naturepl.com:** Fred Bavendam/Minden (tr); David Hall (tl); Brandon Cole (cra). **181 naturepl.com:** Fred Bavendam/Minden (cla, tl, tc); David Hall (bl); Tony Wu (br, tr). **182 Alamy Stock Photo:** Scenics & Science (cra). **Science Photo Library:** CHOKSAWATDIKORN (crb). **183 BluePlanetArchive.com:** Doc White (c). **Science Photo Library:** CHOKSAWATDIKORN (ca). **184 naturepl.com:** Doug Allan (tc). **185 Henk-Jan Hoving/GEOMAR:** (tr). **186-187 BluePlanetArchive.com:** Michael Valos. **187 Shutterstock.com:** Sergey Uryadnikov (br). **188-189 naturepl.com:** Ingo Arndt. **188 Alamy Stock Photo:** Auscape International Pty Ltd (bl); mauritius images GmbH (cra). **naturepl.com:** Ingo Arndt (c); Juergen Freund (cl, tr). **189 Alamy Stock Photo:** mauritius images GmbH (tc); WaterFrame (tr). **naturepl.com:** Juergen Freund (tl). **190 Alamy Stock Photo:** GFC Collection (br); Minden Pictures (tr). **naturepl.com:** Lucas Bustamante (tc); Pete Oxford/Minden (cr, cb). **Shutterstock.com:** kzww (ca). **191 Alamy Stock Photo:** GFC Collection (cb); Minden Pictures (c). **Getty Images:** Chaithanya Krishnan (tc). **naturepl.com:** Pete Oxford/Minden (tr); Mark Moffett/Minden (cra). **Shutterstock.com:** ittisak boonphardpai (br). **192 Alamy Stock Photo:** Anton Sorokin (bl). **192-193 Alamy Stock Photo:** Chris Mattison (c). **Shutterstock.com:** Kichigin (background). **193 Alamy Stock Photo:** Images & Stories (tc); Scubazoo (ftr). **Shutterstock.com:** Ernie Cooper (tr). **194-195 Dreamstime.com:** Kvasay (silhouette). **194 Alamy Stock Photo:** Doug Perrine (bc). **Dreamstime.com:** Balloon18 (l/texture); Lisaalisaill (l). **naturepl.com:** Sean Crane/Minden (crb); Juergen Freund (cra); Pascal Kobeh (c). **Shutterstock.com:** Agami Photo Agency (tr). **195 123RF.com:** agamiphoto (cr). **Alamy Stock Photo:** anthony grote (cl); Scubazoo (ftl, tr). **naturepl.com:** Juergen Freund (tc); Doug Perrine (tl); Mike Perry/Minden (bl). **196-197 naturepl.com:** Adrian Davies (t). **Shutterstock.com:** Fahkamram. **196 Alamy Stock Photo:** blickwinkel (crb). **Getty Images:** Bob Elsdale (cb); Simon Lindley/EyeEm (clb). **197 Getty Images/iStock:** CathyKeifer (crb). **naturepl.com:** Edwin Giesbers (clb). **Shutterstock.com:** Vaclav Sebek (cb). **198-199 Alamy Stock Photo:** Sandra Standbridge. **198 Alamy Stock Photo:** blickwinkel (cl); dpa picture alliance (ca). **naturepl.com:** John Cancalosi (bl); Andy Sands (cb). **199 Alamy Stock Photo:** Joe Blossom (cr); imageBROKER (tl). **Getty Images:** Gary Chalker (br). **naturepl.com:** Sylvain Cordier (ca); Stephen Dalton (cb). **200-201 Warren Photographic Limited**. **202-203 Alamy Stock Photo:** imageBROKER. **202 Alamy Stock Photo:** Nick Greaves (ca, tr). **Shutterstock.com:** Sergey Uryadnikov (tl). **203 Alamy Stock Photo:** Nature Picture Library (tl). **Dorling Kindersley:** Dreamstime.com: David Havel (tr). **Dreamstime.com:** Andrey Gudkov (br). **Shutterstock.com:** Kareen Broodryk (cr); Catchlight Lens (ca). **204 Alamy Stock Photo:** Arterra Picture Library (tl). **Dreamstime.com:** Sergey Uryadnikov (tr). **naturepl.com:** Michael Pitts (cr, bl); Cyril Ruoso (cb). **205 Dreamstime.com:** Andamanse (tl). **naturepl.com:** Mark MacEwen (cr); Tui De Roy/Minden (tr); Michael Pitts (c). **Shutterstock.com:** Sergey Uryadnikov (b). **206 Dreamstime.com:** Callum Redgrave Close (bc/shell); Elena Elisseeva (br). **naturepl.com:** David Tipling (clb). **206-207 Alamy Stock Photo:** Nature Picture Library. **Dreamstime.com:** Antonio De Azevedo Negrão (b/berries); Photoka (b/leaves). **207 Dreamstime.com:** Alexmax (crb); Melinda Fawver (bl). **208 Alamy Stock Photo:** Arterra Picture Library (tl); Steve Proctor (bl); David Hosking (cra). **Shutterstock.com:** Vishnevskiy Vasily (ca). **208-209 Shutterstock.com:** aPhoenix photographer (t); Artiste2d3d (b). **209 Alamy Stock Photo:** imageBROKER (l); Nature Picture Library (c). **naturepl.com:** Pete Oxford/Minden (br). **Shutterstock.com:** Artiste2d3d (l/reeds); xpixel (tl); iliuta goean (cra). **210-211 Getty Images:** Cavan Images. **210 Alamy Stock Photo:** Kevin Elsby (cb); Brian Pollard (clb). **naturepl.com:** Roger Powell (crb). **211 Alamy Stock Photo:** Papilio (crb). **naturepl.com:** Lynn Stone (clb). **Shutterstock.com:** Gerald A. DeBoer (cb). **212 Alamy Stock Photo:** Shravan Sundaram (br). **Dorling Kindersley:** Asia Orlando 2022 (cra). **Dreamstime.com:** Brix24 (clb); Calv6304 (tr); Rck953 (c). **Getty Images/iStock:** Anastasiia_M (cb). **Shutterstock.com:** Evgenii Panov (tl); Vlad Siaber (bl). **212-213 Shutterstock.com:** vectortatu (cb). **213 Alamy Stock Photo:** agefotostock (clb); Larry Geddis (tc); Gabbro (cra); Ivan Kuzmin (cl); Dennis Frates (crb). **Dreamstime.com:** Roman170976 (cr). **Getty Images/iStock:** MicrovOne (tl). **Shutterstock.com:** AP (ca); Agnieszka Bacal (cb). **214 Dorling Kindersley:** Dreamstime.com: Jessamine (fcl/nest). **Shutterstock.com:** Albert Beukhof (cra). **214-215 Getty Images/iStock:** ivanastar (twigs); vtorous (feathers). **Shutterstock.com:** Piotr Krzeslak (b). **215 Dorling Kindersley:** Peter Chadwick/Natural History Museum, London (fcr); Dreamstime.com: Tommason (br). **Shutterstock.com:** Henk Bogaard (tc). **216 Dreamstime.com:** Andrian Muhamad Yusup (tr). **Getty Images:** Education Images (ca, cr); Mark L Stanley (tl). **naturepl.com:** Andy Rouse (bl, c). **Shutterstock.com:** barka (tc). **217 Alamy Stock Photo:** Derren Fox (c); robertharding (ca). **Dreamstime.com:** Ekaterina Elkina (tc). **Getty Images:** Education Images (br); Michael Nolan (tr). **Science Photo Library:** Peter Chadwick (cl). **218 Alamy Stock Photo:** Chris Gomersall (tc); Janet Sheppardson (tr). **Shutterstock.com:** Tony Brindley (cl); Luca Nichetti (cla). **218-219 Alamy Stock Photo:** imageBROKER (background). **Shutterstock.com:** Tony Brindley (c); Elenamiv (c/sky); Luca Nichetti (cb). **219 Alamy Stock Photo:** ap-photo (br). **Shutterstock.com:** BMJ (ca); Jukka Jantunen (tl); Philip Pilosian (cr). **220-221 Shutterstock.com:** Sergey Tarasenko. **220 Alamy Stock Photo:** Danita Delimont Creative (ftl); Raimund Linke (cla). **naturepl.com:** Stefan Christmann (cr, crb); Roland Seitre (cb); Frederique Olivier (bc). **Shutterstock.com:** Roger ARPS BPE1 CPAGB (tl); Jan Martin Will (bl/emperor); Leksele (bl/macaroni); f11photo (bl/fairy); Danita Delimont (tc); Mario_Hoppmann (tr). **221 Alamy Stock Photo:** Samantha Crimmin (br); Michel & Gabrielle Therin-Weise (tr); Steve Bloom Images (cla); Nature Picture Library (ca). **naturepl.com:** Tui De Roy/Minden (c). **Shutterstock.com:** Charles Bergman (bl); Risto Raunio (cra). **222-223 naturepl.com:** Michael & Patricia Fogden/Minden. **224 Alamy Stock Photo:** Octavio Campos Salles (tc, cra). **Shutterstock.com:** Charles Bergman (tr); Rini Kools (bl); Uwe Bergwitz (tl); Split Second Stock (cb). **225 Alamy Stock Photo:** dpa picture alliance (cr); Michael Patrick O'Neill (clb); Octavio Campos Salles (bc); Pulsar Imagens (br). **Shutterstock.com:** Uwe Bergwitz (ca); Ondrej Prosicky (tl); Patrick K. Campbell (cl); Gurkan Ozturk (tc); Ammit Jack (tr). **226 Alamy Stock Photo:** imageBROKER (tl); Robert McGouey/Wildlife (c, cra, cr); William Ragosta (crb). **Dorling Kindersley:** Dreamstime.com: Musat Christian (fcl). **Dreamstime.com:** Petar Zigich (cl). **Getty Images/iStock:** yenwen (ca). **Shutterstock.com:** Sketchart (tr). **227 Alamy Stock Photo:** Nick Upton (br). **Dorling Kindersley:** Dreamstime.com: Jnjhuz (fcl, cl). **Dreamstime.com:** Mikelane45 (cb); Zeninaasya (clb). **Shutterstock.com:** Anna in Sweden (ca); KHilderbrand (tl); Ghost Bear (tr); New Africa (cr); Randy Bjorklund (bc). **228-229 naturepl.com:** Doug Gimesy. **228 naturepl.com:** D. Parer & E. Parer-Cook/Minden (bl). **229 naturepl.com:** Juergen Freund (bc); D. Parer & E. Parer-Cook/Minden (br). **230 Alamy Stock Photo:** FLPA (tc); Anan Kaewkhammul (cr). **Getty Images:** Jami Tarris (bl). **naturepl.com:** Theo Allofs/Minden (br). **Shutterstock.com:** Mo Afridha (c); electra (tl); shaineast (cl); Kayocci (fcl). **231 Alamy Stock Photo:** Auscape International Pty Ltd (c). **naturepl.com:** Mitsuaki Iwago/Minden (cra); Joel Sartore/Photo Ark (cla/joey). **Shutterstock.com:** Craig Dingle (bl); electra (tc, fcl); Kayocci (tr); totajla (cla/sand); Ken Griffiths (bc); shaineast (br). **232-233 naturepl.com:** Suzi Eszterhas/Minden. **234-235 naturepl.com:** Anup Shah (t). **Shutterstock.com:** Fahkamram (background). **234 naturepl.com:** Juergen & Christine Sohns/Minden (crb); Anup Shah (clb, cb). **235 naturepl.com:** Cyril Ruoso (crb); Anup Shah (clb, cb). **236 Alamy Stock Photo:** Elizabeth Cole (bl). **naturepl.com:** Aflo (bc); Yukihiro Fukuda (fbl); Ingo Arndt/Minden (br). **236-237 Getty Images/iStock:** BlackJack3D (ripples); Lemon_tm (t); structuresxx. **naturepl.com:** Mitsuaki Iwago/Minden (tr). **237 Alamy Stock Photo:** AGB Photo Library (bc). **naturepl.com:** Hiroya Minakuchi/Minden (tr); Anup Shah (bl); Yukihiro Fukuda/Minden (br); Cyril Ruoso/Minden (crb). **238-239 Alamy Stock Photo:** volkerpreusser (tc). **238 Alamy Stock Photo:** Arterra Picture Library (cb); Paolino Massimiliano Manuel (br). **naturepl.com:** David Pattyn (cra, c). **239 Alamy Stock Photo:** Andrea Battisti (cr); Manuel Lacoste (ca); FLPA (clb); blickwinkel (bc, br). **naturepl.com:** David Pattyn (cl). **Shutterstock.com:** Massimiliano Paolino (c). **240 Alamy Stock Photo:** BIOSPHOTO (br); Nature Picture Library (bc). **Getty Images/iStock:** Andyworks (tl); Elena Istomina (bl). **naturepl.com:** Eric Dragesco (tr). **241 Alamy Stock Photo:** Sirio Carnevalino (crb); Natural Visions (cl); olandsfokus (cr). **Dreamstime.com:** Dennis Donohue (cb). **Getty Images/iStock:** cooked photos (tl); oleg7799 (cra); ekolara (bc/snarling, bc). **naturepl.com:** Gertrud & Helmut Denzau (bl); Daniel Heuclin (tr); Eric Dragesco (ca). **Shutterstock.com:** istorsvetlana (c). **242-243 Alamy Stock Photo:** imageBROKER. **Shutterstock.com:** Fahkamram (b). **242 naturepl.com:** Klein & Hubert (cb, crb); Ann & Steve Toon (clb). **243 naturepl.com:** Will Burrard-Lucas (cb); Ann & Steve Toon (clb); Charlie Summers (crb). **244 Alamy Stock Photo:** Michele Burgess (br); Mark Levy (tr); KJELL SANDVED/SYLVIA CORDAIY PHOTO LIBRARY LTD (cr). **Getty Images/iStock:** MogensTrolle (tl); UfimtsevaV (cla). **naturepl.com:** Denis-Huot (cl). **245 Alamy Stock Photo:** blickwinkel (bc); Media Drum World (cla). **Dreamstime.com:** Frankandre (tc). **Getty Images:** Paul Souders (cr). **Getty Images/iStock:** Utopia_88 (br); WOLFAVNI (cra). **Shutterstock.com:** Henk Bogaard (cl); Bambang Prihnawan (crb). **246-247 Getty Images/iStock:** Gerald Corsi (b); Pawel Gaul (t). **248-249 Getty Images:** Martin Harvey. **248 Alamy Stock Photo:** Laura Romin & Larry Dalton (clb); André Gilden (tr); Martin Harvey (cr). **Shutterstock.com:** Kiki Dohmeier (cb); Paul Tessier (cl). **249 Alamy Stock Photo:** Martin Harvey (tl). **naturepl.com:** Theo Allofs/Minden (crb). **Shutterstock.com:** Danita Delimont (cb); Serge Goujon (c); Sergey Uryadnikov (clb); Jurgen Vogt (bc). **250 Alamy Stock Photo:** Brian Gibbs (cl). **Shutterstock.com:** Little Things Abroad (c); Madelein Wolfaardt (clb); RovingPhotogZA (cb); sirtravelalot (bc). **251 Alamy Stock Photo:** blickwinkel (tr); Nature Picture Library (tl); robertharding (cl). **naturepl.com:** ZSSD/Minden (cr). **Shutterstock.com:** ArCaLu (br); Stu Porter (bc). **252 Alamy Stock Photo:** Carl Corbidge (ca); John Sirlin (tl); Nature Picture Library (cl, clb); Panther Media GmbH (tr); Nick Rule (fclb); imageBROKER (cb); Natalia Kuzmina (br). **253 123RF.com:** alexandere17 (crb). **Alamy Stock Photo:** Mauricio Abreu (fcla); Saverio Gatto (cla); Jim Varley Photography (ca). **Getty Images:** Munish Palaniappan (cb). **Pierre Landmann:** (tr). **Shutterstock.com:** Wolfgang Zwanzger (cl). **N. N. Shi, R. F. Foelix, N. Yu, and R. Wehner:** (cr, fcr). **254-255 naturepl.com:** Suzi Eszterhas/Minden. **256 Alamy Stock Photo:** Blue Planet Archive (tl, cla); Y Kumar (clb); Hemis (bc); Micha Klootwijk (br). **Getty Images:** Richard Wilbourn (tc). **naturepl.com:** Andy Rouse (bl); Anup Shah (cb). **Shutterstock.com:** BLUR LIFE 1975 (crb); Rudi Hulshof (tr). **257 Alamy Stock Photo:** Helmut Corneli (cb). **Getty Images:** sdominick (crb). **naturepl.com:** Gerrit Vyn (bl). **Shutterstock.com:** Pavel Krasensky (tc); Plotitsyna NiNa (tl); Nicola Simoncini (tr); Ko Sei (clb). **258-259 naturepl.com:** Ch'ien Lee/Minden. **260 Alamy Stock Photo:** Danita Delimont (tc); John Sullivan (tl/spider); David Tipling Photo Library (tr). **Getty Images:** keithsutherland (cl). **naturepl.com:** Guy Edwardes (br); Tui De Roy/Minden (bc). **261 Alamy Stock Photo:** Nature Picture Library (tr); Photomecan (fcr). **BluePlanetArchive.com:** Doc White (br). **Dorling Kindersley:** (b); 123RF.com: Ana Vasileva/ABV (tc). **Dreamstime.com:** Chesampson (tl); Vitor Hugo Artigiani Filho (cra); SI Photography (clb); Dekanaryas (cr). **Getty Images/iStock:** R.M. Nunes (c); sdbower (cb/frog). **Shutterstock.com:** Photoongraphy (cb). **262-263 naturepl.com:** Andy Rouse. **262 Alamy Stock Photo:** Julianna Funk (crb). **Getty Images/iStock:** Jurgita_Zuk (cb). **naturepl.com:** Sergey Gorshkov (clb); Andy Rouse (fclb). **263 Alamy Stock Photo:** Dinodia Photos (cb); imageBROKER (clb); Aditya "Dicky" Singh (crb). **naturepl.com:** Yashpal Rathore (fcrb). **264-265 123RF.com:** rhgdesign (trees). **Shutterstock.com:** HNK (t). **264 Alamy Stock Photo:** Lou Linwei (bl); Minden Pictures (tl); Nature Picture Library (ca). **naturepl.com:** Edwin Giesbers (br); Mitsuaki Iwago/Minden (tr). **Shutterstock.com:** enmyo (cla). **265 Dorling Kindersley:** Dreamstime.com: Emir Hodzic (cla/rocks). **naturepl.com:** Klein & Hubert (ca); Gerry Ellis/Minden (tr). **Shutterstock.com:** Hung Chung Chih (cla); Ondrej Prosicky (tl). **266 123RF.com:** cattallina (c). **Alamy Stock Photo:** Imagebroker (crb); Mira (cb). **Getty Images/iStock:** JMrocek (cr); Remus86 (tl). **Science Photo Library:** Leonard Lee Rue III (tr). **Shutterstock.com:** SZBDesign (br, bl). **266-267 123RF.com:** rhgdesign (trees). **267 123RF.com:** byrdyak (tc). **Dreamstime.com:** Dalia Kvedaraite (c); Khmarskyi Maksym (tr); MartinBergsma (br/trees). **Getty Images/iStock:** Byrdyak (br); ErikMandre (cl); oktaydegirmenci (ca). **268 Getty Images:** DmitryND (br). **Shutterstock.com:** Troutnut. **269 Alamy Stock Photo:** mauritius images GmbH. **naturepl.com:** Danny Green (bl). **270 Alamy Stock Photo:** Frank Fichtmueller (cr). **Dreamstime.com:** Artenz (tr). **Getty Images/iStock:** Binnerstam (br); miralex (tc); Robert Winkler (cb). **Shutterstock.com:** Lasse Johansson (bl). **271 Alamy Stock Photo:** Design Pics Inc (tl). **Dorling Kindersley:** Twan Leenders (bl). **Getty Images/iStock:** Olga Kurbatova (ca). **Shutterstock.com:** Maximillian cabinet (crb); Viesinsh (tr); Hans Verburg (cl); valleyboi63 (c). **Janet M. Storey:** (br). **Paul Sundberg:** (clb). **272-273 Alamy Stock Photo:** Juniors Bildarchiv GmbH. **272 Alamy Stock Photo:** agefotostock (bc); Juniors Bildarchiv GmbH (fbl); Andrew Woodward (bl); Minden Pictures (br). **273 Alamy Stock Photo:** Nature Picture Library (bl, fbr); WaterFrame (br). **Dreamstime.com:** Slowmotiongli (tr). **naturepl.com:** Eric Baccega (bc). **274 Alamy Stock Photo:** robertharding (clb). **Shutterstock.com:** evaurban (cb); Alexey Seafarer (tl); FloridaStock (tr); Eric Isselee (fbr, br). **274-275 Shutterstock.com:** Africa Studio (drift); r2dpr (icicles); sirtravelalot (ice); Christopher Wood (c/snow); Andrei Stepanov (tundra). **275 Alamy Stock Photo:** Gillian Lloyd (cl); Sergey Uryadnikov (tc); robertharding (tr). **Dorling Kindersley:** Dreamstime.com: Mirage3 (br). **Science Photo Library:** POWER AND SYRED (ftr). **Shutterstock.com:** Belovodchenko Anton (clb); MyImages - Micha (c); Alexey Seafarer (cr). **276-277 naturepl.com:** Ole Jorgen Liodden

All other images © Dorling Kindersley

Explore the World with DK Timelines

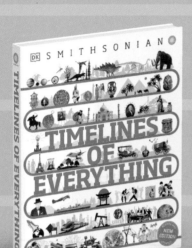

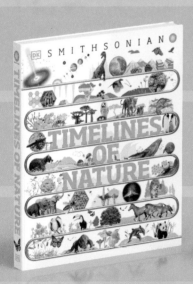

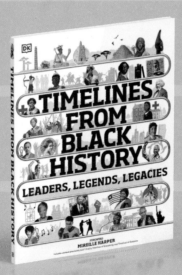

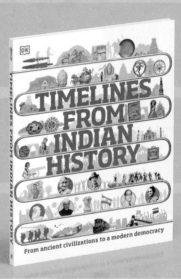

DK For the curious